1986
MK

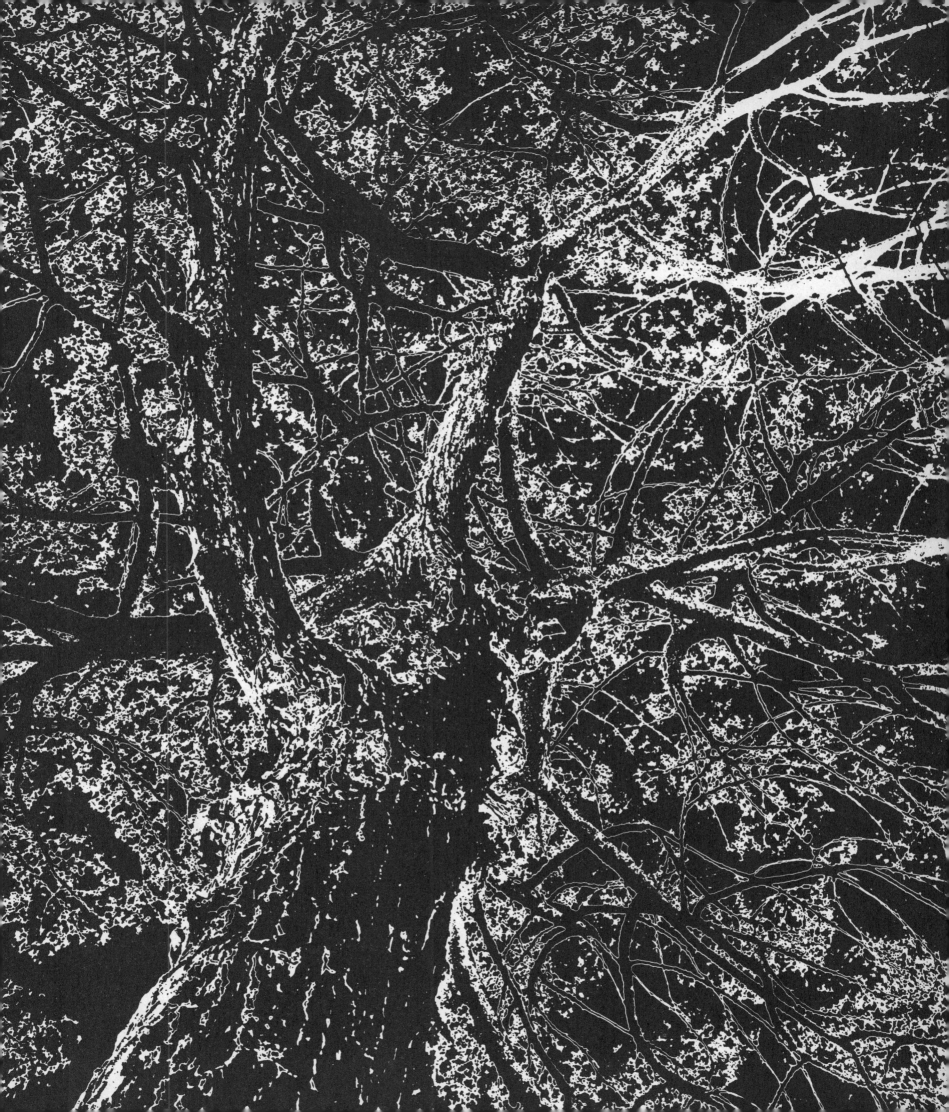

Gogol on Italy   *Who has been in Italy can forget all other regions.*
Who has been in Heaven does not desire the Earth.
Europe compared to Italy is like a gloomy day
compared to a day of sunshine.

Paradise of exiles   *How beautiful is sunset when the glow*
Of Heaven descends upon a land like thee
Thou Paradise of exiles; Italy !

from Shelley, 'Julian and Maddalo', 1819

Umbrella pine on the Palatine Hill, Rome

1 Winter cedes to Spring; Monteroduni, province of Campobasso. In the background the castle of the Pignatelli family.

ROLOFF BENY IN ITALY

The Prophecy of Dante, as seen by Byron

Thou, Italy! so fair that Paradise,
Revived in thee, blooms forth to man restored . . .
Thou, Italy! whose ever golden fields,
Plough'd by the sunbeams solely, would suffice
For the world's granary; thou, whose sky heaven gilds
With brighter stars, and robes with deeper blue;
Thou, in whose pleasant places Summer builds
Her palace, in whose cradle Empire grew,
And form'd the Eternal City's ornaments
From spoils of kings whom freemen overthrew;
Birthplace of heroes, sanctuary of saints,
Where earthly first, then heavenly glory made
Her home; thou, all which fondest fancy paints,
And finds her prior vision but portray'd
In feeble colours, when the eye – from the Alp
Of horrid snow, and rock, and shaggy shade
Of desert-loving pine, whose emerald scalp
Nods to the storm – dilates and dotes o'er thee,
And wistfully implores, as 'twere for help
To see thy sunny fields, my Italy . . .

'The Prophecy of Dante', Canto II, 1819

2 The Angel Gabriel; detail of *The Annunciation and Saints*, triptych dated 1333 and signed by Simone Martini (*c.* 1280–1344), painted for the chapel of S. Ansano in the Cathedral, Siena, now in the Uffizi Gallery, Florence.

(overleaf) Detail of west doorway, Orvieto Cathedral

Anthology drawn from

VIRGIL
CATULLUS
LIVY
OVID
PLINY
ST FRANCIS
DANTE
LORENZO DE' MEDICI
VASARI
CORYATE
SHAKESPEARE
NASHE
EVELYN
GIBBON
BOSWELL
GOETHE
WORDSWORTH
HEINE
CHATEAUBRIAND
BYRON
SHELLEY
GOGOL
STENDHAL
LEOPARDI
TENNYSON
BROWNING
PATER
EDITH WHARTON
BARON CORVO
D'ANNUNZIO
E. M. FORSTER
D. H. LAWRENCE

ROLOFF BENY IN ITALY

Designed and photographed by Roloff Beny
with an epilogue by
Gore Vidal
Text and anthology by Anthony Thwaite
and Peter Porter
Historical notes on the plates by
Brian de Breffny
With 174 colour plates, 122 duotone plates
and 19 line illustrations and maps

THAMES AND HUDSON

Other books designed and photographed
by Roloff Beny
THE THRONES OF EARTH AND HEAVEN
A TIME OF GODS
PLEASURE OF RUINS
TO EVERY THING THERE IS A SEASON
JAPAN IN COLOUR
INDIA
ISLAND CEYLON

To the artists of Italy of all time,
who use marble, wood or clay,
whose brushes paint on fresh plaster or on gilded panels of
wood and linen,
who dream and dream and then erect duomos, palaces and
pavilions of pleasure,
to the romantic hand of varied nature,
and to that particular luminosity of the peninsula
surrounded by glittering seas,
I dedicate this book.

Maps drawn by Hanni Bailey

© 1974 THAMES AND HUDSON LTD, LONDON
PHOTOGRAPHS © ROLOFF BENY, 1974
Reprinted 1983

Text filmset in Great Britain by
Keyspools Ltd, Golborne, Lancs.
Printed and bound in Italy by
Arnoldo Mondadori Editore, Verona.

ISBN 0 500 24089 2

3 Capo Colonna, Calabria; this solitary monument of antiquity is at the tip of a little peninsula, against a background of sky and rolling sea. Near it is the site of Crotone, a celebrated republic of Magna Graecia which at its zenith conquered Sybaris.

3

Jack Wilton on Italian ingenuities

To tell you of the rare pleasures of their gardens, theyr bathes, theyr vineyardes, theyr galleries, were to write a seconde part of the gorgeous Gallerie of gallant devices. Why, you should not come into anie mannes house of account, but hee hadde fish-pondes and little orchardes on the toppe of his leads. If by raine or any other meanes those ponds were so full they need to be slust or let out, even of their superfluities they made melodious use, for they had great winde instruments in stead of leaden spoutes, that went duly on consort, onely with this waters rumbling discent. I sawe a summer banketting house belonging to a merchaunt, that was the mervaile of the world, & could not be matcht except God should make another paradise. It was builte round of greene marble, like a Theater with-out: within there was a heaven and earth comprehended both under one roofe, the heaven was a cleere overhanging vault of christall, wherein the Sunne and Moone, and each visible Starre had his true similitude, shine, scituation, and motion, and by what enwrapped arte I cannot conceive, these spheares in their proper orbes observed their circular wheelinges and turnings, making a certaine kinde of soft angelical murmuring musicke in their often windings & going about, which musick the philosophers say is the true heaven by reason of the grosenes of our senses we are not capable of. For the earth it was counterfeited in that liknes that Adam lorded out it before his fall.

from Thomas Nashe, 'The Unfortunate Traveller', 1594

4 Centuries-old gnarled olive trees in a grove near ancient Medma in Calabria.

Flute player: fresco in a Greek tomb near Paestum
Map of Italy, from Sebastian Münster's
'Geographia', Basel, 1540

FOLD OUT ▷

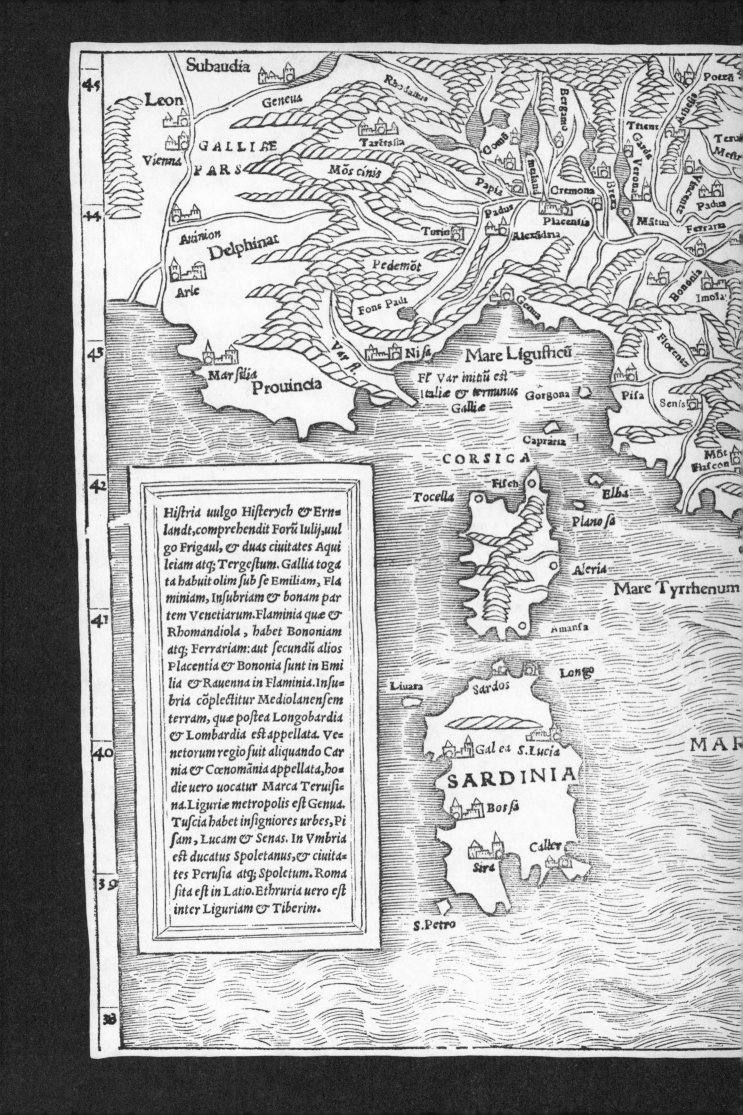

Subaudia

Leon

Geneua

GALLIÆ
PARS

Vienna

Rhodanus

Taretslia

Môs cinis

Comū

Bergamo

Potrā

Athesis

Tricnt

Teruif

Mestr

Garda

Verona

Papis

Melanū

Cremona

Brex

Padua

Auānion

Delphinat

Pedemōt

Turio

Padus

Alexādria

Placentia

Mātua

Ferrara

Arle

Fons Padi

Gema

Bononia

Imola

Florētia

43

Marsilia

Prouincia

Var R.

Nisa

Mare Ligusticū

Fl̄ Var initiū est
Italiæ & terminus
Galliæ

Gorgona

Pisa

Senis

Caprāria

CORSICA

Elba

42

Tocella

Fisch

Plano sa

Aleria

Mare Tyrrhenum

Histria uulgo Histerych & Ern=
landt, comprehendit Forū Iulij, uul
go Frigaul, & duas ciuitates Aqui
leiam atq; Tergestum. Gallia toga
ta habuit olim sub se Emiliam, Fla
miniam, Insubriam & bonam par
tem Venetiarum. Flaminia quæ &
Rhomandiola, habet Bononiam
atq; Ferrariam: aut secundū alios
Placentia & Bononia sunt in Emi
lia & Rauenna in Flaminia. Insu=
bria cōplectitur Mediolanensem
terram, quæ postea Longobardia
& Lombardia est appellata. Ve=
netorum regio fuit aliquando Car
nia & Coenomānia appellata, ho=
die uero uocatur Marca Teruisi=
na. Liguriæ metropolis est Genua.
Tuscia habet insigniores urbes, Pi
sam, Lucam & Senas. In Vmbria
est ducatus Spoletanus, & ciuita=
tes Perusia atq; Spoletum. Roma
sita est in Latio. Ethruria uero est
inter Liguriam & Tiberim.

Amansa

Liuara

Longo

Sardos

Galea

S.Lucia

MAR

SARDINIA

Borsa

Caller

Sira

S.Petro

CONTENTS

DENONTIE SECRETE
CONTRO CHI OCCVLTERÀ
GRATIE ET OFFICII.
O COLVDERÀ PER
NASCONDER LA VERA
RENDITA Ō ESSI.

Foreword
by Roloff Beny

'THE SKY seemed stained and blotted by dark inks, sepia and indigo. Only luminous saffron gray was exposed where the winter sun could penetrate.' This is a blurred quote from a diary kept some twenty years ago when I had left various and beloved nests in Greece, Florence, Venice, Paris, New York, and alighted, coming to rest on a magical curve of the Tiber in Trastevere. Already, a quarter of a century ago, I was bewitched by the unique and legendary light of the Italian peninsula. Here in Rome in my terrace studio I have edited and formed this book on Italy. Every dawn and twilight confirms the poets', travellers', and musicians' appreciation of the ever changing mosaic of light which plays across the skies. On a clear day I can almost see and certainly smell the Mediterranean as the Tiber winds below on its way down to the great Roman port of Ostia. To the east beyond the campanili of Santa Maria Maggiore and Michelangelo's triumphal Campidoglio, the Alban hills are often capped with snow. To the west the dome of Saint Peter's rises like a great shell from the sea, changing form with each variation of light and time of day. Below, in a vast ochre amphitheatre, lying in shattered fragments heaped over five of the celebrated hills of Rome, two thousand years of history sun themselves and refract the light of centuries.

Proust said that 'the mind discriminates in retrospect'. The painter and the writer can take time not just to look but to see and select, perhaps returning many times at different times of the day and night and even through changing seasons. The photographer cannot. He is a lover who remembers but tragically too late. How often a masterpiece of lighting or expression on an unknowing face have been lost during the fraction of time needed to make a lens adjustment. Even worse, magical compositions are retained on the retina long after the moving vehicles of today upon which we depend have shot past and one bemoans the fact that one is not still on foot, donkey, or camel like the travellers of the past. Of course I suffer . . . and yet the seen and untaken photographs are like lyrical dreams, never quite forgotten. They haunt my memory and focus into sharp relief to taunt me with guilt. Unlike the writer and the painter, the photographer is the slave of a machine and sensitized paper and rarely has a second chance.

How I envy the subject of the last plate in this book, Tobias guided by the Archangel Raphael on foot with his faithful dog through a landscape tapestried by wild flowers. The choice of this painting both in the book and on the jacket is

*Letter-box for anonymous accusations,
Doges' Palace, Venice*

17

in no way arbitrary but rather symbolic. Just as the Archangel leads Tobias in this moving parable from the *Apocrypha* to the sacred fish which cures the blindness of his father, I hope to help those who cannot travel – and those more fortunate who do – to recapture and perhaps reassess their own experiences.

Ten volumes would have been easier to edit than one. For every image and every site included, there were a hundred equally valid photographs which were agonizingly returned to the Archive. Now it is up to the reader to explore beyond the limits of this one volume. Italy staggers the traveller with its beloved and familiar landscapes, façades, cloisters, domes, piazzas and human form in marble, wood, and stone. Often the most enduring impression we retain comes unexpectedly even when faced with a known object. My particular quest, I hope evident to the reader, both in the images and anthology, is to reveal the sensual pleasures in all respects of life on this magic peninsula. I recorded an observation about Rome by that romantic but perceptive writer Lesley Blanch which confirms in few words my search:

> Rome, in all its sumptuous, decadent beauty, overblown splendours living in harmony beside an abiding pastoral, or rustic quality. Rome with its wild figs sprouting from high Baroque; its old, old walls cascading with greenery like vegetal fountains – Rome's other fountains. And over all things, that ever shifting glow, brilliant yet soft, turning a rosy wall to orange and every stone to gold.

It is pleasure, sacred and profane, which dominates the entire history of Italian painting, sculpture and architecture – the decorations in the houses of Herculaneum, the joyous tombs of the Etruscans, the raucous entertainment of the Roman amphitheatre and baths, the frankly sensual sculpture of the Renaissance and the later excesses of the Baroque, the pleasure gardens of the popes and the Palladian villas on the Brenta, the pagan spectacle of religious festivals and the sentimental ritual of death, the joyful excursions to mountains, the Bacchanalian harvest of the grape, the *joie de vivre* of the trattorias, sports arenas, super highways and, most of all, the potential of a smile which here has the highest currency value in the world. This is what Italy is all about.

The most mystical visual voyage in Italy is to be alone in the rock-cut sacred galleries at Cumae (plate 102). To enter is like passing through a keyhole to the Pagan past. The inner chamber of the Sibyl is black as the inside of Satan's skull and all around damp and moss pattern the ancient stone like luminous green ink splattered on wet watercolour paper. Beyond the clerestory apertures, hemlock and holm oak muffle the impatient sea and I felt shivers from *The Golden Bough*.

I found Ferrara and Parma, unlike Cumae, or indeed Genoa or Naples, easy to encounter and a delight at every turn. Ferrara, a city of unadorned brick exteriors, whilst hostile and severe on the outside, is rich but never Baroque on the inside – all pure Renaissance like the heavenly frescoes of the Seasons in the Palazzo Schiffanoia. Unhappily they are not included in the book because they were totally covered for restoration. I was allowed to crawl from scaffold to scaffold behind draperies of plastic to behold, at nose length, such wonders as the beggar boy representing the month of March. This was my fate and frustration from the thigh to the boot of Italy . . . hundreds of favourite façades, frescoes, altars, naves, gilded and painted ceilings under wraps . . . necessary, though almost too late, for preserving the monuments of Italy, but heartbreaking for one retracing his steps to resee treasures already familiar twenty years ago. Sometimes the scaffolding afforded me surprising access to an otherwise impossible technical feat. In Bologna, thanks to restorers' ladders, I was able to be on touching level with the powerful reliefs, panel by panel, of Giacomo della Quercia (plates 177–8) on the portal of San Petronio; and the climax was to be able to caress God the Father at its apex ninety feet above the ground. Another exception to test my athletic prowess was when Time-Life commissioned me to photograph the monumental equestrian Colleoni of Verrocchio. I climbed with all my equipment a sixty-foot, free-swinging rope ladder to peer into the piercing eyes of the Condottiere which were reputed to have been inlaid with rubies (plate 271). But perhaps the most haunting night was that spent, again eye to eye, with Giuliano and Lorenzo de' Medici. I floated above the recumbent but alive attendants at the feet of the merchant princes of Florence in the Medici chapel, on a moveable scaffold, tempted to leave the imprint of my hand in the dust of centuries on Night and Day, Dawn and Twilight.

In the capital cities of Italy's many former separate kingdoms I know and cherish the friendship of visitors like myself who came, were conquered, and remained half a lifetime. In Venice I took the photograph, plate 276, from Peggy Guggenheim's home on the Grand Canal on the day of a historic regatta. Her palace, Venier dei Leoni, now houses one of the world's greatest private collections of painting and sculpture, but in the past has housed many remarkable ladies. None more colourful than the fabled Marchesa Casati, whose husband leased it for her capricious extravagances. Once, when her garden, perhaps the largest in Venice, and unfinished white marble palace couldn't hold enough local and Eastern princes, gilded slaves and drugged panthers, she contrived to rent the Piazzetta before the Doge's Palace, arriving last in an entourage of damask-draped gondolas conveying her plumes and golden crinolines, her orchestra dressed in black velvet, ocelot tunics and turbans. Peggy Guggenheim, who now makes her home in this palace, is for me the most generous foreigner, having opened her garden palace and collection as a museum in perpetuity where all the world foregathers. She is one of the last persons to conserve a private gondola and the hour of twilight on the hidden canals is her most sacred moment. As a Venetian by adoption she has expressed her love better than almost any of the centuries of travellers and devotees of this imperilled city in her foreword to the book, *Invito a Venezia*.

. . . As to the Venetians themselves, they are all in love with Venice. With sighs they recount their undying passion for their beloved city. With the rising tide their love mounts and with the receding tide it gently diminishes only to surge forth again when the sea pours back its waters. When Venice is flooded it is even more truly beloved. Then a new ecstasy comes over the inhabitants, as they sweep out the waters from their ground floors, in order to be able to proceed with their daily lives and normal existence. Normal existence is a 'façon de parler'. There is no normal life in Venice. Here everything and everyone floats. Not only the gondolas, launches, barges, vaporettos and 'sandoles' but also the buildings and the people float. One floats in and out of restaurants, shops, cinemas, theatres, museums, churches and hotels. One floats luxuriously with such a sense of freedom, never tormented by traffic or even disturbed by the sound of a claxon. It is this floatingness, which is the essential quality of Venice...'

It would be a great joy for me to edit an anthology of my own friends' impressions of their adopted land who too consider Italy in the words of Shelley, 'A Paradise of Exiles'. Rather, for want of space, I have given Gore Vidal, a neighbour across the Tiber, the last word – in the form of an Epilogue.

My own discovery of Italy will never be ended, but my book is now composed. The night sky above, with its fountains of stars, the Tiber from my terrace in the heat of August challenges the dawns and the dusks of all seasons. May I remind the reader that the book is dedicated to joy in a very troubled world with this quotation from my friend, Dame Rose Macaulay, who was the author of *Pleasure of Ruins*, and from the beginning, the inspiration for many of my books.

The Sybarites they slept away the noon on beds of roses; ... the joys they had, the wines they drank, the palaces, the pleasures, ... and then no more of Sybaris, for Sybaris vanished wholly in a haze of golden opulence and sin ...

Rome, 1974

Detail of marquetry panel, S. Lorenzo, Padula

5 Postcard-seller's stall near the Quattro Canti in Palermo; a panorama of idols dear to the Italians – Pope John XXIII turns his back on a bare-breasted model who contemplates a Madonna and Child over a massive bouquet, Gianni Morandi (above the Pope) and Claudio Villa, stars of the San Remo song festival, kittens, racing cars, old masters, fat babies, healthy lovers, dark Romeos with nordic Juliets, a Carabiniere, St Christopher.

6 Pages in the yellow and blue medieval costume of the Aquila Quarter, one of the 17 groups of which 10 participate annually in the Palio, Siena. Juggling with flags is a traditional part of the colourful ceremonies on each 16th of August which began in the twelfth century.

7 Pages in medieval costume at the Palio, Ferrara.

8 Bathers enjoying the curative waters at Saturnia; since Roman times at least, the people of the surrounding countryside have come to bathe in the hot sulphurous springs of this place and it still retains a pagan atmosphere.

9 Grape festival at Colonna near Rome. Every autumn throughout Italy small towns in the wine-producing regions celebrate the grape harvest and the wine-making.

10 Trulli-dwellers near Locorotondo follow the pall-bearers and mourners on foot in a funeral procession; in the background one of their picturesque conical houses.

11 Students in the Piazza della Signoria, Florence, celebrate the end of the academic year in the Goliardic tradition with costumes, paper-hats, whistles, bells and smoke-bombs.

12 Detail of the altar, Cathedral of S. Lorenzo, Genoa.

13 Church of S. Maria della Salute, Venice, 21 November; acolytes with candles at the feast of the Madonna della Salute commemorating the end of a virulent plague which decimated the city.

14 Bold tomb in the monumental cemetery, S.

Miniato, Florence; a Loved One never to be forgotten.

15 Much-revered effigy of the Madonna del Carmine which is carried through the crowded streets of Trastevere, Rome, during the popular annual festival of No'antri.

16 Fine eighteenth-century reliquary in the form of an arm, the hand holding a feather, containing the arm-bones of St Eustace. Crypt of the Cathedral, Acquaviva delle Fonti, province of Bari.

17 Marzipan lambs in a pastry shop, via Palmieri, Lecce; a traditional Easter sweetmeat in this town.

18 The corpse of St Liberatus in a glass case surrounded by ex-votos. The relic was purchased in the last century by a Duchess Pignatelli and presented to the parish of Roccamandolfi, province of Campobasso, but its ownership was contested by a neighbouring village which frequently sent gangs to steal it.

19 The Italian film director Federico Fellini shooting a scene from his film *Roma* in front of a cardboard mock-up of the Colosseum.

20 'Il Cambio', an elegant restaurant in Piazza Carignano, Turin, patronized by deputies from the nearby Chamber; for fifteen years Cavour ate here, always at the same table.

21 Carabinieri on duty in front of the Spanish Steps, Rome; in the background the pots of azaleas which decorate the stair every spring, displacing the hippies who are there the rest of the year.

22 The glass-roofed Galleria Vittorio Emanuele II in the heart of Milan; the gallery was built 1865–77 – its architect fell to his death from the scaffolding. It is a centre of city life, a favourite meeting place of the Milanese, housing busy cafés, restaurants and shops.

23 A picturesque shop, Campo dei Mori, Venice; the curious statue, one of three, is said to be of one of the three Rioba brothers, Levantine

merchants who lived there in the twelfth century.

24 Detail of the Christmas crib used each year from Christmas to Epiphany in the Church of S. Maria d'Aracoeli, Rome, which is built on the spot where, according to tradition, the Sibyl predicted to the Emperor Augustus the coming of the Son of God.

25 A priest contemplates the purchase of a canary in the beautiful cathedral square, Ascoli Piceno.

26 A wall built of salvaged fragments of an illustrious past, Montecassino.

27 Navvies working near the port in Genoa.

28 Calvary, Monastery of S. Elio, Nepi, province of Viterbo.

29 Rocky inlet at Fiascherino near Lerici. The Bay of Lerici is associated with the sojourn and tragic death of the poet Shelley.

30 Subterranean caves at Castellana, province of Bari, discovered in 1938; they run for over a mile along the course of an ancient river.

31 The peaks of the Pizzocolo range behind Lake Garda, the largest lake in Italy.

32 November in the Gargano, the spur on the boot of Italy.

33 March in Sardinia; a tapestry of wild flowers.

34 June in the Abruzzi; cool beeches and scented broom.

35 The Sardinian coast near the Gulf of Oristano.

36 February – pollarded trees in the plain below the Gran Sasso.

37 April – rural landscape near Civitella, province of Teramo.

38 July – the historic hill-city of Orvieto from the vineyards which produce the famed white wine of this region.

Tennyson remembers his Italian tour

O love, what hours were thine and mine,
In lands of palm and southern pine;
    In lands of palm, of orange-blossom,
Of olive, aloe, and maize and vine . . .

At Florence too what golden hours,
In those long galleries, were ours;
    What drives about the fresh Cascine,
Or walks in Boboli's ducal bowers.

In bright vignettes, and each complete,
Of tower or duomo, sunny-sweet,
    Or palace, how the city glittered,
Through cypress avenues, at our feet . . .

I climbed the roofs at break of day;
Sun-smitten Alps before me lay.
    I stood among the silent statues,
And statued pinnacles, mute as they.

How faintly-flushed, how phantom-fair,
Was Monte Rosa, hanging there
    A thousand shadowy-pencilled valleys
And snowy dells in a golden air . . .

What more? we took our last adieu,
And up the snowy Splugen drew,
    But ere we reached the highest summit
I plucked a daisy, I gave it you.

It told of England then to me,
And now it tells of Italy.
    O love, we two shall go no longer
To lands of summer across the sea . . .

from Tennyson, 'The Daisy', written to his wife Emily in 1853,
remembering their Italian tour of 1851

FOLD OUT ▷

6

7

8

9

10

11

16

17

18

19

20

21

22

23

24

25

26

Heine on
day-dreaming in Italy

Simply letting yourself live is beautiful in Italy. In these marble *palazzi* sighs have a more romantic echo than in our modest brick houses; in the shade of these laurel bushes it is more pleasant to weep than under our gloomy fir trees; it is sweeter to day-dream following the shapes of Italian clouds than under the ash-grey dome of a German sky, a work-day sky in which even clouds take on the solemn and sulky expression of little burghers and yawn with boredom . . .

The people and land of Italy

WHEN, in 1814, Metternich referred to Italy as 'only a geographical expression', he was playing the contemptuous realist. Half a century was to pass before political unity was achieved. For 1,400 years, in fact if not always in name, the peninsula had been a parcel of petty kingdoms, squabbling city-states, turbulent provinces of foreign empires. Sometimes the influence of one of these constituent states spread far beyond its own frontiers: Venice, lamented by Wordsworth in a famous sonnet as once holding 'the gorgeous east in fee', was such a power. But from the time of Theodoric in the late fifth century until Pope Pius IX incarcerated himself in the Vatican in 1870, what the world saw as 'Italy' was a shadow of Roman unification, sharing a language and the ruins of imperial memories, but in most other ways a quarrelsome and divided land.

Those divisions, though nowadays unimportant to the central government, are still there. Italy is a country of regions, with their own landscapes, loyalties, manners and memories. There is a common language, but it is rich in dialects. The topography is perhaps more varied than that of any other European country, with hills and mountains often forming natural frontiers between regions. As for the human impact on the physical, a modern geographer has written: 'In no country in Europe has the imprint of Man on the landscape, with its good and evil consequences, been so marked.'

Again, among European countries it has been continuously and densely settled for the longest period. For a thousand years the lowlands of Lombardy have been enriched with irrigation and intensive work; for two thousand years the uplands of Basilicata have been stripped of their trees and left to the assaults of erosion. Indeed, the contrast between North and South is one of the great divides, not just in terms of geography but in a whole attitude of mind, so that in many ways the two are still mutually exclusive lands, distrustful and despising one another. The *Problema del Mezzogiorno* is not only one of economics, to do with 'redevelopment' or 'public works' or 'credit'; it concerns different loyalties, responses, priorities, sentiments, temperaments. A Sicilian is closer to Africa than he is to Rome. A businessman in Milan shares almost nothing, in traditions, assumptions, responses and affections, with a shepherd in Sardinia. Or as Cavour said while he was dying, soon after the creation of the new kingdom of Italy: 'We are all Italians – but there are still the Neapolitans . . .'.

The Roman Empire established a unity, but it was a unity within which diversity flourished. Roman poets were well aware of the places they came from. Catullus was born in Verona, by origin a Celtic settlement, and it is thought that some of the strange words he brought into the Latin language in his poems are of Celtic origin. Virgil's native place was Mantua, and he gloried in the area to which he himself had brought glory. Ovid celebrated the town of his birth in the remote Abruzzi. Juvenal even became mayor of his town of Aquino, south-east of Rome, at an early age, and set up a shrine in gratitude for the honour given him. Later, the names of many painters direct one immediately to the place of their origin – da Vinci, Veronese, the Bassanos, Pisanello, Caravaggio, Pontormo: a man is known by where he comes from.

But in a sense Italy, in the diversity of its regions and in the wealth of its nature, was discovered not by its own volatile people, not even by its own gifted artists, but by foreign travellers. It was Dr Johnson who said: 'A man who has not been in Italy is always conscious of an inferiority, for his not having seen what is expected a man to see'. Long before Johnson's eighteenth century, however, Italy was a prime goal of the cultivated traveller. In the Middle Ages the pilgrimages to Rome began; but at the same time there were poets, such as Chaucer, who went elsewhere in Italy and who took back with them new literary modes. By the sixteenth century, the country had begun to acquire that heady reputation as a sensualist's haven, so that Thomas Nashe, writing in the person of his 'unfortunate traveller' Jack Wilton, could ironically address an apostrophe to '*Italy* the Paradice of the earth, and the Epicures heaven . . . From thence he brings the art of atheisme, the art of epicurising, the art of whoring, the art of poysoning, the art of Sodomitrie' – dubious but seductive recommendations, reaching their high point in: 'It is nowe a privie note amongst the better sort of men, when they would set a singular marke or brand on a notorious villaine, to say, he hath beene in *Italy*'.

Nashe is here not just indulging in some pleasantly venomous xenophobia (and in the same book he is equally rude about the French, the Spanish, the Dutch and the Danes): he is also smacking his lips, as many northern travellers have done since, at the notion of the earthly pleasures Italy can offer. 'To be entertained of exquisite Italy . . .'. For centuries, enjoyment has been the keynote: of the sun, of the wine, of buildings, ruins, sculpture, paintings, of the commanding and dangerous Alps that straddle the northern frontiers, of the intense and fruitful cultivation of vines, olives, oranges and lemons, and not least the enjoyment – if only at a distance, and through the eye – of the beauty of its women. Travellers of many different temperaments have felt a sudden sense of pleasure at their first discovery of Italy, whether it is Shelley's 'No sooner had we arrived in Italy than the loveliness of the earth and the serenity of the sky made the greatest difference in my sensations', or Henry James's simple but overwhelming 'At last, for the first time, I live'.

Most travellers, and many invaders, have come over the formidable Alpine barrier to reach this garden of delights. This is confused and disputed territory, which even now carries within it unassimilated minorities with their own traditions and languages: French, German and Slav elements, such as the South

Tyrolese of the Trentino and the Alto Adige, and the Ladin speakers of the high valleys of the Dolomites, who preserve their ancient language – akin to the Romansch of Switzerland, and a fossilized remnant of the old Latin tongue – in dwindling isolation. Travel now is easy through the several rail and road tunnels, in themselves monuments of skill and enterprise; but to travellers right down until the late nineteenth century to negotiate this massive conglomeration of rock and ice was risky work. Wordsworth's wondering cry in *The Prelude* – 'We had crossed the Alps' – was not a unique voice. To descend from the passes of the Central Alps in summer was to move from the chill and mists of the mountains to a strong sun, intense light, and the stone walls and tiled roofs of Italy.

Roads were bad, the inns dirty, the food abominable, everywhere there was exploitation, either through simple cheating or through robbery by thieves, highwaymen and pickpockets, the Italians were excitable and treacherous – so ran the northern travellers' tales. Yet still they came, on pilgrimage or political business, to trade or to see the sights; and over the centuries an Italy was created in the mind as well as on the map. After the Alps, it began with the ducal cities of Milan and Mantua, and the plains of Lombardy – those plains of which the English traveller Thomas Coryate wrote in the early seventeenth century: 'As Italy is the garden of Europe, so is Lombardy the garden of Italy . . . It is wholly plaine, and beautified with such an abundance of goodly rivers, pleasant meadowes, fruitfull vineyards, fat pastures, delectable gardens, orchards, woodes, and what not, that the first view thereof did even refollicate my spirits, and tickle my senses with inward joy'.

Then Padua, Vicenza, Verona, Venice: all of them cities of age and substance, but it is Venice which for centuries has caught imaginations, nourished superlatives, elicited ways of trying to describe it, and eluded almost everyone. As Henry James put it: 'The Venice of today is a vast museum where the little wicket that admits you is perpetually turning and creaking, and you march through the institution with a herd of fellow-gazers. There is nothing left to discover or describe, and originality of attitude is utterly impossible'. Guardi and Canaletto have made it so familiar, poets, essayists and letter-writers have evoked its ingredients and its atmosphere so exhaustively, that it is a miracle its first impact – and even subsequent ones – is as strong and surprising as it is. It is a labyrinth, full of intricate lanes and side canals subordinate and tributary to the famous sights, but it is a labyrinth for which every traveller believes he has been given the clue. Even Ruskin, who hated it because it seemed to defy all his aesthetic canons, was obsessed with it.

Venice is a daring man-made invention. Elsewhere in Italy towns and villages more commonly seem to belong to their landscapes, as Florence does, and as so many much smaller places in Tuscany and Umbria do. D. H. Lawrence, who carried on a love-hate affair with Italy for so much of his life, felt this, contrasting the squalor and ugliness of his native Erewash Valley with what he saw in Tuscany, where man had dominated the landscape without trampling on it. The Tuscan imagination created the great sloping disk of Siena, the soaring and bristling towers of San Gimignano, and that hazy, dream-like panorama of domes which is Florence seen from the heights of Fiesole. 'I was bound to admit', wrote Montaigne in the late sixteenth century, 'that neither Orleans, nor Tours, nor even Paris, can boast of environs so richly set with villages and houses as Florence; which with regard to fine houses and palaces, comes first without a doubt'. The rulers of Tuscany valued agricultural improvement as much as more artistic considerations; it is their hand that lies behind the well-tilled uplands, and here it was not thought beneath a nobleman's notice to work the land and improve it: in 1644, the English diarist John Evelyn discovered, to his surprise, that the Duke of Tuscany himself was engaged in the wine trade.

Umbria, fertile and cultivated, was a contrast with what for centuries were the barren stretches of the Campagna as the traveller approached Rome – for many the sole object of pilgrimage. A late eighteenth-century English traveller noted: 'For several posts before you arrive at Rome, few villages, little cultivation and scarcely any inhabitants are to be seen. In the Campagna of Rome . . . no trees, no inclosure, nothing but scattered ruins of temples and tombs, presenting the idea of a country depopulated by pestilence.' But it was Rome itself, for all its surrounding sense of blankness, that had a special resonance – as it was summarized by Shelley,

> at once the Paradise,
> The grave, the city, and the wilderness.

Why this should be so is a matter of history rather than setting, for Rome (despite its famous hills) has no commanding position, and indeed the hills serve to obstruct rather than defend; its river is not really commercially navigable; it has no port; in all directions but that of the sea it is close to mountains that cut it off from the rest of the country. Yet despite all these disadvantages, there was little question but that Rome would be the capital of a united Italy: the presence of emperors and popes for centuries had determined that. It does not need to depend on its neglected environs, for it moved from being the capital of an empire to become the capital of Christendom. Its province is the world.

The Abruzzi was never a place for travellers, and the South itself, with the exception of Naples, was not a place to detain them either; it is only in more recent years that 'the Amalfi drive' has become the easy object of tourism – Sorrento, Positano, Ravello, Amalfi, and such small fishing villages in between as Maiori and Minori. Even Naples, to other travellers as to Gibbon, seemed to have inhabitants who 'dwell on the confines of paradise and hell-fire'. And beyond that were areas even more poverty-stricken, frightening and uncertain – the southern extremities and the islands. True, they had splendid ruins, in those ages that were avid for ruins; but when tastes extended to discover the marvels of the Renaissance – the term itself began to have wide currency only towards the middle of the nineteenth century – the South was seen to have few monuments of the favoured period, and so it was as neglected by followers of art as it had been by anyone fond of order, comfort, and wealth.

For Italy, in its regions and cities, has been as subject to fashion in the minds of foreigners as any other human phenomenon. The roll-call of its painters, sculptors, architects and composers has suffered fluctuations of taste. For centuries, the

Byzantine mosaics of Ravenna, which in the earlier years of our own time were a revelation to Yeats, for example, were considered either 'quaint' or 'disgusting'. One generation would see Raphael as the height of artistic virtue, the next Fra Angelico; while Fuseli, who wrote the first considerable history of Italian art in English, in the early nineteenth century characterized Botticelli with such terms as 'barbarous taste . . . dry minuteness . . . puerile ostentation'. But whatever period or painters or activities were in favour, Italy has always somehow been a magnet, an inspiration, a confirmation, a necessary part of the world of human achievement, to be visited and relished.

Mary McCarthy has described Venice as 'a folding picture-postcard of itself'. The same could be said of Italy as a whole – a succession of glittering impressions, some of them familiar to the point of being clichés, others less well known but falling into place as part of the proper scheme of things. Landscapes, buildings, works of art and particular views alternate, each illuminating and commenting on the other. The representation of credible and actual landscape followed close on the heels of the Italian rediscovery of perspective; and the landscapes are recognizable. The background of Piero della Francesca's *Baptism of Christ* is an authentic Tuscan one, with its serpentine river, its dotted bushes and trees, its tracks and sandy places, and its distant dome-like hills. Tuscan light, bright and distinct, shines through Tuscan paintings, just as the light of Umbria, hazier and more muted, affected the painters of Umbria. And the river winding through Pollaiuolo's *Apollo and Daphne* seems truly the Arno.

There are some places in the world that seem familiar even before one has seen them: seeing them gives a shock of recognition. So it is with Italy. Partly it is, indeed, a visual matter: one has seen so many paintings, so many photographs, read so many descriptions, celebrations, itineraries, watched so many films (from the saccharine romanticism of Hollywood's idea of Rome to the grey realism of post-war Italian cinema), glanced at so many returning travellers' colour slides. But when the experience actually comes, one is not jaded: the expectations are satisfied. And this has a great deal to do with the way in which the places and people seem to combine, in a sense to conspire, in what Stendhal called 'the great art of being happy, which is here practised with this added charm, that the good people do not know that it is an art, the most difficult of all'.

Henry James noted this, in a passage quoted by the liveliest modern Italian interpreter of his people to the outside world, Luigi Barzini. James found himself one day in the small town of Velletri, south of Rome, with nothing to do and nothing to see. It would not seem to have been a propitious or golden moment, one to be commemorated or enjoyed in any way. Yet he wrote this:

There was a narrow raised terrace, with steps, in front of the best of two or three local cafes, and in the soft enclosed, the warm waning light of June, various benign contemplative worthies sat at disburdened tables and, while they smoked long black weeds, enjoyed us under those probable workings of subtlety with which we invest so many quite unimaginably blank (I dare say) Italian simplicities. The charm was, as always in Italy, in the tone and the air and the happy hazard of things, which made any positive pretensions or claimed importance a comparative trifling question ... We lay at ease in the bosom of the past, we practised intimacy, an intimacy so much greater than the mere accidental and ostensible: the difficulty for the right and grateful expression of which makes the old, the familiar tax on the luxury of loving Italy.

Of course one can exaggerate this cosy glow, and it isn't the whole of the story or of the picture: misery, frustration, unscrupulousness and cruelty exist in Italy. But James (who was not, after all, the simplest of men emotionally) was here responding to something which other visitors, less tenuous and less self-examining, have found equally winsome, indeed seductive. Even Ruskin and Lawrence, both of whom separately wrote of 'detesting' the Italians (Ruskin for their 'vociferation', Lawrence for their 'parrot phrases'), could not be indifferent to them; and both of them, despite these fits of exasperation, lived happily for long periods in the place.

There is a continuity in Italy – in the place and in the people – which is remarkable. W. H. Auden, in his preface to the English translation of Goethe's *Italian Journey*, comments on the similarity between Goethe's pre-French Revolution Italy and the country today: 'Is there any other country in Europe where the character of the people seems to have been so little affected by political and technological change?' Churches emerge from the foundations of pagan temples; a religious festival – say of a local saint's day in a town square – seems to take on the characteristics of its predecessors; rows of vines and terraces of olives establish a landscape that has been much the same for six or seven centuries; the beaked prows of fishing boats, with their simple yet not wholly utilitarian shapes, suggest the craft of the fishermen's remote ancestors. Even the faces of men and women suddenly take on an ancient cast, glimpsed in a Renaissance painting or in the portrait busts of judges, matrons, poets and emperors in the Capitoline Museum. (It is a shock to come out of the museum, having seen the dissolute young face of Heliogabalus, and then to find his counterpart strolling down the Via Veneto.) 'Turn but a stone and start a wing ...'. A modern Italian historian, Giuliano Procacci, has written that

> Italy is a land in which everything, from the shape of the fields to the quality and preparation of food, from the types of cultivation to the road system, from the cerebral refinement of the learned to the learned ignorance of the simple, combines to give its inhabitants the sense of an uninterrupted, persistent continuity of work and effort ...

Some might argue that it has been the fate of Italy, since the end of the Roman Empire, to have been on show to the world – coveted for its antiquity, its art, its natural beauty – without ever having had a powerful place in the world's affairs: its one excursion towards such a position, during the twenty years of Fascism, was a disaster. Such an argument, though, must take small account of the ways in which the human imagination is most deeply stirred. Leaving aside all consideration of its political and military leaders (among whom Napoleon, at least ancestrally, must be considered one), a country that has given us Dante, Francis of Assisi, Thomas Aquinas, Galileo, Marconi, Leonardo da Vinci, Michelangelo,

Giotto, Botticelli, Piero della Francesca, Raphael, Monteverdi, Vivaldi, Verdi – to take little more than a dozen of the scores of names that leap immediately to mind – can hardly be said not to have made its mark. And behind these names lies the whole Roman legacy, the presence of which is palpable everywhere in Italy and throughout the minds of Europe and beyond. The traveller in Italy, however, does not need to be reassured by the rhetoric of these proper names. Goethe expressed his rapt devotion not only in his *Journey* but, more concentratedly, in a few lines of a lyric – 'Kennst du das Land wo die Citronen blühen . . .'. And it was Stendhal who perhaps best summed up the appeal of this impossibly rich and complex country: 'The charm of Italy', he wrote, 'is akin to that of being in love'.

Virgil's hymn to his native land

Not the Medean groves or Ganges' streams
Or those of Lydia can equal Italy.
Afghanistan, or India, or far
Arabian isles with incense-breathing sands
Are not its peer. Its black soil did not sprout
With dragon's teeth, to raise a warrior crop,
But luscious fruit and vines from the Campagna
Poured from our fields, cattle and oil
Here found their place in Italy's rich lands . . .
Here Spring gives way to Summer endlessly,
Our flocks bear twice a year, and twice the tree
Offers its apples . . .
See where our cities mount upon the hills,
And rivers flowing by their ancient walls.
Seas on each side, and lakes within – the great
Como, and Garda with its sea-like waves . . .
Our land is full of copper, silver, gold,
And heroes too – Marsians, Sabines, tough
Tribes from the West and tribes of Volscians
Skilled with the spear – and noble families,
Camillus, Decius, Marius, Scipio,
And of them all the chief, Octavius Caesar,
Victor in farthest Asia and our shield
Stalwart upon our native Roman hills.
Hail to thee, land of Saturn, motherland!
For thee I dedicate my art, my verse,
And sing old Hesiod's song through Roman towns.

Virgil, 'Georgics' II, c. 30 BC
translated by Anthony Thwaite

BOOK ONE

SICILY AND THE ISLANDS

Some ancient writers deliver, that Sicilia was in times past conjoined to Italy, but afterwards became an island in this manner. The continent where it was narrowest being continually beaten upon by the violence of the sea on either side, the raging billows in tract of time broke into the earth and so made a way for the water to pass quite through it . . . Others affirm, that the continent being rent asunder by an earthquake, the sea by that means got a footing between both parts thereof. But the poet Hesiod is of another opinion, for he saith that Orion raised up in the open sea that promontory which is near to the mountain of Pelorus, and on it built a temple to Neptune, at this day exceedingly honoured by the inhabitants thereabout. After the finishing of which work he went into Euboea, where he obtained an immortal name, and for the fame that went of him was numbered amongst the stars.

Diodorus Siculus, 1st century BC, translated by H. C., Gent, 1653

39 Looking across the Strait of Messina from Pellaro in Calabria to Sicily. Near the mouth of the Strait are Scylla and Charybdis, the treacherous rock and whirlpool dreaded by Greek and Roman mariners.

53

Sicily and the islands

Most travellers, in the present as well as in the past, begin their Italian journey in the north. To the Germans, the French, the English, the gateway to Italy is the Alps. But by origin the point of entry can as significantly be seen to be through the southern extremities – Sicily, Sardinia, the Campanian coast. These areas still share more, in their landscapes and climate, with Greece and with North Africa than they do with the heartland of Italy. The Bronze Age of the nuraghi is stamped on the face of Sardinia in a way that is true of no prehistoric remains on the Italian peninsula. Sicily is like a triangle severed from Greece while hot, sharing something too with the Greek colonies of eastern North Africa. *Magna Graecia* is no mere historical term for these ancient segments of Italy's southernmost outposts. When Rome was no more than a group of forested hills above the Tiber, Greek colonists had built the temples of Akragas (Agrigento), Segesta, Selinunte, and cities that were vigorous and civilized, the distant but faithful manifestations of Corinth and Crete.

But Sicily, Sardinia, and the smaller islands too (Capri, Procida, Ischia, the Aeolian islands) all mark something else as well: the historical advance and retreat of invading and occupying cultures, so that each shows the tidal remains of a succession of influences. Each is a palimpsest, a scrawled-over map of history, an assembly of layers and juxtapositions rich both in heritage and in confusion. There is no such thing as a specifically Sicilian culture and little of a Sardinian one, but an accretion and amalgam of diverse cultures: the early immigrant Sicels in both Sicily and Sardinia, Phoenicians, Greeks, Carthaginians, Romans, Vandals, Byzantines and Saracens, Normans and Angevins, Spaniards and Austrians. Gateway and crossroads, pawn and prize – such metaphors grope towards defining these beautiful but also recalcitrant and forbidding islands.

Staying in Palermo on his journey through Sicily, Goethe wrote on 13 April 1787: 'Italy without Sicily cannot be understood; Sicily is the key to everything'. Here is an archetypal landscape of rugged and inhospitable mountains (including the huge, graceful, yet still sullenly flaring sweep of Etna) contrasted with those gentler regions that inspired Theocritus and the whole pastoral tradition. But the Greek settlers who built their cities there mainly favoured the middle ground and lived on high but not unfriendly plateaus and ridges, away from the malarial plains and valleys. The idea of the acropolis, transplanted from Greece,

Detail of bronze doors, Monreale Cathedral, Sicily

seems to foreshadow those later hilltop clusters of Tuscany, just as the Sicilian Greek 'tyrants' (such as Timoleon, Dion, Hieron II of Syracuse) seem early ancestors of the princes and dukes of the medieval and Renaissance city-states. And is there a single such prince or duke who, on the mainland, created anything as magnificent, cosmopolitan and enlightened as Roger II did, centuries before, in his court at Palermo?

Yet Sicily's position in the heart of the Mediterranean, a stepping-stone between Africa and Europe, made it a disputed battleground: not a place where one would expect a continuity of culture but a setting for abrupt ends and equally abrupt new starts. The life of the ordinary Sicilian over the centuries has characteristically been one of defence against invasion, days of rural poverty and serfdom, sickness and misery. Out of this common ground great monuments have risen; some of them – such as the serene temple at Segesta, beautifully isolated and open to the sky – seem to belong indisputably to the landscapes in which they are set. But in a sense every building, every work of art, in Sicily is a fresh beginning, and has been born from a struggle.

Conquest and exploitation have thus marked Sicily's history. What has been exploited is a rich agriculture. Sheep and, even more, horses have been notably raised on the island since very early times: the prancing horses on the superb Sicilian coinage are not merely numismatic emblems. Sicily, together with such North African provinces as Numidia, was the granary of Rome. Vines, olives and honey-bees provided much produce for the Roman Empire. So the bloody struggles in antiquity between Carthaginians and Greeks, and then Carthaginians and Romans, were not over a territory of doubtful value – as was so with Sardinia – but a real economic prize.

This particular non-European invader dominates almost three centuries. The great commercial ambitions of Carthage looked across the Mediterranean enviously to Sicily. Carthage had been founded on the North African coast more than a generation before the earliest Greek colonies were established on Sicily, and the island seemed ripe for conquest, split as it was between the separate dictators of Gela, Syracuse, Agrigento, and so forth. In the same year (480 BC) that the Spartans and Athenians put a stop to the Persian advance towards the heartland of Greece at Thermopylae and Salamis, a Carthaginian fleet under Hamilcar crossed the sea with an army of over 100,000, swept into Sicily through their own Cartha-ginian outpost of Panormus (modern Palermo), and besieged the city of Himera on the north coast. But the Greeks, though with smaller forces, had more cunning tactics, destroyed the Carthaginian ships drawn up on the beach, and took thous-ands of prisoners. Almost seventy years later, however, another Carthaginian army had better success, and conquered most of Sicily, leaving only Syracuse – which itself had defeated the notoriously disastrous Athenian expedition only a few years earlier. By the beginning of the fourth century BC, the heyday of Greek Sicily was over.

What the Greeks achieved on the island can be seen splendidly but mutely, in the ruins of Segesta, Selinunte, Agrigento and Taormina: mutely because so much of the Greek inheritance is bound up with famous men who lived, sometimes temporarily, on the island – Plato, recruited as an ornament of Dionysius's intellectual court at Syracuse; Empedocles, poet, philosopher, doctor, musician and engineer, who was born at Agrigento; from the same city, Archimedes the geometer, whose '*Eureka!*' has earned him a place in the vocabularies even of those many people who know nothing of the suddenly discovered principle which made him exclaim the word; and Pindar in his Odes celebrated the richness, beauty and skill of these cities and their inhabitants. They had no real political unity, except to repel a common invader; indeed they were fiercely parochial in all matters of political standing. But they provided a stimulating and congenial milieu for poets, philosophers, scientists and artists of many sorts. All this, as well as the noble temples and theatres, is the inheritance of Greek Sicily.

Roman Sicily's story is more depressingly one of war, pillage, insurrection and exploitation. Twice the Carthaginian outposts and their allies were put down, during the two Punic wars; there were risings of slaves; the governor Verres ground down the people with taxation – and as a result was brought to trial and became the subject of one of Cicero's most famous speeches; Sextus Pompey rebelled against the central government of Octavian, and was crushed. Yet at the same time its beginnings as a holiday centre can be seen. Sicily, according to Cicero, was Rome's 'suburban retreat', there were mineral baths at Sciacca, hotels on the slopes of Etna, and professional guides doing a busy trade with tourists at Syracuse. The magnificent theatre at Taormina as we see it is at least as much a creation of the Romans as of the Greeks, with its great natural backdrop of Etna and the sea. Much later, at the end of the third century AD, the luxurious country house of Piazza Armerina, with mosaics which are the finest domestic examples in the whole of the Roman Empire, is a sign of the opulence that was still possible on the island after all the exigencies that preceded it.

Among the many succeeding invasions, those of the Saracens and the Normans were the strangest; the second drove out the first, but – wittingly or not – adapted their own severer northern styles and mingled them with the Muslim richnesses, so that what we see in Palermo is a unique blend. After the Byzantine stagnancy, the Saracens had brought all the skills – and the tolerance – of Arab civilization in its golden period; irrigated terraces, cotton, citrus fruit, date palms, and the papyrus that still densely fringes the banks of the Ciane River near Syracuse. In the middle of the tenth century, there were over three hundred mosques in Palermo; there were parks, gardens, orange-groves, fountains. It was one of the biggest cities in Islam, and probably the most pleasant. And even after it was besieged and conquered by the Normans in 1071–72, the new rulers followed a regime of tolerance, order and peace that extended its enlightenment for another century. Roger II's palace at Palermo, and in particular its Palatine Chapel, is the finest palpable monument to this period, blending Arab and Norman in a way that seems to go deeper than superficial architectural style. Not far away, the Duomo of William II at Monreale takes the process a stage further, with its contrasts between gold and marble, polychrome and serene white. The loss of Sicily haunted the Arab mind for centuries: to those who had known it, it was a golden land, the Great Good Place. As the Arab poet Iqbal put it:

O Sicily you are the glory of the ocean . . .
You were the cradle of this nation's culture,
Whose fire like beauty burnt the world.

Yet what grew from it was something even finer, a centre of excellence and humanity, based on the solid practicalities of Roger II's rule, which was an inspiration to the rest of Europe.

Nothing comparable could follow it. Yet when the Angevin kings conquered Sicily in the thirteenth century (a short-lived episode, culminating in the massacre of the French known as the Sicilian Vespers), and in their turn were succeeded by rulers from Aragon and Castile, Sicily continued to show an eclecticism, a chameleon-like ability to absorb styles of art without losing its own character. The seventeenth- and eighteenth-century villas of Bagheria, poised above the sea, are the florid and sometimes grotesque survivors of late Spanish rule, a show of suburban wealth that often transcends the vulgarity of its origins and is elevated to a specially-labelled style of its own: Sicilian Baroque. And when the island was united with Naples and became part of an independent kingdom under the Bourbons, such fancifulness and extravagance took a new direction from the new rulers, with elements of whimsical *chinoiserie* and the like that rival the roughly contemporary caprices of the Prince Regent at Brighton.

Yet how far all this seems from the toughness and resilience of Sicily and the other islands: a toughness and resilience that is symbolised in the native rock – the black, glassy, volcanic obsidian – of the neighbouring islets of Lipari, Vulcano, Stromboli and the rest. Valued throughout prehistory as a material for finely polished tools, it is indigenous and enduring. The Aeolian islands are the solid, craggy remnants of volcanic eruptions, and however much they have been developed in recent years into holiday places – particularly Lipari – they, like Sicily, keep their ancient and uningratiating character.

This is even more true of Sardinia, which has been called the hermit of Italy. Long a penal settlement and a place of malarial exile, its modern emergence as an escapist tourist resort along the Costa Esmeralda is frail-rooted. Its ruined nuraghi (about 6,500 of them scattered all over the island, particularly towards the west) seem its natural, though mysterious, emblems. Massive, conical, sometimes with complex outworks, they have a strength that impressively survives even their frequent part-dismantlement: they have long been a source of ready-dressed stone. Built between about 1300–500 BC, there is nothing quite like them anywhere else in the world. These reddish-brown fortified houses, gaunt and silent towers, stand like beacons on the scorched plateaus. They have the strange and remote presence of the bronze figurines of the same period – beckoning warriors, horned and helmeted, or men poised with bows and arrows, or a mother and child, the mother's right hand lifted in prayer.

What followed the nuraghic people was a number of Phoenician trading settlements (such as at Nora, south-west of Cagliari, and Tharros, on Capo San Marco), and then widespread penetration and settlement by the Carthaginians right across the western half of the country. But – as ever – the Carthaginians left little to look at. It must have been them that D. H. Lawrence had in mind when, setting out for his irritable, comic, captivating tour round the island, he wrote: 'Sardinia, which has no history, no date, no race, no offering'. The slate has been rubbed almost clean. More surprisingly, the Romans too made scant lasting impact; the amphitheatre at Cagliari is the most impressive survivor. For both Carthaginians and Romans, Sardinia was a gaol-farm, an estate run by prisoners and slaves: what Cary has called 'settlements of the Botany Bay type'. And thereafter raids and sporadic occupation by Vandals, Pisans, Aragonese – a debased version of what happened to Sicily, with none of the high and surprising peaks that mark Sicilian history.

It is one of the ironies of the economics of modern travel that these islands are probably better known today by foreign tourists (particularly by chilly northerners seeking the sun) than many parts of mainland Italy. For Capri and Ischia, this has been rediscovery rather than an entirely new enterprise: in ancient times, too, they were the holiday resorts of the rich, and celebrated as such. Indeed, they have never had a significant life of their own. But Sicily, though it was loved by cultivated Romans of the late Republic and early Empire as a pleasantly archaic place, full of Greek statues and a people speaking mellifluous Greek, has for centuries had a different image – an island inhabited by small, dark, part-Arab folk, wretched in their poverty, fierce in their family and clan loyalties, and given to feuds and internecine brotherhoods. Even now, the past bears down on the present in Sicily, sometimes in ways that seem merely decorative and charming: the Opera dei Pupi in Palermo, for example – a tiny theatre in which the ancient exploits of the Knights of France against the Saracens are enacted by abruptly jerking and jingling puppets, with naivety but without self-consciousness. Watching these theatrical simplicities, one might be patronising – until one thinks of the remoteness of the events they celebrate, and the fact that they are still part of the island's consciousness, glimpsed in Arab tower and Norman fortress.

Certainly the survival of traditional dress, dances, handicrafts – the obvious outward manifestations of the islands' special history and tastes – has been helped by the arrival of tourists eager for souvenirs for the camera and for the shelf. But one need not go far from the favourite holiday centres in Sicily and Sardinia to find such things surviving without subsidy or applause. A goatboy will still be wandering across the hillside with his flock, playing his pipes among myrtles and mimosas, just as Theocritus memorialised him centuries ago. Even older is what Lawrence fancied he saw in the eyes of Sardinians: 'eyes of soft, blank darkness, all velvet, with no imp looking out of them. And they strike a stranger, older note: before the soul became self-conscious: before the mentality of Greece appeared in the world'.

The landscapes and buildings and people of the islands have qualities found nowhere else in Italy, and nowhere else is there a stronger feeling of antiquity: Lawrence wasn't being only fanciful or tendentious. In their hills, the poet feels both inspired and separate – perhaps inspired *because* separate:

> How marvellous to make art
> Out of stringing such things together!

Sea, ruins, limestone, bees,
Such emptiness, set apart
From the neat urbanities,
Under such a sky, in such weather . . .

The goat-bells come closer now,
And a man is rounding them up:
The only man here but me.
Well, anyway, that was how
It seemed for a moment. Now stop
Believing you're really free

Or would want to live here if you were.
The notes are just notes. The art
Is the art of what you can say.
The goatherd gives a long stare.
I say, 'Buon giorno', and start
Back down the track, away.

At the mouth of the Strait of Messina that lies between Sicily and the south-western tip of the Italian mainland are the rock of Scylla and the whirlpool of Charybdis: the sixheaded sea-monster, ravenous for ships, and the sucking, man-devouring female hurled into the sea for stealing the cattle of Hercules. That they exist more powerfully in the imagination than in geographical fact is what one should expect from the magic of art, for their reality is that of Homer's and Virgil's remembered poetry. But the separateness of Sicily and the other islands *is* plain fact, however it came about; and of this Virgil has something to say too. He must have stood on the north-eastern tip of Sicily (the ancient Pelorus, the modern Punte del Faro):

Once, so they say, these two were a single land:
And then came a spasm which split them and tore them apart
(Thus do the ages bring violent flux to the earth),
And the sea rushed in with a shout and divided them both –
Italy-Sicily – cutting their coasts away,
The sea splitting their cities and fields with a strait.

This strait and narrow seas, however easily spanned today by steamer and hydro-foil, have determined both the strengths and the limitations of the Italian islands: fierce pride dominated by a succession of ruthless outsiders.

*Interior of atrium, Temple of Concord,
Agrigento, Sicily*

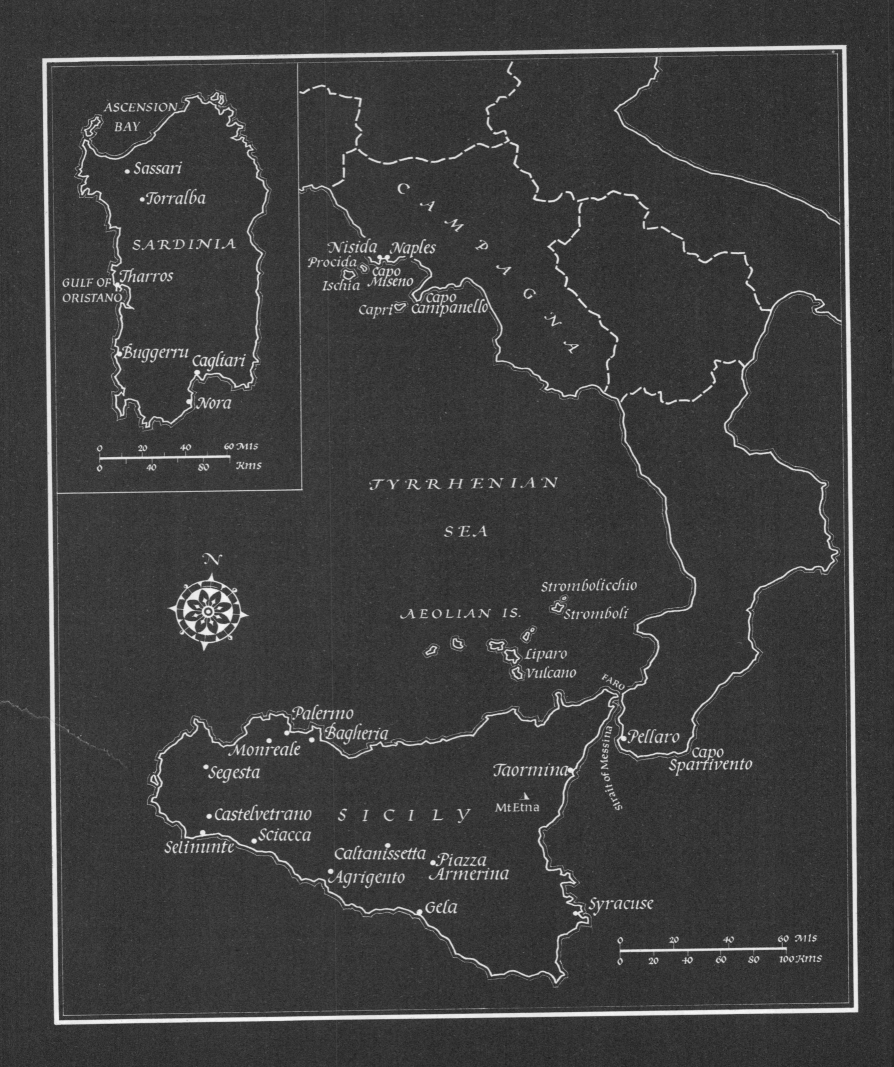

ASCENSION BAY

• Sassari

• Torralba

SARDINIA

GULF OF
ORISTANO   • Tharros

• Buggerru   Cagliari
                 •

              • Nora

0   20   40   60 Mls
0   40   80   Kms

CAMPAGNA

Nisida Naples
Procida • Capo
Ischia   Miseno
         Capri • Capo
                   Campanello

TYRRHENIAN

SEA

N

Strombolicchio

AEOLIAN IS.   • Stromboli

          Liparo
          Vulcano

                              FARO

Palermo
Bagheria   Strait of Messina   • Pellaro

Monreale   Capo
• Segesta   Taormina   Spartivento

• Castelvetrano   SICILY
   • Sciacca   ▲ Mt Etna
Selinunte

        Caltanissetta • Piazza
                         Armerina
        • Agrigento

                • Gela   • Syracuse

0   20   40   60 Mls
0   20   40   60   80   100 Kms

40 The Greco-Roman theatre at Taormina, Sicily, originally built by Greek colonists in the third century BC, later altered by the Romans. Behind the ruined scena rises the snow-covered peak of Etna.

41 Agrigento, one of the richest and most beautiful of the Greek cities of Sicily. In the foreground is the Temple of Olympian Zeus; behind it that of Hercules.

42 The Temple of Hera, Agrigento, fifth century BC, at the extreme east end of the temple area.

43 The Temple of Concord, Agrigento, fifth century BC. Its fine state of preservation is due to the fact that it was used as a church in the Middle Ages.

44 Sheep grazing on the hill-side near the lonely, unfinished Temple of Segesta, Sicily, sole survivor of a once great city.

45 Shepherds still tend their sheep in a way hardly different from those of classical times.

46 Islands in the Bay of Naples: Nisida (now joined to the mainland by a causeway), Procida and Ischia.

47 Seats in the theatre at Segesta, looking out across the hills to the distant sea.

48 Venus Anadyomene – 'Venus rising from the water' – in the National Museum, Syracuse: a second-century BC Roman copy of an original by Praxiteles.

49 Papyrus growing near the Fountain of Cyane, Syracuse, the only place in Europe where this North African plant grows naturally.

50 The Temple of Segesta, Sicily, late fifth century BC, one of the grandest and most mysterious of Doric temples.

51 Outer wall of the theatre at Taormina. This part of the theatre, as the use of brick and of the round arch demonstrate, belongs to the Roman period.

52, 53 Mosaics from the villa at Piazza Armerina, Sicily, among the masterpieces of Roman art.

Hunters corner a boar, kill it and carry it off on a pole.

54 Two giant figures, representing Tunisian prisoners, the work of Gaspare Lo Guercio in 1668, from the Porta Nuova, Palermo.

55 Palermo Cathedral, the south-east corner. Begun in 1169, the building is a mixture of Norman, Islamic and Gothic styles; the clock tower on the right was added in 1840.

56 The ruined staircase of the once splendid Palazzo Bonagia, Palermo, destroyed by bombing in the Second World War.

57 Animal heads from the fountain of the Piazza Pretoria, Palermo, erected in Florence in 1555 and moved to Sicily eighteen years later.

58 Capri and Punto Campanella, from the slopes of Mount Costanzo, a setting for luxurious relaxation since the days of the Emperor Augustus.

59 The Faraglioni – three great rocks, one with a natural arch through which boats can pass – off the Punta Tragara at the south-eastern tip of Capri.

60 Strombolicchio, one of the Aeolian Islands, which once served as a stronghold.

61 Part of the village on Stromboli, now practically abandoned in the face of the still active volcano.

62 Lemon-pickers: two brothers, gardeners at La Mortella, on the Isle of Ischia, residence of the composer Sir William Walton.

63 The Nuraghe Sant'Antine, Sardinia – one of the thousands of prehistoric conical huts, built of unmortared stone, which are peculiar to Sardinia.

64, 65 Young man and woman dressed for the Ascension Day festivities at Sassari, Sardinia.

66 Melons in the market of Buggerru, Sardinia.

67 Nave and apse of Monreale Cathedral, showing the great apsidal mosaic of Christ Panto-

crator above the Virgin and Child, saints and apostles.

68 Mosaic showing Christ with angels, prophets and Evangelists, in the dome of La Martorana, Palermo, a Norman church dating from 1143.

69 The nave of Monreale Cathedral; mosaics between the windows depict the story of the Fall; beneath them the Sacrifice of Isaac and scenes from the life of Joseph.

70 Mosaic figures of St Mercury and St George, Eastern soldier-saints, in the Cathedral of Monreale, last and most splendid of the Norman cathedrals of Sicily; begun in 1174 under William II.

71 The Santissima Trinità, Delia, near Castelvetrano, Sicily, a small .church built by the Normans on a Byzantine plan in the late twelfth century.

72 The mirrored ballroom of the Villa Palagonia at Bagheria, Sicily, added by the eccentric Prince Ferdinando Francesco Gravina about 1746.

73 Sicilian Baroque at its most extravagant: stucco decoration of the oratory of S. Zita, Palermo, by Giacomo Serpotta.

74 Baptismal font of 1610 in the sixteenth-century Chiesa Madre, Castelvetrano, Sicily.

75 The Chinese Palazzina, built in 1799 as a hunting lodge for the Bourbon monarchs of Naples and Sicily; it stands in the park of La Favorita, Palermo, and was designed by Venanzio Marvuglia.

76 The ceiling of the king's bedchamber in the Chinese Palazzina, painted with delicate *chinoiserie* scenes.

77 Part of the inlaid marble altar frontal in the church of St Agata, Caltanissetta, Sicily, a work commissioned by the Jesuits in the mid-eighteenth century.

78 A seventeenth-century Baroque side altar in the church of S. Giuseppe dei Teatini, Palermo, with marble carved to a lace-like delicacy.

Goethe at the theatre, Taormina

Whatever shape it may have had originally, Art has assisted Nature to build this semicircle which held the amphitheatre audience . . . If one sits down where the topmost spectators sat, one has to admit that no audience in any other theatre ever beheld such a view. Citadels stand perched on higher cliffs to the right; down below lies the town . . . Straight ahead one sees the long ridge of Etna, to the left the coast line as far as Catania or even Syracuse, and the whole panorama is capped by the huge, fuming, fiery mountain, the look of which, tempered by distance and atmosphere, is, however, more friendly than forbidding.

May 7th 1787 : Italian Journey,
translated by W. H. Auden and Elizabeth Mayer

Etna

A haven is there, sheltered from every wind,
Ample and calm – but Etna erupts close by,
Over and over hurling its smoke at the sky,
Fuliginous billows splattered with white-hot cinders,
Firing its salvos of flame to the furthest stars . . .
Thus, when Enceladus turns from the pain at his side,
Sicily quakes and rumbles, the smoke like a tent.
That night we hid in the forest, fearing these furies,
Unable to see what caused the terrible noise;
The stars were all quenched, no light shone down from the sky,
There was only a thick fog that covered the heavens
And clouds muffling the moon deep in the night.

Virgil, Aeneid, Book III, 30–19 BC
translated by Anthony Thwaite

FOLD OUT ▷

Ciane

Over what lands and what oceans the goddess wandered
It would take long to tell. When everywhere else had been searched in,
To Sicily she returned, and at last came towards the Ciane.
The nymph would have told her all, but she was changed into water,
And so, though she wished to speak, she lacked both lips and a language.
Still, with what powers she had the nymph produced her evidence,
Showing – what the mother knew well – there on the sacred waters
Persephone's girdle floating, just where it chanced to have fallen.
Seeing it, knowing at once her daughter indeed had been stolen,
Straight from her unkempt hair the goddess tore out great handfuls,
Beat on her breasts with her fists, over and over again.
Ignorant where her child was, she called all lands ungrateful,
But Sicily above all, where she had found these traces.
So with an angry hand she broke in pieces the ploughshares,
Destroyed both farmers and cattle, called on the fields to be traitors,
Blighted the seed in the furrow. Sicily, famous and fertile,
Languished, fertile no longer: crops never came to the harvest,
Blasted with too much heat or rotten with heavy torrents;
Baleful the stars and the winds, ravenous the birds for the seedlings;
Grasses and tares and thistles choking the miserable wheat.

Ovid (43 BC–AD 17), Metamorphoses, Book V, translated by Anthony Thwaite

Pleasures of island solitude

Sad though I am at my old friend going away,
Yet I approve his choice of living by empty Cumae
Where he will be the Sibyl's solitary neighbour.
The place is next door to Baiae, fine sands and pleasant seclusion.
Better Procida's rock than the stinking noisy Subura!

Juvenal (AD 60–140), Satire III,
translated by Anthony Thwaite

Agrigentum

Acragas, high on its steeps and its walls spread wide,
Loomed in the distance, once breeder of marvellous horses.

Virgil, Aeneid, Book III, 30–19 BC.
translated by Anthony Thwaite

Goethe at Agrigentum

I swear that I have never in my whole life enjoyed such a vision of spring as I did at sunrise this morning. The new Agrigento stands on the site of the ancient citadel, which covers an area large enough to house a city. From our windows we look down over a wide, gentle slope, now entirely covered with gardens and vineyards, so that one would never guess this was once a densely populated urban quarter. All one can see rising out of this green and flowering area is the Temple of Concord near its southern edge and the scanty ruins of the Temple of Juno to the east. All the other sacred ruins, which lie along a straight line between these two points, are invisible from this height. At the foot of the slope, looking south, lies the shore plain, which extends for about two miles till it reaches the sea . . .

It is easy to imagine what a stupendous sight the rising tiers of Agrigento must have looked from the sea . . . The slender architecture of the Temple of Concord, which has withstood so many centuries, already conforms more nearly to our standard of beauty and harmony than the style which preceded it – compared to Paestum, it is like the image of a god as opposed to the image of a giant.

April 25th 1787 : Italian Journey, translated by W. H. Auden and Elizabeth Mayer

Goethe at Segesta

The site of the temple is remarkable. Standing on an isolated hill at the head of a long, wide valley and surrounded by cliffs, it towers over a vast landscape, but, extensive as the view is, only a small corner of the sea is visible. The countryside broods in a melancholy fertility; it is cultivated but with scarcely a sign of human habitation. The tops of the flowering thistles were alive with butterflies; wild fennel, its last year's growth now withered, stood eight or nine feet high and in such profusion and apparent order that one might have taken it for a nursery garden. The wind howled around the columns as though they were a forest, and birds of prey wheeled, screaming, above the empty shell.

April 20th 1787 : Italian Journey, translated by W. H. Auden and Elizabeth Mayer

'Street in Agrigentum'

There a wind endures that I remember
burning in the manes of horses, slanting
in races across the plains, a wind
that stains the sandstone, wears away the heart
of mournful columns, thrown down on the grass.
Antique soul, grey with rancour, you go back
to join that wind, breathing the delicate moss
covering the giants who have fallen from heaven.
How solitary you are
within the space still left to you! And all the more
you grieve to hear the sound that moves far off,
a breadth of sound that moves towards the sea
where Hesperus already touches dawn:
the mouth-organ now quivers at the lips
of the waggoner as he climbs
up the hill made clean by the moon,
slowly among the murmuring saracen olives.

Salvatore Quasimodo (1901–1968), translated by Anthony Thwaite

Goethe's arrival in Palermo

I cannot begin to describe the way in which this Queen of the Islands has received us – with mulberry trees in their freshest green, evergreen oleanders, hedges of lemon trees . . . In a public garden I saw great beds of ranunculi and anemones. The air is mild, warm and fragrant. Furthermore, the full moon rose over a promontory and was reflected in the sea, and all this after being tossed by the waves for four days and nights!

April 3rd 1787 : Italian Journey
translated by W. H. Auden and Elizabeth Mayer

Goethe, sailing towards Sicily from Naples

Daybreak found us between Ischia and Capri and about a mile from the latter, as the sun rose magnificently behind the crags of Capri and Cape Minerva . . . By about four in the afternoon we lost sight of Vesuvius, but Cape Minerva and Ischia were still visible. As evening drew near, they too disappeared. The sun sank into the sea accompanied by clouds and a streak of purple light a mile long . . . Now there was no more land to be seen, the horizon was a circle of water and the night sky was lit up by the moon.

March 30th 1787 : Italian Journey,
translated by W. H. Auden and Elizabeth Mayer

Leaving Sicily for Sardinia

Strangely large in mass and bulk Monte Pellegrino looks: and bare, like a Sahara in heaven: and old-looking. These coasts of Sicily are very imposing, terrific, fortifying the interior. And again one gets the feeling that age has worn them bare: as if old, old civilisations had worn away and exhausted the soil, leaving a terrifying blank-ness of rock, as at Syracuse in plateaus, and here in great mass.

D. H. Lawrence : Sea and Sardinia, 1923

The Aeolian Islands

Between the Sicilian coast and the island of Lipari
Another island soars up, expelling smoke from its bastions.
Deep in its rock is a vast volcanic cavern
Hollowed out by Cyclopean fires; and there you may hear
The ringing of anvils, the roaring of molten metal,
And a hot pulse of flame that steadily beats from the furnace.
This is the place of Vulcan, the isle of Vulcano.

Virgil, Aeneid, Book VIII, 30–19 BC
translated by Anthony Thwaite

'Islands'

Your islands appear,
they rise little by little
or blaze out with one blow,
the clear-cut profile,
the archipelago,
lands open to sun, to mists,
founded on nothing,
fearful of a single breath,
with so much life left behind,
such a sea crossed, recrossed.

Bartolo Cattafi (b. 1922),
translated by Anthony Thwaite

64

65

Two Arab poets on the loss of Sicily to the Normans

Weep as you will your tears of blood,
O grave of Arab civilisation.
Once this place was alive with the people of the desert,
And the ocean was a playground for their boats . . .
O Sicily you are the glory of the ocean . . .
You were the cradle of this nation's culture,
Whose fire like beauty burnt the world . . .
Tell me your pains, I too am immersed in pain,
I am the dust of that caravan of which you were the destination.
Fill the colours in the pictures of the past and show them to me;
Make me sad by telling the tales of past days.

Iqbal, 'Bang-i Dara':
translated by G. D. Gaur

O Sea! You conceal beyond your further shores a veritable
Paradise. In my own country I knew only joy, never misfortune.

There, in the dawn of my life, I saw the sun in his glory. Now,
in exile and in tears, I witness his decline . . .

O that I could embark on the crescent moon, fly to the shores of
Sicily and there crush myself against the breast of the sun!

Ibn Hamdis, refugee from Syracuse:
translated by John Julius Norwich

'They were going to a ball'

The ballroom was all golden; smoothed on cornices, stippled on door-frames, damascened pale, almost silvery, over darker gold on door panels and on the shutters which covered and annulled the windows, conferring on the room the look of some superb jewel-case shut off from an unworthy world.

Giuseppe di Lampedusa, 'The Leopard', 1958, Chapter VI,
translated by Archibald Colquhoun

Nelson to Lord Hobart: December 22nd, 1803

God knows, if we could possess one Island, Sardinia, we should want neither Malta, nor any other: this which is the finest Island in the Mediterranean, possesses Harbours fit for Arsenals, and of a capacity to hold our Navy, within 24 hours' sail of Toulon. Bays to ride our Fleets in, and to watch both Italy and Toulon, no fleet could pass to the Eastward between Sicily and the Coast of Barbary, nor through the Faro of Messina: Malta, in point of position, is not to be named the same year with Sardinia . . . And, my Lord, I venture to predict, that if we do not – from delicacy, or commiseration of the lot of the unfortunate King of Sardinia – the French will get possession of the island. Sardinia is very little known. It was the policy of Piedmont to keep it in the background, and whoever it has belonged to, it seems to have been their maxim to rule the inhabitants with severity, in loading its produce with such duties as prevented the growth . . . The country is fruitful beyond idea, and abounds in cattle and sheep – and would in corn, wine and oil. In the hands of a liberal Government, and freed from the dread of the Barbary States, there is no telling what its produce would not amount to. It is worth any money to obtain, and I pledge my existence it could be held for as little as Malta in its establishment, and produce a large revenue.

BOOK TWO

APULIA BASILICATA CALABRIA CAMPAGNA

O my Lord Jesus Christ, two graces do I pray Thee to grant unto me ere I die: the first that while I live I may feel in my body and in my soul, so far as is possible, that sorrow, sweet Lord, that Thou didst suffer in the hour of Thy bitterest Passion; the second is that I may feel in my heart, so far as may be possible, that exceeding love wherewith, O Son of God, Thou wast enkindled to endure willingly for us sinners agony so great.

St Francis's prayer before receiving the stigmata, 1224, from 'The Little Flowers of St Francis', Part II

79 Simple wayside Calvary near Roccamandolfi, province of Campobasso; on the cross are the instruments of the Passion, the naive work of the village carpenter.

Apulia, Basilicata, Calabria, Campagna

SOUTHERN ITALY, that part of it romanticized as a place of eternal sunshine, everlasting mid-day – the Mezzogiorno – is also as accurately seen as a place of degradation, of the stagnation of antiquity. The Sibyl at Cumae was one of the most potent presences of ancient times: yet Petronius, writing some time towards the middle of the first century A D, makes Trimalchio in the *Satyricon* say: 'I actually saw the Sibyl at Cumae with my own eyes. She was hanging in a bottle, and when the boys asked her in Greek, "What do you want, Sibyl", she replied, also in Greek, "I want to die".'

Cumae, the temples and labyrinths of which Virgil ascribed to Daedalus, the genius who had constructed the Cnossos labyrinth, was close to oblivion by the time of the *Aeneid*. Juvenal called it a ghost town, its ruined sanctuaries already eight centuries old. Its Greekness was as strange and foreign to these Roman poets as the Great Wall of China. What had begun as a place for the inspired and primitive practices of ritual, part of that cult of the irrational which is as much a part of the Greek spirit as the lucidities of Greek science and speculation, had become a goal for gaping tourists almost two thousand years ago.

For centuries southern Italy has seemed a distinct and separate place even to other Italians. The frontier of the Southern Kingdom at Torre del Epitafia is one of the oldest in Europe, and though of course it has not been an actual frontier since the unification of 1860, the differences of mind and character that it marks are still real ones. As much as Sicily and Sardinia, but without the obvious explanation of literal isolation, Campania, Calabria and Apulia have tenaciously (sometimes with miserable stubbornness) kept their special qualities: grandeur and sluttishness, conspicuous wealth in the middle of wretched poverty, a devotion to ease and pleasure in a setting cruel sometimes to the merest subsistence. If *dolce far niente* is the motto of the South, it has more often been said with resignation than sung with joy.

Yet these disapproving negatives, which may be simply the residue of a northern puritan work-ethic, don't by any means wholly catch the spirit and flavour of the Italian South. Even if one excludes as wholly Greek, and therefore exotic, such monuments as the magnificent Doric temples of Paestum (so well preserved because for centuries the malarial mosquito effectively prevented anyone living in the area and robbing the buildings for stone), there are still those thoroughly

Monumental gate-fountain near the quayside, Naples

Roman flies-in-amber, the engulfed and then revealed cities of Pompeii and Herculaneum; the great castles of the Normans and Angevins, such as the Castel del Monte and the Castel Nuovo; the superb Byzantine Cattolica at Stilo; and from the later Spanish and Bourbon periods, it is enough simply to point at the extraordinary palace of Caserta, outside Naples – the largest palace in Italy (unless one counts the Vatican), and a rival to Versailles. All these, so various and so distinct, are as much a part of the South as the beggars, the exploitation, the lassitude and the dirt.

These southern lands were by nature munificent. Campania in particular was prodigiously fertile, with a volcanic soil rich in minerals and retentive of moisture even during drought. For the Romans, its vineyards produced some of their favourite wines: Falernian, Sorrentine, Vesuvian. Cicero called it 'the most beautiful estate of the Roman people', and in his *De Lege Agraria* passionately argued against it being split up into separate smallholdings: 'the source of your wealth, an adornment in peacetime, a support in war, the basis of your revenues, the granary of your legions, the relief of your grain supply – will you allow all this to perish?' It was one of Virgil's favourite landscapes, and his own supposed epitaph celebrates his resting-place in 'Parthenope', a traditional name for the area round Naples:

> Mantua gave me birth, Calabria snatched me away:
> Now Parthenope holds me, who sang of fields, flocks, wars.

And it was Virgil more than anyone else who tried to keep alive the mysterious and legendary past symbolized in the megalithic recesses of Cumae.

There were practical uses too, apart from the agricultural wealth. At Cape Misenum and Poteoli (modern Pozzuoli) were great Roman naval bases. Capua was a busy centre for the manufacture of bronze weapons, carpets and tapestries: Virgil called it 'the greatest and richest city in Italy'. And the visitor today to Pompeii and Herculaneum is aware, even in their silent and dusty vistas, of the busy-ness and bustle of streets, shops and market-places.

Vesuvius, thirty miles in circumference and rising to a height of over 4,000 feet, dominates the Bay of Naples; Goethe called it 'a peak of Hell rising out of Paradise', and ascribed to its influence the characteristic resignation of the area:

> The Terrible beside the Beautiful, the Beautiful beside the Terrible, cancel one another out and produce a feeling of indifference. The Neapolitan would certainly be a different creature if he did not feel himself wedged between God and the Devil.

The eruption of August AD 79 quickly became one of the great historic moments of destruction, comparable in its effect on the imagination to the Lisbon earthquake or the bombing of Hiroshima. Pliny's account memorializes it; but countless travellers since have been equally struck by what survived the deluge. Even Stendhal, less eager for antiquities than many before and since, was moved to write in April 1817:

> The strangest sight I saw in all my wanderings has been Pompeii. Here the traveller may feel himself transported bodily into the realms of antiquity; and

he whose mind is trained, however ill, to believe naught but what is plain and proven, may discover in a flash more solid truth than the most ingenious of scholars. There is indescribable pleasure to be had from meeting face to face with this self-same antiquity, concerning which one has read such countless volumes.

Close by, Naples itself lies on the edge of its astonishing bay within sight of Vesuvius. Originally a Greek colony ('new city'), neither its Greek nor its Roman periods have left much behind. Conquered by Goths and Byzantines, it achieved its modern character under the Normans and the Hohenstaufen Emperor Frederick II and his Angevin successors, such as Charles I of Anjou, who made it the capital of the Kingdom of the South; but, even more, under the two centuries of Spanish (Aragonese) rule, followed by the Bourbon Kingdom of the Two Sicilies, to which we owe Caserta. Seen now from the main Rome–Naples road, Caserta seems an incongruous giant dumped down in a broad plain, encroached upon by farms, houses and small factories. But in its size and lavishness it represents the Golden Age of the Neapolitan South, a time when Naples rivalled Rome in wealth, power and certainly in enlightenment. But it could not last, and from there the road was only downhill, through the notorious 'King Bomba' (whom Gladstone saw as a ruler under whom 'the negation of God is erected into a system of government'), to the squalor, poverty and violence that disgusted outsiders – Italians as well as foreigners – see today.

A more peaceful and smiling southern Italy is apparent along the bays of Sorrento and Salerno. Here, though it is difficult to imagine today, Amalfi was a great maritime republic, a rival to Genoa and Pisa in its eastern ventures. The churches of the Amalfi coast still have something of the exotic glitter of mosques about them, and the Arab world never feels very far away: the splendid bronze doors of the Cathedral of Sant'Andrea in Amalfi were commissioned by the head of the Amalfitan colony in Constantinople, and were manufactured there some time before 1066 by a Syrian. The Norman-Saracenic style dominates the little hilltop town of Ravello close by, itself ruled independently for over seven centuries: here the Palazzo Rufolo and the Villa Cimbrone have a special quality of strangeness in their tropical gardens, and indeed the Rufolo became the famous inspiration of Wagner's magic garden of Klingsor in the second act of *Parsifal*. The juxtaposition (rather than blend) of styles and objects in these favoured great houses, high above the clear blue bay, is an illustration in miniature of the eclecticism that, as much in Sicily and Sardinia, marks southern Italian art and architecture. Dominated by successive waves of foreigners (not always conquering ones: the Villa Cimbrone as we know it was the product of a peaceful English peer and his cultivated if eccentric valet), churches, houses and towns are a patchwork of modes and manners.

Under and beside all this imported wealth and beauty is the southern peasant, working his terraces and vineyards, herding his sheep and goats. He cultivates, and has cultivated for centuries, a fruitful field. Goethe, always the practical man where plants and their growth were concerned, wrote: 'Here the soil produces everything, and one can expect from three to five harvests a year. In a really good year, I am told, they can grow maize three times in the same fields'. And of Naples itself, his stolidity was even moved to say: 'Naples is a paradise; everyone lives in a state of intoxicated self-forgetfulness, myself included. I seem to be a completely different person whom I hardly recognise. Yesterday I thought to myself: Either you were mad before, or you are mad now.' But the peasants of the Campanian fields and the street-folk of Naples have always had a more stringent life, naturally, than the foreigners who have observed them. The English poet Samuel Rogers, staying in Naples in February 1815, among all the delights he recorded in the city, noted laconically in his Journal on 25 February: 'A dead Lazzarone found on the staircase of an English Lady here one morning'.

The three southernmost areas – Apulia, Basilicata and Calabria – are the spur, heel, instep and toe of the familiar Italian 'boot': they range from the dry limestone plains of the Apulian shepherds to the steep Lucanian mountains and the thick Calabrian forests inland. These are the least known and poorest provinces of Italy, but here too there are striking remnants of a more glorious past; and in Apulia the great aqueduct has begun to bring back the prosperity the place once knew. These are chiefly known as the regions of the Emperor Frederick II and his son Manfred; but earlier, on the bank of the river Ofanto, was fought one of the most celebrated battles of antiquity: Cannae, where Hannibal's armies slaughtered 60,000 Romans. And there are the great cathedrals of Troia and Trani, with blended elements of Saracen and that Pisan Romanesque style which is quite distinct from both the Germanic Gothic of the Italian north and the French Gothic of the Neapolitan churches. Finally, deep down on the heel, are the golden lime-stone Baroque buildings of Lecce – a Baroque that is entirely its own, the product of two architects in particular, Zimbalo and Cino, who here created a style that can perhaps be called intrinsically southern Italian.

No famous tourists of the past noted these regions or places: no Goethe or Ruskin, no Shelley or Byron, wrote of them in their journals or memorialized them in their poems. We have to look much further back to find much mention of them – to Virgil, for example, who himself died at Brundisium (modern Brindisi), and who described the fierce watersnakes of Calabria in a vivid passage in his *Georgics*:

> Take note of that wicked watersnake who in Calabrian woods
> Journeys swiftly erect, with a scaly back,
> A lean underbelly, and spotted with blotches all over.
> While rivers are rushing along, while the earth is all wet,
> In springtime he lives in ponds and by river-banks, keen
> To feast off fishes and frogs for ever and ever.
> But when the marshes are dry and the sun bakes the soil
> He hurries to land, furious his fiery eyes,
> Darts through the fields, wild with his thirst and the heat.
> May I never sleep out of doors or lie in the grass
> Where he has cast off his skin and is sallying forth
> Renewed in his vigour, leaving his young ones behind;
> Stiff in the sun he moves, his tongue flicking out.

But it would be wrong to take this as a mark of ancient dislike of the whole area. As Gilbert Highet has said, in Virgil's time 'Tarentum, now little more than a naval base, was a beauty spot as renowned and almost as exotic as Rio de Janeiro'; and Horace in one of his Epistles contrasted 'peaceful Tarentum' with the noise and bustle of 'imperial Rome'. Yet succeeding generations, right down until very recent times, have seen the extreme southern mainland as mighty, savage and isolated landscapes. It will not be easy for new schemes of land reclamation, land reform, new roads, hydro-electric plants and the like to shift these older images: Virgil's watersnake is truer to the modern picture even now.

Indeed, despite the beauty and interest that can be found in some of these southern outposts, it is inevitably to Naples and its environs that one returns: 'See Naples and die' has become a hoary and perhaps meaningless old tag, and to approach it today through its proliferating, grimy, cluttered outskirts is a depressing experience. But nothing can change its position beside its astonishing bay, nor can anything compete with the roar, the babble, the smell, the sheer sense of resilient life, which one is bathed in and subjected to in its narrow streets and sprawling buildings. Away from all that, there are the marvellous collections in its National Museum – not just the treasures accumulated in the Farnese collection (such as the Titians and the ancient sculptures) and the long years of scavenging from Pompeii and Herculaneum, but also the magnificent excavated pottery found in tombs all over southern Italy – possibly the finest collection of Greek pottery in the world, a fit illustration in a single art-form that this was indeed *Magna Graecia*.

These Greek vases are the frail relics of a vanished culture. Elsewhere, on both a large scale and a small one, the past asserts itself, from the huge, naked stone octagon of Frederick's Castel del Monte to the fairy-tale conical *trulli* within sight of it on that Apulian plateau: both of them are emblematic of the resilience of both prince and peasant, close to the rock, the earth, the found objects of antiquity – that primal world celebrated by recent writers as well as by the classics, by outsiders such as Norman Douglas as well as by natives such as Andrea Giovene, whose two volumes of *The Book of Giuliano Sansevero* are an idyll on a lost world, a primitive, poverty-stricken society of olives, ancient tombs, ancient loyalties, suffused with the spirit of a church that has accommodated pagan, pre-Christian elements in its colours, festivities and rituals. Despite the encroachments of the modern world, it is still a place where (in Auden's 'Good-bye to the Mezzogiorno') the sun's

> unwinking
> Outrageous eye laughs to scorn any notion
> Of change or escape, and a silent
> Ex-volcano, without a stream or a bird,
> Echoes that laugh.

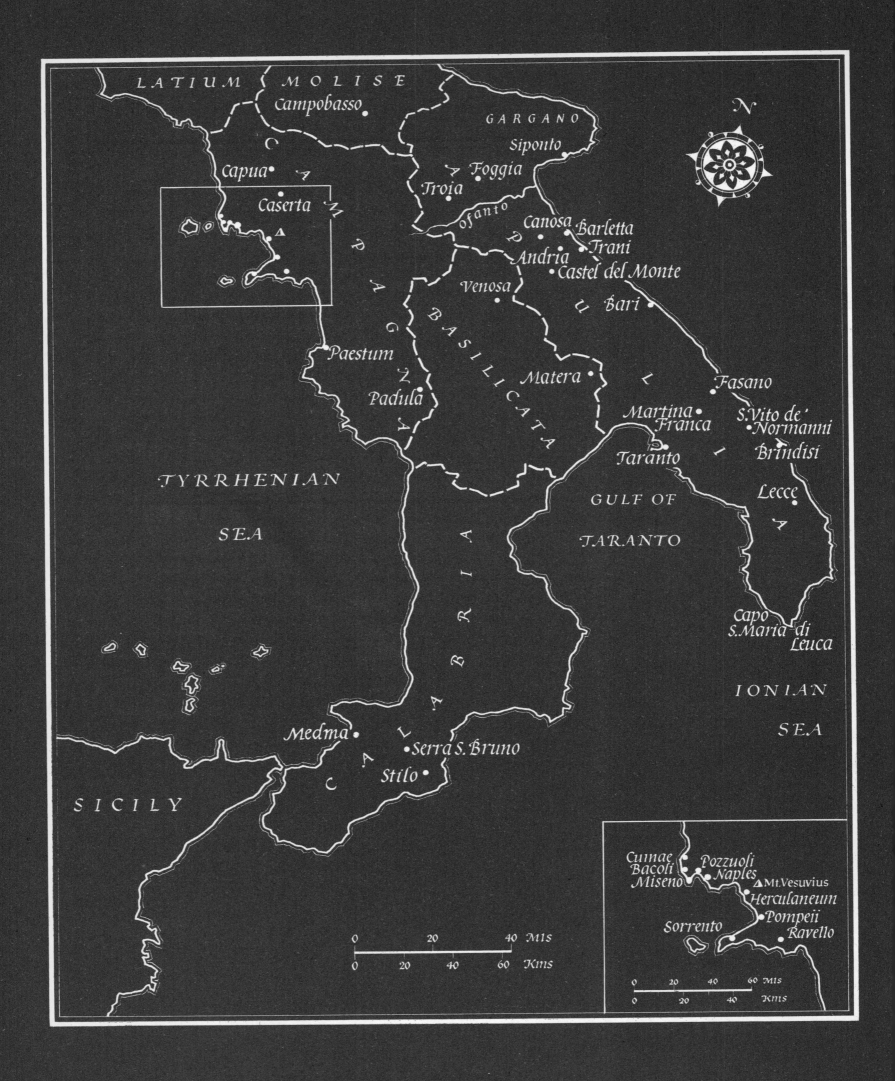

Pliny on Campania

In what terms to describe the coast of Campania taken by itself, with its blissful and heavenly loveliness, so as to manifest that there is one region where Nature has been at work in her joyous mood! And then again all that invigorating healthfulness all the year round, the climate so temperate, the plains so fertile, the hills so sunny, the glades so secure, the groves so shady! Such wealth of various forests, the breezes from so many mountains, the great fertility of its corn and vines and olives, the glorious fleeces of its sheep, the sturdy necks of its bulls, the many lakes, the rich supply of rivers and springs flowing over all its surface, its many seas and harbours, and the bosom of its lands offering on all sides a welcome to commerce, the country itself eagerly running out into the seas, as it were, to aid mankind.

'Natural History', Book III, chapter 5, 1st century AD

Samuel Rogers by the Tyrrhenian Sea

How many suns have risen from behind the mountains, & set in the Tyrrhene sea, throwing these gigantic shadows aslant the green and briary floor! since in these temples gods were worshipped – Is it true that they remained buried for ages in the night of woods, till a young painter or a shepherd fell in with them? Now the sea-breeze, & the mountain-breeze sweep thro' them – Now the fisherman of Salerno as he passes, sees them standing on the desert plain under the mountains, & pilgrims visit them from the corners of the earth, & the little towns that hang upon the mountains like an eagle's eyrie look down always upon them . . .

March 4th 1815, 'Italian Journal'

FOLD OUT ▷

CARLO III

GIOACCHINO MURAT

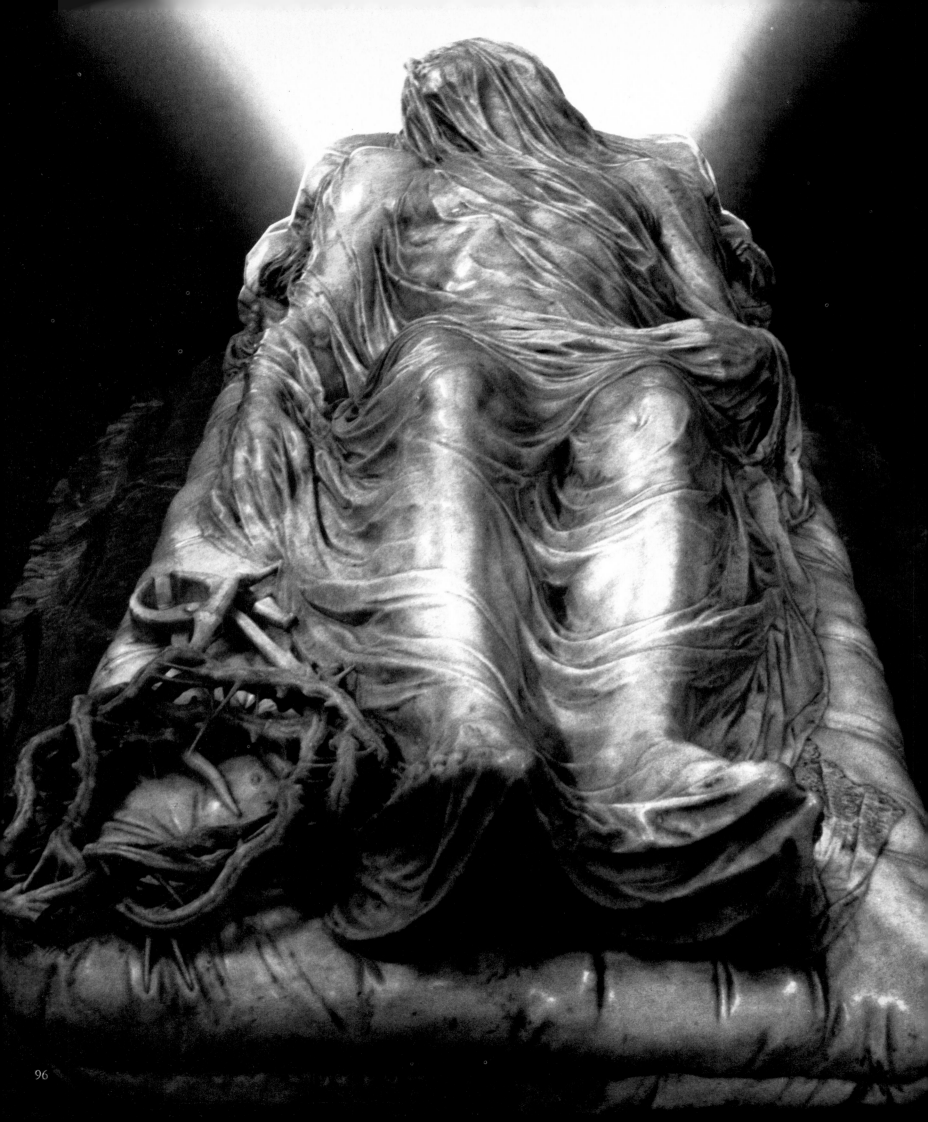

Chateaubriand on the Bay of Naples

Every morning, as soon as day began to break, I would go to an arcade that extended along the shore. The sun rose in front of me over Vesuvius; it illumined with its tenderest flames the hills of Salerno, the azure sea dotted with white sails of the fishermen . . . Flowers and fruit moist with dew are not as suave or as fresh as the Neapolitan landscape emerging from the shadows of night . . . Some climates perhaps are dangerous to virtue from their extreme voluptuousness. And is not that what the ingenious myth means, in which it is related that Parthenope was built over a siren's grave?

from 'Les Martyres', 1809

Virgil on Cumae

When you have reached it safely, this city of Cumae,
And mysterious Avernus whose waters are deep in a wood,
There you will find a prophetess who from her cave
Spells out your destiny, writing the words on leaves.
She arranges them all in recesses, methodical, left
In scrupulous order – but if the door opened, allowing
A breeze to run riot among them, she never would deign
To seize the blown leaves and restore them. Therefore those men
Who come to consult the Sibyl detest her abode
And go away ignorant of what they came to discover.
But the delays, the impatience of friends, the fair wind
Propitious for journeys, the urge to depart – none of these
Should distract you from begging the Sibyl's advice. You must hope
That at last she will speak of your future, rapt and inspired.

Virgil, 'Aeneid' Book III, 30–19 BC
translated by Anthony Thwaite

George Gissing on the burial of Alaric the Goth at Cosenza

Do the rivers Busento and Crati still keep the secret of that 'royal sepulchre, adorned with the splendid spoils and trophies of Rome'? It seems improbable that the grave was ever disturbed; to this day there exists somewhere near Cosenza a treasure-house more alluring than any pictured in Arabian tale. It is not easy to conjecture what 'spoils and trophies' the Goths buried with their king; if they sacrificed masses of precious metal, then perchance there still lies in the river-bed some portion of that golden statue of *Virtus*, which the Romans melted down to eke out the ransom claimed by Alaric. The year 410 AD was no unfitting moment to break into bullion the figure personifying Manly Worth. 'After that', says an old historian, 'all bravery and honour perished out of Rome'.

from 'By the Ionian Sea', 1901

Shelley on Naples

Naples! thou heart of men which ever pantest
Naked, beneath the lidless eyes of heaven!
Elysian City, which to calm enchantest
The mutinous air and sea: they round thee, even
As sleep round Love, are driven!
Metropolis of a ruined Paradise . . .

from 'Ode to Naples', 1820

Goethe in Naples

I won't say another word about the beauties of the city and its situation, which have been described and praised so often. As they say here, *'Vedi Napoli e poi muor !'* – See Naples and die! One can't blame the Neapolitan for never wanting to leave his city, nor its poets singing the praises of its situation in lofty hyperboles: it would still be wonderful even if a few more Vesuviuses were to rise in the neighbourhood.

March 3rd 1787: 'Italian Journey',
translated by W. H. Auden and Elizabeth Mayer

I have forgotten to tell you about another characteristic of the Neapolitans, their love of creches, or *presepe*, which, at Christmas, can be seen in all their churches. These consist of groups of large, sumptuous figures representing the adoration of the shepherds, the angels and the three Magi. In this gay Naples the representation has climbed up on to the flat roof tops. A light framework, like a hut, is decorated with trees and evergreen shrubs. In it the Mother of God, the Infant and all the others stand or float, dressed up most gorgeously in a wardrobe on which the family spends a large sum. The background – Vesuvius and all the surrounding countryside – gives the whole thing an incomparable majesty.

May 27th 1787: 'Italian Journey',
translated by W. H. Auden and Elizabeth Mayer

Goethe at Paestum

In the distance appeared some huge quadrilateral masses, and when we finally reached them, we were at first uncertain whether we were driving through rocks or ruins. Then we recognised what they where, the remains of temples, monuments to a once glorious city . . . At first sight they excited nothing but stupefaction. I found myself in a world which was completely strange to me . . . But in less than an hour I found myself reconciled to them and even thanking my guardian angel for having allowed me to see these well-preserved remains with my own eyes.

March 23rd 1787: 'Italian Journey',
translated by W. H. Auden and Elizabeth Mayer

Stendhal in Naples

And so here we are at last, snugly established in the Palazzo degli Studi; step out of the door, turn left, and there before you lies the via di Toledo – one of the principal goals of all my journey, the busiest, most joyous thoroughfare in the entire universe. Yet would you believe it? For five mortal hours we trudged from inn to inn, vainly imploring shelter; there must be fully two or three thousand English tourists in the place; and when I finally ferreted out a lodging, it proved to be an eyrie perched up seven flights of stairs. Yet, for all its disadvantages, it faces the San-Carlo, and I can look out over Vesuvius and the sea.

February 9th 1815: from 'Rome, Naples and Florence'

Stendhal at Caserta . . .

I have just ridden thirty miles, and all to no purpose. Caserta is no better than a barracks set in a landscape as unpromising as that of Versailles. Because of the danger of earthquakes, all the walls of the palace are built five foot thick; in consequence – as at St Peter's – the apartments stay warm in winter and cool in summer. Murat attempted to complete this edifice: the paintings which adorn it are even drearier than those of Paris, but the general scheme is more grandiose.

April 5th 1815: from 'Rome, Naples and Florence'

and Goethe, with another view of Caserta

The new castle is a palace worthy of a king, a huge quadrilateral building like the Escorial with a number of inner courtyards. Its location is extraordinarily beautiful – upon one of the most fertile plains in the world with a park extending to the feet of the mountains. From the latter an aqueduct carries a whole river to supply the castle and surrounding countryside with water. This can be released to hurl itself over some artificially arranged rocks in a stupendous cascade. The gardens are beautifully laid out and in perfect harmony with a region that is itself a garden.

March 14th 1787: 'Italian Journey',
translated by W. H. Auden and Elizabeth Mayer

Shelley on Pompeii

I stood within the city disinterred;
And heard the autumnal leaves like light footfalls
Of spirits passing through the streets; and heard
The mountain's slumberous voice at intervals
Thrill through those roofless halls . . .

from 'Ode to Naples', 1820

Leopardi on Vesuvius and the ruins of Pompeii

One thousand and eight hundred years have passed
since all the peopled places vanished, crushed
by flaming force, and yet the peasant, still
intent on nurturing a vine that's starved
in dead and ashen earth, is watchful still –
lifting his eyes high to the deadly peak
that's no more peaceful now than then,
still threatening himself, his kin, his goods
poor though they are.
                Poor wretch, sleepless all night
he lies upon the hovel's roof, again
starts up and watches the insidious course
of terrifying lava, pouring out
from fertile womb to sandy slopes, and shines
all round Capri and Naples port and on
Mergellina. If he should see it come,
or hear the water groaning in his well,
he'd wake his children, shake his wife from sleep,
and snatching up whatever he could find
flee – looking back at what was once his home,
his little field that kept famine away,
prey to the molten tide that, crackling, comes
and covers everything so lastingly.

Pompeii, obliterated, comes to light,
like an entombed skeleton that greed
or piety have dragged back to the air;
and from the empty forum, standing up
between smashed columns, the traveller may gaze
long at the forked peak and its fuming tip,
still threatening the ruins scattered round.

from 'The Broom' ('La ginestra'), 1836
translated by Anthony Thwaite

Samuel Rogers at Pompeii

As we looked down into the vintner's shop & on the jars inclosed in the counter cased with various bits of Marble, I thought I saw the man serving his customers – & as the shadows of evening came on, & standing alone, I looked up the street of tombs towards the city-gate, the strange silence & deserted air of the place almost overcame me . . . A single horseman was coming down the narrow street, & the hollow reverberation of his horse's hoofs made it still more dreary to the ear.

March 1st 1815, 'Italian Journal'

EGO SVM PR ALFA NOVI et A et O SIMS

LVC

QVATTVOR HI LEG VM PIA MVNDO IVSSA DEDRVNT · SVBIVGA PVEM XI NEDIT MAXR

BOOK THREE

ABRUZZI
LATIUM
MOLISE
UMBRIA

Rome is the great object of our pilgrimage . . . My temper is not very susceptible of enthusiasm, and the enthusiasm which I do not feel I have ever scorned to affect. But at the distance of twenty-five years I can neither forget nor express the strong emotions which agitated my mind as I first approached and entered the *eternal City*. After a sleepless night, I trod with a lofty step the ruins of the Forum; each memorable spot where Romulus *stood*, or Tully spoke, or Caesar fell, was at once present to my eye; and several days of intoxication were lost or enjoyed before I could descend to a cool and minute investigation.

Autobiography of Edward Gibbon, 1796

120 The Arch of Constantine, Rome; this majestic fourth-century arch has served as a model for triumphal arches throughout the world.

Abruzzi, Latium, Molise, Umbria

The ocean hath his chart, the stars their map,
And Knowledge spreads them on her ample lap;
But Rome is as the desert where we steer
Stumbling o'er recollections.

Thus Byron in *Childe Harold*; and the traveller knows what he meant. For almost 2,500 years Rome has been a city of importance, and its supreme position both as the centre of the Roman Empire and the seat of papal government is only a part of that importance. Yet it is a confusing place, not always ready to yield up its beauties or its secrets, and there is no authentic map or chart of the sort Byron was looking for. No city can have been more written about, and none more thoroughly buried under a silt of literature and comment.

Two areas in particular have the power of stirring the sort of 'recollections' Byron wrote of: the Capitol and the Forum. But each is distinct, not only in its ancient function but also in the way each represents a different kind of survival. The Capitoline Hill of the Romans had as its pride a huge temple built on Etruscan foundations, the Temple of Jupiter Optimus Maximus; today nothing remains of it above ground, and the design of the Piazza del Campidoglio as we see it is the work of Michelangelo in the sixteenth century. Yet the whole structure and lay-out are a Renaissance wax-impression of the classic past as they wanted to remember it, dominated at its centre by the equestrian statue of Marcus Aurelius, superbly vivid and commanding.

The Forum, on the other hand, is a wilderness of ruins hemmed in by later buildings and roads, a sunken garden of antiquities stragglingly isolated in the centre of Rome. Standing on the terrace behind the Senators' Palace on the Capitoline Hill, one looks towards the distant Arch of Titus and the Colosseum, and the slopes of six of the seven hills of ancient Rome: the Quirinal, Viminal, Esquiline, Palatine, Coelian and Aventine. And in between are the columns of temples and palaces, the triumphal arches of emperors, fallen masonry and marble. It is a confused and confusing sight, a grandiose reminder of glory and transience: 'sacred to eternity', maybe, as Shelley put it, but remorselessly separate from all the Romes that have followed.

Horse-tamer and obelisk, Quirinale, Rome

Claude, the not-quite-autobiographical 'hero' of Arthur Hugh Clough's *Amours de Voyage*, affected to be disappointed by what he saw in mid-nineteenth-century Rome:

All the foolish destructions, and all the sillier savings,
All the incongruous things of past incompatible ages,
Seem to be treasured up here to make fools of present and future . . .
Rome, believe me, my friend, is like its own Monte Testaceo,
Merely a marvellous mass of broken and castaway wine-pots . . .
'Brickwork I found thee, and marble I left thee!' their
                                        Emperor vaunted;
'Marble I thought thee, and brickwork I find thee!' the
                                        Tourist may answer.

Certainly the boast of Augustus seems belied by the dominance of brick almost wherever one finds traces of imperial Rome; but the fact is, of course, that much of the marble veneer clamped or cleated onto the ancient walls has been removed over the centuries and been reworked and re-used elsewhere. The sheer size, however fragmentary and detached from their intended use, of the Colosseum, the Baths of Caracalla, the basilica of Maxentius, compel the wonder, if not the admiration, of any traveller less jaundiced than Clough's Claude. And in two prominent monuments – the variously named Castel Sant'Angelo or Hadrian's Mausoleum, and the Pantheon – there is a sense of massive continuity unique among all remains of the ancient world.

What Hadrian intended as a burial place for the imperial family became fortress, papal refuge, papal palace, prison, barracks, and – eventually, and inevitably – a museum. Here the Borgias planned and plotted, and on the top of its great pillbox the archangel Michael, sheathing his sword, was reputedly seen by St Gregory in the year 590 – a vision that marked the end of an epidemic of plague and gave the place its alternative name. The Pantheon, like several other churches in Italy, is a consecrated Roman building; but it is unlike all the others in its state of preservation and its fidelity to its original structure. The immense vault, with its shaft through the cupola open to the sky, seems to trap the whispered echoes of the ages. Founded by Agrippa in the Augustan age, and today substantially as it was rebuilt by Hadrian in the second century A D, its grand simplicity and the fact of its survival as the most complete important building of the ancient world are equally moving.

Elsewhere, one sees history in strata or piecemeal, and continuity in the patchwork of changing uses and styles. 'Adapted', 'enlarged', 'renovated', 'restored' are key verbs in any Rome guide-book. One of the most surprising but also one of the most satisfying adaptations is the spacious ellipse of the Piazza Navona, its shape and space determined by the stadium of Domitian that preceded it, so that what we see now is a Renaissance and Baroque scheme of spaciousness and leisure imposed on an ancient one. Bernini's fountain of the rivers, plumb in the centre, itself includes a Roman obelisk imitating Egyptian work; and the children who always seem to throng the Piazza Navona hurtle about it as if in imitation of chariots.

Sometimes one literally steps down through receding ages, and the notion of the past being like layers piled on top of one another becomes actual. Such is the case at the church of St Clement, now the base of gentle and helpful Irish Dominicans. Here one moves down through the church itself, with its fine twelfth-century mosaics and its carved marble from six centuries before, and finds much earlier Roman walls, the walls of fourth-century basilica, first-century houses, and – oddest of all – a complete small Mithraic temple of the late second century, with its slaughtered bull in marble. And this is sixty or so feet below the present level, deep under a church that celebrates other sacrifices and other ritual meals. In the dark and dank chamber of the temple of Mithras, there is an almost oppressively heavy sense of the weight of Rome's tortuous and often bloody past.

Yet on the surface – and Rome is as much a city of surfaces as of depths – the place as we know it is modern; if by 'modern' we use the label as traditional historians do, and distinguish between 'ancient', 'medieval' and 'modern'. Bramante arrived in Rome in 1500, and he and his successors (such as Michelangelo and Vignola) superimposed a Neo-classic stamp, to be followed in its turn by the Baroque of Borromini and Bernini. These styles and their derivatives determined what we call Rome today. There are hundreds of more recent buildings, of course, but in an odd way they seem to have a more neutral impact than the jarring juxtaposition of old and new in many cities. Still, one makes a special exception for the monument to Victor Emmanuel, that brilliantly cold and almost absurd allegorical 'Altar of Italy', with its chariots leaping and rearing above the skyline from so many vantage points. It is so big, so white and so unlikely that it hardly seems real.

The palaces of Rome, on the other hand, however large they are (and some of them, such as the Rospigliosi, the Colonna and the Doria, are enormous), and whatever transmutations they have undergone since they were first built, are after all great houses and not great stunts. Some of them are now museums or galleries (such as the sumptuous Borghese), some are embassies or institutes, some (such as the Quirinal) are official residences, or government buildings (such as the Madama). Close to Rome are such princely villas as the Villa Lante and Caprarola, by the lake of Vico – late Renaissance masterpieces of formality and symmetry, with 'secret gardens', elegantly harnessed water, and an atmosphere of classic repose. They were built to impress, and indeed they succeed in this. Each has its own copious history, and a book could be devoted to each; many have been already. What they represent is something like 250 years (roughly, 1500–1750) of immensely wealthy princes, cardinals and popes, who lavished their wealth on architects and artists, and on gardens and collections of *objets d'arts* with which to surround and fill them.

The *ur*-version of all these, in scale and show if not in concept, lies outside Rome: Hadrian's Villa at Tivoli. Here the emperor wanted to create not only a great palace but an area which would show in reproduction the finest buildings of his whole empire. What began as an outdoor museum of full-size facsimiles became a quarry for antiquarian plunder, its statues and columns now scattered all over Italy, and indeed all over the world. It was the fad or fantasy of the most powerful man in the universe; it seems haunted by the presence of Antinous, the boy Hadrian loved; and now it is a garden of ruins – incomparable ruins, but still ruins.

Strangely, this obsession with collecting, with accumulating the treasures of a dominated world, seems reflected in a quite different way in the Vatican. Put in the balance in one scale the basilica of St Peter and in the other the collections of the Vatican museums and galleries, and which would weigh the heavier? From some of the finest productions of the Egyptian and Etruscan civilizations to some of the most famous pieces of Greek and Roman sculpture, and from the master-pieces of Raphael to Michelangelo's ceiling in the Sistine Chapel, the Vatican encompasses a whole history of culture – and of patronage – in itself. Its Library and archives are crammed with codices, incunabula, early copies of Virgil, letters written by Henry VIII, manuscript poems by Michelangelo and Petrarch. The approach to the City across the Piazza of St Peter, Bernini's majestic open entrance hall, is calculated to instil awe if not reverence (reverence is perhaps more proper in St John Lateran, 'the cathedral of Rome and the world'), and that emphasis is kept up within the great church itself, an amalgam of workmanship and funerary monuments that underline, if nothing else, the worldly achievement of the papacy.

But behind Rome and the Vatican and all their works is a hinterland just as profoundly Italian. To the north, the Etruscan tombs of Tarquinia hide beneath their small carapaces, among what Lawrence called 'the rough nothingness' of their hillside, the paintings of a civilization remote not only in time from the concerns of Augustus, Hadrian, Septimius Severus, Renaissance prince and Renaissance pope. The banquets, the hunting and fishing, the pleasure in sport and in music that these frescoes celebrate seem to embody a way of life closer to what the ordinary Italian has known for centuries. Distant they may be (and Lawrence set them up in opposition to what he saw as the dreariness of the Romans), but they still have a pervading sense of real lives being lived – and enjoyed.

The uplands and plateaux of the Molise and the high mountains of the Abruzzi run back from these coastal regions of Latium and Rome. But the traveller north is more likely to head into Umbria, to its cities of Orvieto, Spoleto and Perugia, and to Assisi. Orvieto too has its Etruscan necropolises, but – apart from its fine setting high above the valley – its real distinction is its Duomo, with its façade of many-coloured marble and mosaic and, most of all, its astonishing Signorelli frescoes of the Last Judgment; in them, a tortured sense of cruelty and a virile delight in the human form seem to strive for the upper hand, as malevolent and grimacing demons grapple with the damned, sometimes dive-bombing them gleefully like fiends from a twentieth-century horror comic. Coming out into the sun and the peacefulness of the buildings grouped round the Duomo square, it takes a few moments to disengage oneself from Signorelli's powerfully haunted and haunting images within.

Spoleto, partly ringed by its pre-Roman walls, has been seen as the type-case of a community that spans continuously the two and a half millennia of Italian history: Vellumbres, Etruscans, Romans (and, though they failed to conquer it, Hannibal's Carthaginians) knew it and left their traces behind. As a Lombard capital, it dominated central Italy. Today, it draws on the talents of the world for its summer theatre festival, in its incomparable setting at the foot of Monte Luco. Perugia, so much a living product of the late Middle Ages, also has earlier roots: the Roman inscription designating the town *'Augusta Perusia'* can still be seen over one of its gates, and the tiny circular church of S. Michele Arcangelo on its northern outskirts is at least as old as the sixth century AD. Indeed Perugia, busy and bustling though it is, was never designed for motor traffic, and it must be the most frustrating of all Italian cities to negotiate by car. Its towers, spires and castellations as delineated in Bonfigli's fifteenth-century fresco still seem astonishingly recognizable today, the spire of S. Giuliana in particular looming up in the picture's foreground. The Via dei Priori, dominated by the simple grandeur of its Palazzo dei Priori, sweeps into the Corso Vanucci with all the swaggering assurance of a thoroughfare that knows it was intended for pleasurable walking and not for busy wheels.

The wheels of tourists – more particularly, of pilgrims – spin eastward, in charabancs from all over the world, to Assisi. Yet exploited and self-exploiting though the place has been and is, it defies its commercializing and cheapening, and in an uncanny way asserts even now the spirit of the man who made it famous. The massive Basilica of St Francis stands like a fortress on its ridge by the town (Goethe referred to it disparagingly as 'a Babylonian tower'), witness of the speed with which St Francis became the centre of a cult; for within two years of his death his devoted follower, Brother Elias, and Pope Gregory IX had come together to found this memorial church. But it is within the Basilica, and more particularly in the Giotto frescoes in the upper church, that one has some sense of Francis's dignity, gentleness and simplicity; for example, in the familiar muted colours – browns, blues and greens – of that detail showing him preaching to the birds. Even more, the Hermitage at Carceri and the church of St Damian, both just outside Assisi, seem to combine the appropriate humility and mysticism.

They are qualities that one finds not only in these places of special religious association but throughout the landscapes of Umbria: qualities that pervade the Umbrian school of painters, such as Perugino and Pinturicchio, in whom what might be called the negative virtues of stillness and restraint are suffused with a deep spirituality. Todi's central piazza, with its austere Gothic buildings, and Gubbio's rising tiers of terraced towers and churches, are only two of the towns in this region that give one a strongly present sense of what an Umbrian city-state of the Middle Ages must have been like. They belong to their landscape, not assertively but as if by nature. Beyond them, to the north in Tuscany, are the more strongly willed and ambitious marks of man's discovery of himself in the Renaissance. Here in Umbria man seems to have made a pact with the terrain, adapting both it and himself in a common cause.

To the west, the province of the Abruzzi is harsher country, mountainous and thickly forested; and it is an odd irony that out of it came the most sophisticated, hedonistic and sensual of the Roman poets, Ovid: he was born at Sulmo, the modern Sulmona:

Sulmo is where I came from, a third of Paelignia.

173

Small, it is true, but healthy and running with brooks . . .
Perhaps a stranger, as he looked at the low city walls
Of Sulmo, so river-surrounded, so small in size,
Might think to himself: 'Yes, little indeed you are,
But from you a great poet came, and made you great'.

This is loyal and respectful boasting by the local boy who made good, for the Abruzzi could not hold such a one. Reputations were then, and are now, made in Rome. From Rome stemmed the whole concept of the City, the Eternal City, with all the weight of its political and spiritual force. Writers and artists might shudder at its noise and its machinations, but more often than not they depended on its patronage. Its name and fame have spread through two and a half millennia to people who have never known it, whose lands have never been part of its empire, and who have variously seen it as inspiration, template of the heavenly city, oppressor and ogre. Even in a land as regionally distinct and self-aware as Italy, Rome transcends all regions. All roads lead there, as the apophthegm has it; and whatever shadow it may seem to be of its past, the words of Ausonius are still resonant – 'First among cities, the home of the gods, is Rome the golden'.

Claudian on the greatness of Rome

A city greater than any upon earth, whose amplitude no eye can measure, whose beauty no imagination can picture, who raises a golden head amid the neighbouring stars and with her seven hills imitates the seven regions of heaven, mother of arms and of law, who extends her sway over all the earth and was the earliest cradle of justice, this is the city which, sprung from humble beginnings, has stretched to either pole, and from one small place extended its power so that upon it the sun never sets.

'De Consulatu Stilichonis', late 4th century AD

In the Campagna

The champaign with its endless fleece
    Of feathery grasses everywhere!
Silence and passion, joy and peace,
    An everlasting wash of air –
Rome's ghost since her decease.

Such life here, through such lengths of hours,
    Such miracles performed in play,
Such primal naked forms of flowers,
    Such letting nature have her way
While heaven looks from its towers!

from 'Two in the Campagna', Robert Browning, 1880

FOLD OUT ▷

123

Byron on the ruins of Rome

Oh Rome! my country! city of the soul!
The orphans of the heart must turn to thee,
Lone mother of dead empires! and control
In their shut breasts their petty misery.
What are our woes and sufferance? Come and see
The cypress, hear the owl, and plod your way
O'er steps of broken thrones and temples, Ye!
Whose agonies are evils of a day –
A world is at our feet as fragile as our clay.

The Niobe of nations! there she stands,
Childless and crownless, in her voiceless woe;
An empty urn within her wither'd hands,
Whose holy dust was scatter'd long ago;
The Scipios' tomb contains no ashes now;
The very sepulchres lie tenantless
Of their heroic dwellers: dost thou flow,
Old Tiber! through a marble wilderness?
Rise, with thy yellow waves, and mantle her distress.

The Goth, the Christian, Time, War, Flood, and Fire,
Have dealt upon the seven-hill'd city's pride;
She saw her glories star by star expire,
And up the steep barbarian monarchs ride,
Where the car climb'd the Capitol; far and wide
Temple and tower went down, nor left a site:
Chaos of ruins! who shall trace the void,
O'er the dim fragments cast a lunar light,
And say, 'here was, or is', where all is doubly night?

'Childe Harold's Pilgrimage', 1818, Canto IV, stanzas 78–80

Dickens on the Colosseum

To see it crumbling there, an inch a year; its walls and arches overgrown with green; its corridors open to the day; the long grass growing in its porches; . . . to see its Pit of Fight filled up with earth, and the peaceful Cross planted in the centre; to climb into its upper halls, and look down on ruin, ruin, ruin, all about it; . . . the temples of the old religion, fallen down and gone; is to see the ghost of old Rome.

'Pictures of Italy', 1846

Shelley on the Forum

The Forum is a plain in the midst of Rome, a kind of desert full of heaps of stone and pits; and though so near the habitations of men, is the most desolate place you can conceive. The ruins of temples stand in and around it, shattered columns and ranges of others complete, supporting cornices of exquisite workmanship, and vast vaults of shattered domes distinct with regular compartments, once filled with sculptures of ivory or brass. The temples of Jupiter, and Concord, and Peace, and the Sun, and the Moon, and Vesta, are all within a short distance of this spot. Behold the wrecks of what a great nation once dedicated to the abstractions of the mind! Rome is a city, as it were, of the dead, or rather of those who cannot die, and who survive the puny generations which inhabit and pass over the spot which they have made sacred to eternity . . . Wide wild fields are enclosed within it, and there are grassy lanes and copses winding among the ruins, and a great green hill, lonely and bare, which overhangs the Tiber. The gardens of the modern palaces are like wild woods of cedar, and cypress, and pine, and the neglected walks are overgrown with weeds . . .

Letter to Thomas Love Peacock, 1818

Goethe in Rome

As I rush about Rome looking at the major monuments, the immensity of the place has a quietening effect. In other places one has to search for the important points of interest; here they crowd in on one in profusion. Wherever you turn your eyes, every kind of vista, near and distant, confronts you – palaces, ruins, gardens, wildernesses, small houses, stables, triumphal arches, columns – all of them often so close together that they could be sketched on a single sheet of paper. One would need a thousand styluses to write with. What can one do here with a single pen? And then, in the evening, one feels exhausted after so much looking and admiring.

November 5th 1786: 'Italian Journey',
translated by W. H. Auden and Elizabeth Mayer

John Evelyn at St Peter's

I visited St Peter's, that most stupendious and incomparable Basilicum, far surpassing any now extant in the world, and perhaps, Solomon's temple excepted, any that was ever built. The largeness of the piazza before the portico is worth observing, because it affords a noble prospect of the Church . . .

Evelyn's Diary, 1644

Virgil on Rome

I, in my ignorance, used to think that Rome
Was like the market town to which the shepherds
Went with their lambs and kids to sell them there.
In this way I learned how dogs are like their puppies,
Goats like their kids, and all large things like small.
Rome lifts her head above all other cities,
High as the cypress above the trees it dwarfs.

Eclogues I, c. 37 BC
translated by Anthony Thwaite

Samuel Rogers in Rome

Of Antient Rome its roads & aqueducts, its walls & watchtowers, its seven hills,
its campagna, & the mountains that skirt it, the river that crosses it & the sea that
opens beyond it, still remain to us. Many of these things are not only unchanged
but unchangeable. The snow at this moment shines on Soracte, the Tiber winds
along from the Apennines to the Tyrrhene sea, & the sun still continues to rise
and set in the same places. What materials then are left for the Imagination to
work with!

December 11th 1814, 'Italian Journal'

Stendhal in the Sistine Chapel

I have just returned from the famous Sistine Chapel after hearing the Papal Mass,
for which I had managed to secure myself the best place available, on the right,
just behind Cardinal Consalvi; and I may now claim to have heard the celebrated
castrati of the Sistine choir. No, forsooth! Never did I, in all my days, endure so
daemonic a caterwauling! This was the most excruciating cacophony I have
encountered these ten years. During the whole space of two hours that the Mass
lasted, I spent full ninety minutes in unbelieving astonishment, feeling my pulse,
examining whether I were not sick of some disease, enquiring of my neighbours'
reactions. Unhappily, however, these neighbours of mine were English tourists –
folk for whom *fashion* is a most implacable master: they replied to my puzzlement
by quoting passages of Burney. My mind being fully made up concerning the
music, I found delight and compensation in the manly beauty of the ceiling and
in Michelangelo's *Last Judgment*; meanwhile I studied the features of divers
Cardinals.

August 1st 1817: from 'Rome, Naples and Florence'

Assisi

Assisi, in your deepest calm,
The soul, intent, has never slowed.
But in the mind and without harm
The Tescio burst and overflowed.

The parched white river twists with thirst,
Furious, and furious too the boughs
Of olive-trees that seem to burst
Like flames the twisting banks arouse.

The hot convulsions of the breath
Whitening into prayers at night
I saw come slowly freshening,

And Francis, tortured unto death
By devils lurid in the light,
Upon the rose thorns, racked and bleeding.

Gabriele D'Annunzio (1863–1938),
translated by Anthony Thwaite

Shepherds in the Abruzzi

September. Let us go: a time for going.
Now the Abruzzi shepherds leave their pens
And travel towards the sea, wild breakers blowing
Up from the Adriatic, green as those
Pastures upon the mountain, drinking thence
The chilly springs whose taste forever goes
Back to their native land, to quench their thirst
However far they go . . .

Gabriele D'Annunzio (from 'I pastori'),
translated by Anthony Thwaite

Byron on the poets of Latium

And near, Albano's scarce divided waves
Shine from a sister valley; – and afar
The Tiber winds, and the broad ocean laves
The Latian coast where sprung the Epic war,
'Arms and the Man,' whose re-ascending star
Rose o'er an empire . . . and where yon bar
Of girdling mountains intercepts the sight
The Sabine farm was till'd, the weary bard's delight.

'Childe Harold's Pilgrimage', 1818, Canto IV, Stanza 174

154

159

BOOK FOUR

EMILIA
TUSCANY
THE MARCHES

Nothing in this state is ill-proportioned, nothing improper, nothing incongruous, nothing left vague; everything occupies its proper place, which is not only clearly defined but also in the right relation to all the others.

Leonardo Bruni (1369–1444) on Florence, from 'Laudatio Florentinae Urbis'

159 *Madonna with Pomegranate*, 1406/08; a master-piece of the great Sienese sculptor Jacopo della Quercia (1374–1438), Museum of the Duomo, Ferrara.

Emilia, Tuscany, the Marches

WHILE ROME gave the Western world its order of government and its chief religion, Tuscany and its capital city, Florence, made an equally important bequest to Italy herself – the classical Italian language. Written Italian is derived from the dialect of Tuscany, and Italians from all parts of the country use it to this day in their writing, whatever they may speak at home. Tuscan emerged as the dominant regional dialect in the late Middle Ages: it was the language of poets and scholars such as Dante, Petrarch, Boccaccio, of philosophers and humanists such as Leon Battista Alberti, Leonardo Bruni and Pico della Mirandola, and it lived just as vitally in the down-to-earth words of the chronicler Villani, the gossipy anecdotes of Vasari's *Lives of the Artists*, and the *Autobiography* of Benvenuto Cellini. Later writers who were not Tuscan-born, Tasso and Ariosto among them, wrote in Tuscan; and by the end of the Renaissance it had become the official language of Italy.

This measured, liquid and realistic tongue is a true daughter of the city of Florence, the noblest of all city states since Periclean Athens. Only Venice, among the great cities of Italy, has kept as much of the physical presence of her former glory. Sitting in the hot green valley of the Arno like a magnificent cup in its saucer, the city manages to be both light and sombre, grandiose and human. Though its achievements lie in the distant past, Florence is not a ghost city, just as Tuscany is still a rich and working province. Here, in Florence itself, in Pisa nearby, in the small towns of the Casentino and Mugello, eastwards to Arezzo and north again to the lands of Romagna and the Marches – this was the birth-place of the Renaissance, and therefore of modern Europe as we know it.

It is still a countryside of small farms, vineyards, walled cities and steeply wooded hills. Tradition says that Florence was a Roman settlement, and the City of the Lily was always the most assiduous imitator of the ancient Roman virtues and Republican spirit. Chancellors of Florence asserted time and again in their writings and their speeches that the Florentine Commune was guided by the same principles that moved Cicero. In the dark days at the end of the fourteenth and beginning of the fifteenth century, Florence stood alone in defence of republican independence against the absolutism of the Viscontis in Milan. Of course, Florence had her patricians, and no more than Athens before her could she be described as a democracy in the modern sense; but whatever the excesses of the

Campanile and dome of Cathedral, Siena

popolo grasso, the *popolo minuto* counted, and even the Medici preferred to rule fifteenth-century Florence as influential private citizens, not dukes or lords.

It was this harking back to Rome, and ultimately to Greece, which led to the Renaissance itself. 'Rebirth' is an accurate term for the movement which was pioneered in Florence, since the great humanist theorists and scholars who inspired the artists of the *Quattrocento* were trying to bring back to life the classical world they loved so much. Many of the essential texts were not available to learned men as late as the end of the fourteenth century. One great Florentine, Poggio Bracciolini, discovered long-lost Latin manuscripts while on business for the Pope, and Cosimo de' Medici, *Il Vecchio*, kept the shop of Vespasiano da Bisticci continuously at work transcribing texts and commentaries. Yet there was nothing academic about this: they loved the past because they needed it. And all the while the practical energy of a great people was building a powerful and beautiful city, adorned with fine churches and works of art, but essentially a trading community using its wealth to make its own life richer and more rewarding.

Artists of Botticelli's and Michelangelo's generations owed much to the scholars and commentators who had preceded them, but these men in turn were the heirs of the practical discoverers who can claim as big a hand as any in the development of the Renaissance. Giotto revolutionized European art in the early years of the thirteenth century, and his and Brunelleschi's and Donatello's amazing achievements owed as much to their inborn genius and wonderful eye as they did to humanist theory. But the mark of Florence at this time was its tolerance – everyone could do his own thing, as the modern vernacular puts it. Donatello might be amused by Uccello's passion for perspective at its most impractical, but he would never have questioned Uccello's right to pursue it wherever it took him. For more than four centuries this mercantile city raised and attracted the most renowned body of great artists in the history of the world.

A large part of the art they produced is still in place in the city they beautified, due to the paternalism and tyranny of the later Medici. In 1530, the Florentine Republic died, when the Spanish troops of the Emperor Charles V entered the city. The Grand Dukes had their virtues, and even find some supporters among historians, but the only thing the modern lover of Florence can say in their favour, especially after wandering through the Pitti Palace or the later rooms of the Uffizi gallery, is that they protected Florence's incomparable heritage of art and finally bequeathed it to the state. Florence went to sleep at the end of the sixteenth century, but when she was awoken in the nineteenth – by Ruskin and Burckhardt, among others – it was with the same miraculous sense of her beauty intact which the Sleeping Beauty had.

To see great works of art *in situ* is incomparably more moving than to look at them collected into museums. Even in Florence, convenience and security have ordained that many pictures and pieces of sculpture should be moved from their original sites, but it is extraordinary how many have not. The smaller churches are especially rewarding – Ghirlandaio's frescoes of the life of St Francis in Santa Trinità; the fourteen groups of statues in niches of the walls of Orsanmichele, and Orcagna's tabernacle inside; Rossellino's and Desiderio's tombs of Bruni and

Carlo Marsuppini in Santa Croce; the Cardinal of Portugal's chapel in San Miniato, with Baldovinetti's Annunciation; a veritable *catalogue raisonné* of the life-work of Andrea del Castagno in the Cenacolo di Sant'Apollonia. The greatness of Florentine art is not just grounded in the life of the city but can be seen still to be there.

People coming to Florence for the first time are often surprised by its unrelenting aspect, its lack of the picturesque. So many of the buildings look like fortresses, which indeed they were. Even along the banks of the Arno, where the prevailing style for *palazzi* is less sombre, there is a shut-up look, an unwelcoming solidity perhaps addressed to the treacherous river which is always ready to overflow its banks. Florence had no natural defences, so it became a city built of the strongest stone, a fortress on an undefended plain.

Compare Florence's great rival, Siena. As one drives into this supremely beautiful city, one passes an enormous and repulsive fortress-arsenal built by Cosimo I, Grand Duke of Tuscany, to keep the rebellious Sienese in order. But Siena itself, perched high above the plain, is not made up of sombre town houses of the Florentine sort: it seems to have relied on its God-given defences. The Cathedral in Siena has no architectural wonder to recommend it, such as Brunelleschi's dome on Santa Maria del Fiore in Florence, but it is much more attractive. However, Siena lost the war with Florence, and the defeated can fall back on charm more easily than the victorious. Florence was at all times a serious city, and its buildings proclaim the fact. The Palazzo Vecchio and the Bargello still have shades of the prison-house about them, and what private dwelling anywhere in the world looks as hard and unadorned as the Pitti Palace?

Honouring the intellect made Florence the obvious home of the Renaissance; at the same time, suspicion of intellectual flamboyance led to that remarkable anticipation of the Reformation, Savonarola's theocratic rule, which turned Europe's most audacious community into an attempt to reproduce the City of God on earth. All the strains of idealism, intellectual fervour, love of science, and even, it must be admitted, pedantry can be seen in the marvellous procession of great paintings and sculpture produced in Florence between the lifetimes of Giotto and Michelangelo. Princes and tyrants throughout Italy sent to Florence for artists to beautify and dignify their territories. Florence, in her turn, attracted famous men from all over Europe, often sending them back to their homelands *ex officio* Florentines and spreaders of the true gospel of the Renaissance. And all this happened in a bourgeois republic, which owed its success to its powers of adapting itself to practical circumstances.

The wealth of Florence sprang from the wool trade; and this forced the Florentines to make a study of the provision of credit in order to facilitate trade – so Florentine traders became bankers to the papacy and the whole of western Europe. The great city families, the Medici, Strozzi and the rest, were arrogant, but they were never too proud to trade. The old aristocracy hardly survived the internecine quarrels between Guelph and Ghibelline which were endemic to every Italian state. Dante, a White Guelph, could not get beyond the state of mind which made faction inevitable. Festering in exile, he hoped for the overthrow of

223

the rulers of his home city. Within fifty years of his death, the new men were in charge, those who believed not in a Europe of feudal dependence but in an emergent world of independent states, modelled on the Roman Republic.

Cosimo de' Medici, *pater patriae*, saw that this dream could not last – there were too many sharks in the troubled waters of Italy. Absolutism was returning to Europe in the wake of revived central governments in France and Spain. Cosimo and his grandson, Lorenzo the Magnificent, sought to guide Florence through these difficult times by pursuing a policy of the balance of power. They succeeded remarkably well, but history would not make a special case for Florence. She enjoyed freedom long enough to open the gates of learning and imagination, and then she was eclipsed. With her sank the Renaissance, and it is a dreadful irony that, by 1600, she was better known in England as the scene of bizarre court murders, such as Webster dealt with in *The White Devil*, than as the mother-city of Bruni, Alberti and Leonardo.

There has always been a bias in art history in favour of Tuscany, which is hardly surprising, since Tuscan achievements were so great. Before the rise of Florence, Pisa was one of the great maritime republics and founder of the most impressive school of sculpture in Europe. Niccolò, Giovanni and Andrea Pisano worked in most of the important Italian cities. Pisan Gothic architecture can still be seen in that extraordinary grassy rectangle on the outskirts of the city, known as the Piazza dei Miracoli, made up of the Cathedral, the Baptistry, the Leaning Tower and the Campo Santo. Inside the latter is a great fresco of 'The Triumph of Death', a veritable guide to the best in Italian Gothic painting and the inspiration for one of Liszt's more grisly compositions.

Siena, though subdued by Florence – and even more by the plague – has always seemed favoured by fortune: the Sienese were a proud and skilful people. She gave birth to that obstinate girl, Catherine, who became the patron saint of Italy. Her painters of the schools of Duccio, Sassetta and Simone Martini shared with Giotto pre-eminence in all Italy. And the countryside around Siena is among the most attractive in the peninsula. The road from Florence runs through the Chianti, dotted with dark fir trees, vineyards and villas, passing monasteries, fortresses and farms; and in the distance the traveller sees an isolated hill town or castle dominating the landscape. San Gimignano is the most famous of these hill towns, largely because it has preserved so many of its medieval towers, strongholds of its warring citizens, but up close appearing to be bleak stone funnels. The jewel of the Sienese countryside is Pienza, an attempt to realize that typical Renaissance concept, the ideal city, portrayed by both Alberti and Piero della Francesca. The great humanist Pope, Pius II, was born in this small village, and after elevation to the papacy he beautified his birthplace and made it the seat of his administration. Today it is the best of ghost towns, haunted by the spirits of papal exiles who had had to leave Rome for an idealized existence in the heart of the Tuscan countryside.

West of Siena and Volterra lies the almost uninhabited Maremma, salty and malarial marsh: north of Lucca are the beaches on which Shelley was washed up, fronting the lagoons where Puccini loved to shoot duck. Following the Arno upstream from Pisa to Florence, one travels through the Florentine *contado* or heartland: here are the villas of the Medici, the Vespucci and the Carducci families. The world-famous academies, attended by Poliziano, Pico and Lorenzo himself, were conducted at the Medici villa at Careggi, or at Marsilio Ficino's villa next door. The later Medici villas, Cafaggiolo, Poggio a Caiano and Petraia, are on a larger scale but are still delightful country houses by comparison with the opulence of French country châteaux in the Loire valley. This, again, points to a quality in the Florentine enlightenment – everything was on a human scale. Florentine *grandezza* lay in the mind, not in some Versailles-like triumph.

Among her dependent cities, Florence always had loyal allies as well as bitter enemies. Arezzo and Prato are two of the most important. Today Arezzo attracts visitors chiefly because of its cycle of frescoes by Piero della Francesca, telling the story of the Legend of the True Cross, perhaps the most magnificent series of paintings in the world. But it was also the birthplace of the monk Guido, who invented musical notation, of Petrarch, Bruni, Vasari, and that delightful but scandalous writer Pietro Aretino. It looks dusty in the summer sun, yet it still glows with a tingling immediacy which is the mark of the Italian Renaissance.

The place-names which echo through history from the environs of Florence are many. Sometimes we know them in different contexts – as with Vallombrosa, whose drifting autumn leaves came to Milton's mind when he was writing his masterpiece in England. Usually we recall them attached to great artists, local boys who left the countryside, often as apprentices, and came to their maternal city to create masterpieces which would make her and their own villages immortal: Leonardo from Vinci, Mino from Fiesole, Andrea from Castagno, Desiderio from Settignano, Giuliano from Sangallo, Jacopo from Sansovino. Genius was commoner in Florence than ordinariness, and in spreading outwards to the rest of Europe it changed the very nature of the world we live in.

North of Tuscany is Emilia Romagna, the most central of Italy's provinces, and a part much disputed and marched over by mercenary armies. Towards the sea, the Romagnol lords were especially warlike and treacherous, notably the rulers of Ferrara, Ravenna and Rimini. Ravenna had been the glorious capital of the late Roman Empire, as the mausoleum of Galla Placidia and the churches of San Vitale and the two Sant'Apollinari remind one. The ageless brightness of the mosaics survives; little remains of the ferocious da Polenta family, except the new tomb given the remains of Dante who died in Ravenna under their protection. Outside the city, the abbey of Pomposa keeps its dignified vigil by the sea, waiting for time to restore the glory it lost to the malaria mosquito. Rimini is a brief oasis of Renaissance splendour among a desolation of modern beach development: the spirit of Sigismondo Malatesta must have quietened, not to be poisoning the camping sites. The Tempio Malatestiano is probably Alberti's most ambitious building, though unfinished, and the whole of Sigismondo's obsessional world glitters on unrepentantly.

Inland from Ravenna, controlling the flat and fertile plain between Bologna and the river Po as it divides for its sluggish progress through its Adriatic delta, lies the ancient fortified city of Ferrara. During late medieval times and during the High Renaissance, it was the seat of the Este family, one of the great names in

Italian history. At the height of its power, Ferrara, like Mantua, was protected by marshes and flooded channels, but recent draining has recovered much richly alluvial land, and modern Ferrara is the centre of a thriving agricultural district, with the consequent advantage of being renowned for the excellence of its food and cooking. Ferrara is the opposite of most North Italian cities, since it was neither built as an exercise in Renaissance town-planning nor built around some vantage point for defence. Its prominent buildings are thus dispersed throughout the city and, though impressive, they do not present a pattern of power or symmetry.

The Este dynasty was dispossessed from Ferrara by Pope Clement VIII in 1597 and took their rule (and many priceless works of art, including the pictures assembled by Isabella d'Este, the world's first great collector in the modern sense) to nearby Modena. But they left behind superb symbols of their long rule – the incredible moated castle, the Palazzo Schifanoia, perhaps best translated by borrowing from Potsdam its title 'Sans Souci', and the palace of Lodovico Sforza 'Il Moro', an Este son-in-law. The castle is a proper home for a tyrant, and here Niccolò III had his son Ugo and second wife Parisina murdered in the early fifteenth century, thereby giving Italy a story to rival that of Paolo and Francesca.

But Niccolò's sons, Lionello, Borso and Ercole I, raised the Ferrara court to a height equalled only by Florence and Urbino. The poet Ariosto was a senior government official in the service of the Estes, and though Byron accused the Dukes of Ferrara of mistreating him, it was while he lived in the city that he composed *Orlando Furioso*. Artists attracted to the Ferrara court included Piero della Francesca and Pisanello (whose medallion for Lionello d'Este is among the most exquisite works of art of the Renaissance). Cosmè Tura, one of the most original of *Quattrocento* painters, was a native of the city and his work still survives in the museum of the Duomo and in the Schifanoia Palace. The faded frescoes of Tura and Cossa in the Hall of the Months bring to life the buoyant and extrovert personality of Borso d'Este for whom they were painted. They do not have the deep domestic naturalness and grandeur of Mantegna's similar series for the Gonzagas in Mantua, but they convey even better the high-spirited confidence of a great Renaissance ruler at home in the world he had inherited.

Ferrara is the birthplace of the reforming monk Savonarola, though his end came in Florence. Its intellectual life attracted Pico, Guarino and Tasso, and it is only just that the sisters Isabella and Beatrice d'Este should be among the most celebrated blue-stockings in history. It was for the Duke Ercole I that Josquin des Près wrote those works which are peaks of Renaissance music, the motet *Miserere mei Deus* and the Mass, *Hercules Dux Ferrariae*. Its glory may have departed along with the power of the Estes, but Ferrara is a dignified city, confident that its name will always be respected among lovers of civilization.

Along the road to Modena and Reggio is a site which is a monument to another great and indomitable woman – the castle of Canossa, seat of the Countess Matilda, who ruled almost all Tuscany in the eleventh century. The ruins of Canossa are still a place of pilgrimage for people raised on the story of the humbling of the Holy Roman Emperor, Henry IV, who in January 1077 was forced to wait barefoot in the snow until granted absolution by Pope Gregory VII. Unfortunately for Italy, the struggle between Pope and Emperor had not yet entered its bitterest stage, and the internecine misery of the Guelph and Ghibelline factions lay in the future.

Modena, the second home of the Este family, lives almost wholly in the past. The Ducal Palace, from which Mary of Modena set out to become the wife of the Duke of York and so briefly Queen of England, is enormous but out of proportion. The true gem of this severely unmodern town is the Cathedral, a masterpiece of Romanesque architecture, with a bell tower christened 'La Ghirlandina' for the decorative bronzework which festoons the weathercock. The outside of the Cathedral is carved with reliefs of scenes from the Bible, including Adam and Eve and Noah's Ark, and the interior, beautifully lit by a great rose window, contains much fine work in marquetry. In organization the Cathedral is highly original and ahead of its time, for a building begun in 1099.

The rich countryside of the Po valley has made each of its important towns and centres famous for local foods, and so spread their names across the globe. None is more celebrated than Parma, of the glazed and richly cured ham and dried Parmesan cheese. But Parma is more than a stopping-place for gourmets; it is a sombre and well-preserved city, the former capital of yet another of Italy's art-loving ruling families, the Farnese. Originally a Roman family, the Farnese established themselves in Parma and in nearby Piacenza in the fifteenth century. Their days of power were later than was the case with many of the great families, and they reached their height under the patronage of the royal house of Spain. One Duke of Parma, who died young, was the Spanish Governor of the Netherlands who drew up his army on the coast at Ostend to be ferried to England by the Spanish Armada of 1588. His equestrian statue and that of his son Ranuccio stand outside Piacenza's Palazzo del Comune, generally known as 'Il Gotico'. Parma's distinguished sons are more remarkable than those of most towns of its size – Correggio and Parmigianino among painters, the printer Bodoni and the composer Verdi, who was born in the little town of Roncole near Busseto just outside the city. Another great name belongs to Parma by proxy, that of Stendhal. People still come to look for the famous Charterhouse, and the citizens are willing enough to find candidates for them. Unfortunately, there was no such building outside the imagination of the author of *La Chartreuse de Parme*.

The main buildings of Parma make a group as remarkable in their way as those on Pisa's Piazza dei Miracoli. The Cathedral, the Baptistery and the Church of St John the Evangelist form the heart of the city. The first two are Romanesque with Gothic additions, and the third is Renaissance with a Baroque façade. In a cupola of the Cathedral, Correggio's frescoes of the Assumption, with their incomparable airborne grace and delicacy of colouring, fully warrant Titian's remark that if the dome were filled with gold it would still fall short of the paintings' proper price.

San Giovanni has another series of Correggio masterpieces, and also frescoes by his pupil Parmigianino depicting the Adoration of the Magi. The charm of this master's etiolated figures and gentle demeanour is doubly attractive if one considers the excesses of the Mannerist painters who followed him. The Baptistery is surely the most beautiful in Italy. Octagonal, as are so many baptisteries, this exquisite building consists of five storeys of colonnades, and is crowned with a Gothic arch. The Farnese theatre, a masterpiece of interior design constructed of wood in a manner similar to the Teatro Olimpico in Vicenza, shares with that masterpiece of Palladio and his pupil Scamozzi's Teatro Olimpico at Sabbioneta the title of the oldest surviving theatre in Italy. Parma has the reputation of being the most operatically minded Italian city, and the regular audience at its Teatro Regio is feared by all singers, each member being a fastidious connoisseur.

Not far from Parma, but belonging more properly to the more distant city of Mantua, is another ghost town, Sabbioneta, the magnificent folly of Vespasiano Gonzaga, a scion of a junior branch of the Gonzagas. It was his whim, as it was Pope Pius II's before him, to turn a country village into an ideal metropolis. The passing of their power has left both Sabbioneta and Pienza much as they were four hundreds years ago – models of Renaissance humanism and idealized pomp. Vespasiano Gonzaga invited scholars and artists to his 'little Athens', and he lived out his patrician life in the manner recommended by Castiglione, with a ducal palace, a Summer Palazzo del Giardino, and a family church, the Incoronata. All of this is now stripped of its splendour, the population having faded away, leaving only the lineaments of Vespasiano's dream.

The greatest city of the Romagna, and one of the most famous in Italy, is Bologna. Its university claims the title of the oldest in the country. Its Philharmonic Society was the first musical academy to award a diploma to the young Mozart, and its school of wind players and composers carried baroque trumpet and string music throughout Europe. Bologna is a flourishing modern city, in which the towers of medieval faction rise among agreeable arcades and attractive streets. Only San Gimignano can boast more extraordinary fortified towers than Bologna's Torre degli Asinelli and Torre Garisenda. Among the great churches of Bologna are San Domenico (where the saint, that grim Spanish watchdog, is buried) and San Petronio. To think of Bologna is to think of San Petronio, one of the largest churches in Christendom, which, if its original plans had matured, would have been the most extensive church in the world. As with so many buildings begun in the Age of Faith, it is unfinished, with naked brickwork on the upper half of the façade. The central door is the work of the greatest of Sienese sculptors, Jacopo della Quercia. Inside the vast disposition of this giant among Gothic basilicas, it is easy to imagine the virtuoso trumpeters and string players of the seventeenth and eighteenth centuries astounding all creation with the antiphonal fanfares of Torelli and his followers. Inside the more modest San Domenico, guarding St Dominic's last resting place, stands an angel by Michelangelo, one of the earliest and most restrained of his works. The Pinacoteca is full of fine paintings, including the oddity of a Last Judgment by a fifteenth-century Bolognese painter which suggests the writhing stylization of Tantric art.

South of Ravenna, in the Marches, lies Urbino, where the Renaissance world touched its apogee. Duke Federico of Montefeltro inherited this small hilly town in the early years of the fifteenth century. In retirement, he built the ducal palace and made it a centre of learning and the arts. It is enormously impressive today; the rooms are spacious and light, the intarsia is a model of daring perspective allied to good taste, the atmosphere is human and controlled. The Duke's cult of personality was highly developed, and his initials in one form or another decorate each room, yet one feels that he had something to draw attention to. The world was a book which all sane men could read, and one had to write something in the pages before one departed. Duke Federico invited great men to his court and was rewarded by having other great men born and trained in his own remote territory – Bramante, Raphael and Castiglione among them.

Every ruler of a city or a duchy could beautify his domain in the time of the High Renaissance, and almost all did. A year stopping off at towns and villages in this part of Italy would not exhaust the legacy of two centuries' imagination and daring. There have been great achievements since, and remarkable manifestations of faith (the little town of Loreto beyond Urbino, with its world-famous pilgrims' shrine, testifies to the persistence of Christian inspiration); but their heyday was that springtime of rebirth which awoke not only Italy but the whole of Europe out of its cold slumber of superstition and ignorance.

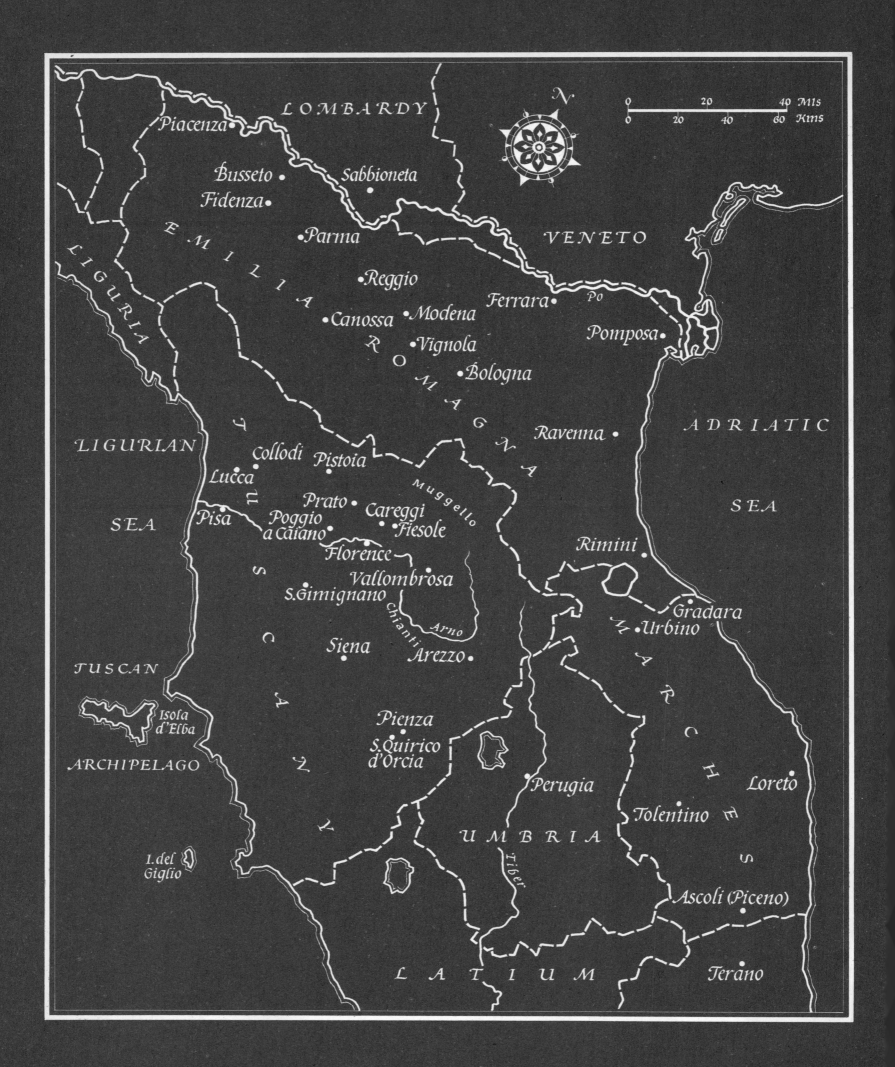

231

Dante meets Francesca da Rimini

The land where I was born sits by the seas,
  Upon that shore to which the Po descends,
  With all his followers, in search of peace.

Love, which the gentle heart soon apprehends,
  Seized him for the fair person which was ta'en
  From me, and me even yet the mode offends,

Love, who to none beloved to love again
  Remits, seized me with wish to please, so strong,
  That, as thou seest, yet, yet it doth remain.

'The Inferno', 1300–1310, Canto V,
translated by Byron

The ghosts of Pisa

I have got here into a famous old feudal palazzo, on the Arno, large enough for a garrison, with dungeons below and cells in the walls, and so full of *Ghosts*, that the learned Fletcher (my valet) has begged leave to change his room, and then refused to occupy his *new* room, because there were more ghosts there than in the other . . . The house belonged to the Lanfranchi family, (the same mentioned by Ugolino in his dream, as his persecutor with Sismondi) and has had a fierce owner or two in its time. The staircase etc. is said to have been built by Michel Agnola.

Byron to John Murray, Pisa, 1821

FOLD OUT ▷

On the nature of things

Great Mother of Aeneas, and of Love;
Delight of mankind, and the powers above;
Who all beneath those sprinkled drops of light
Which slide upon the face of gloomy night,
Whither vast regions of that liquid world
Where groves of ships on watery hills are hurled,
Or fruitful earth, doth bless, since 'tis by thee
That all things live which the bright sun does see . . .

Lucretius (c. 98–55 BC), 'De Rerum Natura',
translated by the Earl of Rochester

'This intimate alliance of the mind'

There come from time to time, eras of more favourable conditions, in which the thoughts of men draw nearer together than is their wont, and the many interests of the intellectual world combine in one complete type of general culture. The fifteenth century in Italy is one of these happier eras, and what is sometimes said of the age of Pericles is true of that of Lorenzo: – it is an age productive in personalities, many-sided, centralised, complete. Here, artists and philosophers and those whom the action of the world has elevated and made keen, do not live in isolation, but breathe a common air, and catch light and heat from each other's thought . . . and it is to this intimate alliance of the mind, this participation in the best thoughts which that age produced, that the art of Italy in the fifteenth century owes much of its grave dignity and influence.

Walter Pater, 'The Renaissance', 1878

Art and morals

Sigismondo, of the noble family of the Malatesta but illegitimate, was very vigorous in body and mind, eloquent, and gifted with great military ability. He had a thorough knowledge of history and no slight acquaintance with philosophy. Whatever he attempted he seemed born for, but the evil part of his character had the upper hand. He was such a slave to avarice that he was ready not only to plunder but to steal. His lust was so unbridled that he violated his daughters and his sons-in-law. He outdid all barbarians in cruelty. No one felt safe under his rule. Wealth or a beautiful wife or handsome children were enough to cause a man to be accused of a crime. He hated priests and despised religion. He had no belief in another world and thought the soul died with the body. Nevertheless he built at Rimini a splendid church dedicated to St Francis, though he filled it so full of pagan works of art it seemed less a Christian sanctuary than a temple of heathen devil-worshippers. In it he erected for his mistress a tomb of magnificent marble and exquisite workmanship with an inscription in the pagan style as follows, 'Sacred to the deified Isotta.'

Sigismondo Malatesta, described in the Commentaries of Pius II (1405–64)

Humanist in springtime

Welcome to May
with its wild banner waving!

Welcome to Spring
that moves men to love,
and you girls, inspiring
your lovers, yourselves made
lovely with roses and flowers
bred in Spring hours,

Come to the haunted shade
of the cool green bowers –
There is safety among
so many youths and maids;
The world is young
and burns with love in May.

The youths are armed with love,
the girls will yield their love
in sweet surrender:
theirs are the hearts to render,
they give them up and say
do not wage war in May!

Angelo Poliziano (1454–94),
translated by Peter Porter

190

Siena at sunset

Fonte Branda I last saw with Charles Norton, under the same arches where Dante saw it. We drank of it together, and walked together that evening on the hill above, where the fireflies among the scented thickets shone fitfully in the still undarkened air. *How* they shone! moving like fine-broken starlight through the purple leaves. How they shone! through the sunset that faded into thunderous night as I entered Siena three days before, the white edges of the mountainous clouds still lighted from the west, and the openly golden sky calm behind the Gate of Siena's heart, with its still golden words, 'Cor magis tibi Siena pandit,' and the fireflies everywhere in sky and cloud rising and falling, mixed with the lightning, and more intense than the stars.

John Ruskin, 'Praeterita', 1889

A nineteenth century view of the Magnificent

In a villa overhanging the towers of Florence, on the steep slope of that lofty hill crowned by the mother city, the ancient Fiesole, in gardens which Tully might have envied, with Fiscino, Landino and Politian at his side, he [Lorenzo il Magnifico] delighted his hours of leisure with the beautiful visions of Platonic philosophy, for which the summer stillness of an Italian sky appears the most congenial accompaniment.

The prospect from an elevation of a great city in its silence is one of the most impressive as well as beautiful we ever behold. But far more must it have brought home seriousness to the mind of one, who, by the force of events, and the generous ambition of his family, and his own, was involved in the dangerous necessity of governing without the right, and, as far as might be, without the semblance of power; . . . If thoughts like these could bring a cloud over the brow of Lorenzo, . . . he might restore its serenity by other scenes which his garden commanded. Mountains bright with various hues, and clothed with wood, bounded the horizon, and, on most sides, at no great distance; but embosomed in these were other villas and domains of his own; while the level country bore witness to his agricultural improvements, the classic diversion of a statesman's cares.

Henry Hallam, 'History of Literature', 1839

Tombstones in Santa Croce

In Santa Croce's holy precincts lie
Ashes which make it holier, dust which is
Even in itself an immortality,
Though there were nothing save the past, and this,
The particle of those sublimities
Which have relapsed to chaos: here repose
Angelo's, Alfieri's bones, and his,
The starry Galileo, with his woes;
Here Machiavelli's earth return'd to whence it rose.

Byron, 'Childe Harold's Pilgrimage', 1818, Canto IV, stanza 54

Shelley's funeral pyre

We have been burning the bodies of Shelley and Williams on the sea-shore, to render them fit for removal and regular interment. You can have no idea what an extraordinary effect such a funeral pile has, on a desolate shore, with mountains in the background and the sea before, and the singular appearance the salt and frankincense gave to the flame. All of Shelley was consumed, except his *heart*, which would not take the flame, and is now preserved in spirits of wine.

Byron, in a letter to Thomas Moore, Pisa, 1822

The childhood of Andrea Castagno

Andrea was born on a small farm called Castagno, in the Mugello, and took that as his surname when he came to Florence. His father died when he was a little child and left him in the care of an uncle, who set him to herd his cattle. One day he sought shelter from the rain in the house of a journeyman painter who was doing a small job for a countryman, an oratory or a tabernacle. Andrea watched in rapt admiration. He had never seen such a thing and he looked attentively at the work and how it was done. A sudden inclination was born in him which became a passionate desire for art, and he began scratching drawings of animals on stones and walls. The report of this reached the ears of a Florentine gentleman, Benedetto de' Medici, who had the boy called before him and questioned him. He asked him if he would like to become a painter. To this Andrea replied that he wanted this more than anything in the world. So Benedetto took the boy to Florence and placed him with one of the best masters.

Vasari, 'Life of Castagno', 1550

The Triumph of Death, Campo Santo, Pisa

Orcagna painted gentlefolk of every degree seated in a flowery meadow beneath a delicious grove of orange trees. Cupids hover over the young girls of the party shooting their arrows at the maidens. Knights and nobles listen to music or watch dancers who rejoice in the gladness of their youth and love. Orcagna here portrayed Catruccio Castrucani, lord of Lucca, a handsome youth wearing an azure blue cap and holding a falcon on his hand. Here is depicted everything the world has to offer of joy and delight, as far as space would permit and according to the high requirements of art.

Vasari, 'Life of Orcagna', 1550
(The painting attributed by Vasari to Orcagna is now credited to Francesco Traini.)

Florence in the picture

Presently Mr Eager gave a signal for the carriages to stop, and marshalled the party for their ramble on the hill. A hollow like a great amphitheatre, full of terraced steps and misty olives, now lay between them and the heights of Fiesole, and the road, still following its curve, was about to sweep on to a promontory which stood out into the plain. It was this promontory, uncultivated, wet, covered with bushes and occasional trees, which had caught the fancy of Alessio Baldovinetti nearly five hundred years before. He had ascended it, that diligent and rather obscure master, possibly with an eye to business, possibly for the joy of ascending. Standing there, he had seen the view of the Val d'Arno and distant Florence, which he had afterwards introduced . . . into his work.

from E. M. Forster, 'A Room with a View', 1908

Up at a villa

What of a villa? Though winter be over in March by rights,
'Tis May perhaps ere the snow shall have withered well off the heights:
You've the brown ploughed land before, where the oxen steam and wheeze,
And the hills over-smoked behind by the faint gray olive trees.

Is it better in May, I ask you? You've summer all at once;
In a day he leaps complete with a few strong April suns!
'Mid the sharp short emerald wheat, scarce risen three fingers well,
The wild tulip, at end of its tube, blows out its great red bell,
Like a thin clear bubble of blood, for the children to pick and sell . . .

All the year long at the villa, nothing to see though you linger,
Except yon cypress that points like Death's lean lifted forefinger.
Some think fireflies pretty, when they mix i' the corn and mingle,
Or thrid the stinking hemp till the stalks of it seem a-tingle.
Late August or early September, the stunning cicala is shrill,
And the bees keep their tiresome whine round the resinous firs on the hill.

from Robert Browning, 'Up at a Villa – Down in the City', 1880

Leonardo Bruni homesick

When I was there I lived with the greatest happiness and ease of mind, both because of the amenity and pleasures of the city and because of the polished manners of my friends . . . especially if they are devoted to the study of humane letters which seems to me to have deserted all other cities like shabby houses and betaken itself to our Florence as to some shrine of the muses. There is no place in the world to compare with the splendour of Florence or the urbanity of the Florentines.

Leonardo Bruni (1369–1444), in a letter to Coluccio Salutati, when lying sick at the Papal Court of Viterbo

Andrea del Sarto to his wife

You smile? why, there's my picture ready made,
There's what we painters call our harmony!
A common grayness silvers everything, –
All in a twilight, you and I alike
– You, at the point of your first pride in me
(That's gone you know), – but I, at every point;
My youth, my hope, my art, being all toned down
To yonder sober pleasant Fiesole.
There's the bell clinking from the chapel-top;
The length of convent wall across the way
Holds the trees safer, huddled more inside;
The last monk leaves the garden; days decrease
And autumn grows, autumn in everything.

Robert Browning

Shelley at Lucca

They from the throng of men had stepped aside,
And made their home under the green hill-side.
It was that hill, whose intervening brow
   Screens Lucca from the Pisan's envious eye,
Which the circumfluous plain waving below,
   Like a wide lake of green fertility,
With streams and fields and marshes bare,
   Divides from the far Apennines – which lie
Islanded in the immeasurable air.

from 'The Boat on the Serchio', 1821

194

197

Luca Signorelli to his son

They brought thy body back to me quite dead,
Just as thou hadst been stricken in the brawl.
I let no tear, I let no curses fall,
But signed to them to lay thee on the bed.

Then, with clenched teeth, I stripped thy clothes soaked red;
And taking up my pencil at God's call,
All night I drew thy features, drew them all,
And every beauty of thy pale chill head.

For I required the glory of thy limbs,
To lend it to archangel and to saint,
And of thy brow for brows with halo rims;

And thou shalt stand, in groups that I shall paint
Upon God's walls; till, like procession hymns
Lost in the distance, ages make them faint.

Eugene Lee-Hamilton (1845–1907)

A masque of Death

The spectacle was called The Triumph of Death. The chariot was prepared by Piero himself, and with such secrecy that not a whisper got abroad. The completed work was disclosed and presented at one and the same moment. The triumphal car was draped in black cloth, with skeletons and crosses painted on it. It was drawn by coal-black buffaloes. Within the car stood a colossal figure of Death, scythe in hand, while around him were covered tombs which opened when the procession halted. At the sound of a wailing summons, moaned through trumpets, the figures of the dead raised themselves half out of their tombs, and seated their skeletal forms thereon while they sang the words: *Dolor, pianto, e penitenzia . . .*

Vasari, 'Life of Piero di Cosimo', 1550

Epitaph

Fummo già come vo'sete,
Vo'sarete come noi.
As you are, so once were we;
As we are, so shall you be!

Placard on a float of corpses in a Florentine Carnival

Henry IV at Canossa

And so he came, as he had been commanded. The castle stood within three walls, and once he had been admitted within the second wall, he passed the whole day, barefoot and fasting from that morning until evening, in expectation of the Roman pontiff's decision. All his cortège remained outside; he had put aside all regal honours and had nothing about him of kingly dignity. Thus he passed the next day, and again the third day. Finally, on the fourth day he was granted audience and after much discussion between them of this and that point, the excommunication was conditionally lifted from him.

Lambert of Hersfeld, 'Annals', late 11th century

Este dukedom

Ferrara! in thy wide and grass-grown streets,
Whose symmetry was not for solitude,
There seems as 'twere a curse upon the seats
Of former sovereigns, and the antique brood
Of Este, which for many an age made good
Its strength within thy walls, and was of yore
Patron or tyrant, as the changing mood
Of petty power impell'd, of those who wore
The wreath which Dante's brow alone had worn before.

Byron, 'Childe Harold's Pilgrimage', 1818, Canto IV, stanza 35

Youth

Youth is beauty mixed with pleasure,
Flying on the swiftest feet;
Taste that sweetness while it be sweet,
Tomorrow's an uncertain measure.

*Lorenzo de' Medici (1449–92), from 'Canzone di Bacco',
translated by Peter Porter*

BOOK FIVE

LIGURIA LOMBARDY PIEDMONT

At the bottom of Mt Cenis, vines begin to appear, and I perceived those of Italy to be planted in rows and espaliers, with corn and fruit trees between them. In France it is different . . . There was a violent west wind at our backs the whole day, which so overwhelmed us with dust it destroyed the pleasure I should otherwise have had in approaching the beautiful city of Turin, and in having all Italy before me, after being so long a sojourner in the wild countries of Bresse, Swisserland and Savoy. Upon our arrival at the gates, the custom-house officers examined us very gently, and with great civility. In Italy at last!

Dr Charles Burney, 'The Present State of Music in France and Italy', 1771

215 Window of Queen Maria Teresa of Sardinia's oratory, Royal Palace, Turin. Eighteenth century.

297

Liguria, Lombardy, Piedmont

Detail of wrought-iron gates, Palazzo Reale, Turin

IN MANY WAYS modern Italian life is dominated by the great industrial cities of Turin and Milan, capitals of the provinces of Piedmont and Lombardy. With Rome, they form the triumvirate of Italian economic and administrative life, but it is all too easy to ignore them in favour of more picturesque and historic parts of Italy. Yet each is the centre of a rich and fascinating countryside, and Milan, particularly, is characteristic of that energy and resourcefulness which are as much part of the Italian personality as *dolce far niente* or classical serenity.

Milan was a greaty city in the Middle Ages, fortress and base of the Visconti and Sforza dynasties, apex of the plain of Lombardy for more than a millennium. While Venice and Florence have survived into the modern world without becoming truly part of it, Milan has grown steadily since Napoleon's occupation to become the commercial centre of North Italy. It is the home of modern Italian architecture, of banking and publishing, and the centre of organized politics. It can be said to hold the soul of contemporary life in the peninsula – the practical and the ideal combined, the patriotic and the forward-looking. Alessandro Manzoni, the most loved of Italian authors, was born and lived most of his life in Milan: his spirit invests the busy Milanese atmosphere to this day – the Saturday afternoon crowds strolling and chatting in the enormous glass-roofed Galleria Vittorio Emanuele II, the solid middle-class families of the suburbs, and the great international businesses. Living with history is something the Milanese are good at: they know they are the heart of Italy. They have nourished Bishop Ambrose, the Viscontis and Sforzas, Manzoni, Verdi and the partisans of the Second World War. Italy has given so much to the world: Milan represents what it has kept for itself.

The Piedmontese have often been described by their fellow-Italians as hard, rough and self-reliant, and they needed such qualities to affect the unification of Italy in the last century. The Risorgimento owed much to the government of early nineteenth-century Turin: the shrewd Cavour tempering Mazzini the idealist and Garibaldi the man of action. Now that its royal house has gone, Piedmont seems a little less like the Prussia of Italy it once was, but the solidity and respectability of its towns and villages, the massive formality of Turin itself and the miracle of the Fiat company, remain to testify to a hard-working Northern ethic which sets the province apart from the rest of the country. Its very name suggests a wariness:

people living at the foot of the Alps were always ready for invaders, whether Teutonic or French. The mountains did not represent freedom to them but danger. The Alps still seem to hang over Turin menacingly: looking along the straight lines of the streets, often the eye ends in a prospect of snow-covered peaks. This, even more than Milan, is the home of modern Italian naturalism. The heroes of the stories of Cesare Pavese move inexorably from their small villages steeped in tradition to the factories and football-fanaticism of Turin.

A grander world lives on in the palaces and town houses which have a sombre ornateness peculiar to the province. The great buildings designed by the architect Juvarra – the façade of the Madama Palace, the Juvarra Chapel and the Stupìnigi Hunting Lodge – combine opulence with fine detail to produce an effect of claustrophobic richness. We are in the northernmost part of the South, Germania in Italia as it might be, the chief representation of the Industrial Revolution in a country which gave birth both to the Renaissance and the Counter Reformation. Piedmont has always attracted English sympathizers, but they were of a very different sort from the poets, art lovers and divines who flocked to Venice, Florence and Rome. They were often men of action, statesmen or engineers: Turner, Browning and Ruskin looked elsewhere.

Liguria, the province immediately south of Piedmont, is dominated by the great port of Genoa, but encompasses the full sweep of the littoral running from the Bay of Spezia to the Italian Riviera. Modern seaside resorts and unchanged fishing villages alternate along the superb foreshore. In the eleventh and twelfth centuries, Genoa and Pisa were deadly enemies and these were the waters they fought over. Yet it is far easier to characterize Pisa than to begin to describe Genoa. There is no important city in Italy which is so misunderstood and undervalued. This may be due to the lack of great names in Genoese history, and especially to the dearth of native Genoese artists. Apart from Columbus, who was born in the city, Andrea Doria, Simone Boccanegra and Niccolò Paganini just about complete the tally: an admiral, a plebeian patriot celebrated by Verdi, and a violinist believed to be in league with the Devil – these are the only Genoese who are famous outside Italy. Yet their native city was, for more than five hundred years, a prosperous, powerful maritime republic, contending on equal terms with Venice and the Ottoman Empire.

Nor did it suffer the humiliations of many of its rivals. In the nineteenth century, Genoa was the chief port of Italy and today remains a thriving trading centre and metropolis. There are magnificent buildings in Genoa, and the city is famous for its love of comfort and good food, but one looks in vain for the Genoese equivalents of the painters, architects, writers and printers who enriched Venice. Perhaps Genoa was the Carthage of Italy: it lived fully in itself and imported the art it required. *Genova la Superba* was revealed when Doria's fleet sailed out, or when the visiting merchant looked out over a magnificent harbour stocked with foreign vessels. The city was and is superbly placed: seen from the heights which rise above it, or from the mole, it bears comparison with Naples viewed from the Castle of St Elmo or the Castel del' Ovo. Although most of the thoroughfares are narrow and steep, Genoa has one of the finest streets of palaces in Europe – the

Strada Nuova, which so astounded Rubens when he saw it in 1607. This was one of the first great city thoroughfares deliberately planned and laid out by an architect to dignify not just the houses which fronted it but the whole city itself.

Elsewhere, many of the villas and palaces have been submerged in the industrial suburbia which now surrounds the city and its harbour. One of the earliest of the great Genoese villas is still much as it was – the Palazzo Doria on the harbour front, built for the Admiral in 1529. In 1644, John Evelyn, the diarist, described the marble terraces and the aviary, 'wherein grew trees of more than two feet in diameter, besides cypresses, myrtles, lentiscuses and other rare shrubs' and 'two other gardens full of orange-trees, citrons and pomegranates, grots and statues.'

Genoese *villeggiatura* survives around the great port, and the continued prosperity of the city makes it less dependent on visitors than many comparable Italian centres. Genoa has not been popular in Italy: an old Tuscan proverb asserted that it had 'a sea without fish, mountains without trees, men without honour, and women without modesty'. But nobody ever denied that Genoa was rich and self-confident, and the curious may find a strange proof of this in the celebrated Staglieno cemetery, with its fantastic Victorian monumental sculptures. Genoa the Proud may not be anyone's favourite Italian city, but it would be a good nomination for the least self-conscious one.

History moves impartially, destroying, erasing and restoring. In Milan it has been especially quixotic, so that the world of the early Christian Church can be felt more readily within the industrial and commercial complex of the modern city than the more recent epoch of the Middle Ages. The Basilica of Sant'Ambrogio was consecrated during the lifetime of St Ambrose himself, and includes a shrine with the bodies of early martyrs and the most remarkable ninth-century gold altar, masterpiece of the Milanese goldsmith's art. More wonderful than the treasures it contains is the impression it makes on visitors. Here the rite of the Western Church was first formulated, and here Augustine approached his conversion. The sombre church, with its decorated apse and ancient crypt, has been added to and much restored, so that it now stands as the greatest example of Lombard Romanesque architecture. More than this, though, it radiates the purposefulness and directness of the early Christian congregation.

Very different in effect is the great Duomo, the colossal apotheosis of Italian Gothic. In truth, there is not much Italian Gothic for it to excel, and the enormous structure, with its 3,000 statues inside and out, can strike the jaundiced observer as rather like the biggest wedding cake ever baked. It was begun quite late, in 1386, at the order of Gian Galeazzo Visconti, and the architect must have taken his inspiration from across the Alps in Northern Europe. Being such a giant work of art in itself – a sort of Fabergé cathedral magnified a hundred thousand times – it contains few art treasures. The people of Milan love it, and the world recognizes Milan by its unmistakable outline, but there are many churches in Christendom one would rather worship in or look at.

Milan has a rich collection of palaces and museums, including the famous Brera Art Gallery, perhaps the most spacious and beautifully displayed collection in Italy. Here are the Mantegna *Dead Christ*, a superb if morbid study in deep perspective, Piero della Francesca's noble altar-piece for Duke Frederick of Urbino, the most refined Crivelli in the world, and a characteristically sinister Caravaggio of the Supper at Emmaus. There are Botticelli and Pollaiuolo master-pieces at the Poldi-Pezzoli Museum, and an interesting collection of Italian Victoriana which includes a stained-glass window honouring Dante which is as sentimental as Mendelssohn.

The heart of medieval Milan is the great fortress of Castello Sforzesco, begun not by the Sforzas but by their predecessors, the Viscontis, at the end of the fourteenth century. It is everything the fevered imagination could demand of a fortified citadel. Moated, towered and grim, it encloses pleasant courtyards and extensive galleries and chambers. The tower is every child's fantasy of the perfect sandcastle. Close up, all sense of the picturesque falls away, and one sees only the scale and weight of the enormous structure. No building in Italy impresses so profoundly with its unswervable devotion to power. In an age of intercontinental missiles and citizen armies, the Castello Sforzesco still symbolizes ruthless strength and *Machtpolitik*. Our age has tamed it to make museums of art works and musical instruments. The effigy of Gaston de Foix, soldier and friend of Milan, rests here, close to one of Michelangelo's most transcendental Pietàs.

For three hundred years Milan represented autocracy, and fought to bring all North Italy under her control. Yet the great Milanese tyrants, Barnabò and Gian Galeazzo Visconti and Francesco Sforza, were men of culture and patrons of art. When Leonardo da Vinci felt himself unappreciated in Florence, he went to the Sforza court at Milan. His siege machines, fortifications and monuments for the Duke all came to nothing, but Milan does possess the most famous work he ever produced – his fresco of the Last Supper in the monastery of Santa Maria delle Grazie. Three hundred years later, Milan became the musical capital of Italy, with La Scala the senior theatre of the musical world. Rossini, Bellini and Donizetti all triumphed at La Scala, and it was here that the young Verdi witnessed the overwhelming success of his third opera, *Nabucco*. Milan shared with Turin in the glory of the Risorgimento: Napoleon, that man of ambiguities, had already nourished Milanese liberalism while suppressing national identity. The city emerged at the unification of Italy as the real capital of the northern half of the kingdom, and quickly became the economic heart of the country.

The countryside around Milan is dotted with the villas and estates of the patrician families, such as the Borromeos, who contributed not only generations of civil rulers and cardinals to Milanese life but also one of Italy's best-known saints, Carlo Borromeo. Immediately south of the city is the famous Certosa of Pavia, the superb abbey of the Carthusians which Gian Galeazzo intended as the Visconti family mausoleum. Pavia University was one of the dozen great centres of learning in the Middle Ages: farther back still, it was in Pavia that Theodoric the Ostrogoth imprisoned the philosopher Boethius.

The great and fertile plain of Lombardy stretches away from Milan eastwards and southwards through the rice and grain fields, a flat and humid terrain dominated by lines of Lombardy poplars, those upright sentinels of a warring past. The canal systems of the Po and its tributaries nourish many great cities, including Mantua (not only birthplace of Virgil but seat of the Gonzaga family), Crema, Cremona and Piacenza. Each has its heritage from the Middle Ages and Renaissance, its celebrated native sons and intense local pride. Small villages and towns which seem scarcely more than entries on the map speak of victories and defeats long ago, or of men of genius who ventured beyond their homes to the greater glory of Europe.

North of Milan are the great Italian lakes, Maggiore, Como and Garda, with their attendant smaller lakes like deep moons sunk in the foothills of the Alps. For thousands of years every propitious circumstance of climate, situation and natural beauty has drawn people to the villas, houses and towns which flank their shores. The poet Catullus used to retire to Sirmio (modern Sirmione) on Lake Garda, while Lake Maggiore was for generations the favoured place of relaxation of the rulers of Milan. Near Stresa on Maggiore are the Borromean islands, immaculate villas riding at anchor on the blue waters of the lake. Isola Bella is a testament to the ingenuity of man, especially when he is bent on making a place of delectation for himself. What was once a rocky pinnacle is now a palace and garden-pavilion rising above terraces reaching to the water. Here, in the Lakes, are the banks of flowers so strangely missing from most Italian gardens. Isola Bella is largely the same today as when Fontana created it for the Borromeo family in the middle of the seventeenth century. Bishop Burnet of Salisbury saw it in 1685 and wrote: 'the whole Island is a garden . . . and because the figure of the Island was not made regular by Nature, they have built great Vaults and Portica's along the Rock, which are all made Grotesque, and so they have brought it into a regular form by laying earth over those Vaults'. It is a man-made miracle, a Neo-classic temple of beauty which has naturalized Nature itself. Other great villas are the Villa d'Este at Cernobbio on Lake Como, and the remote and beautiful Villa Cicogna at Bisuschio, one of the best preserved of old Italian country houses.

So far north, the character of the cities acquires a more restrained tone, a guarded charm which is also to be found in the personality of their people. Varese, Lecco, Bergamo and Brescia are not fully in the Alps but nestle among the foothills: shortage of space is almost a required attribute, and each 'old town' with its winding streets, sudden abbreviated piazzas and one-way traffic systems positively rejoices in its confinement. Bergamo is the jewel of North Italian cities. The Bergamask which Shakespeare and Debussy honoured is no more theatrical than the spiralling, tall-fronted city itself. The condottiere, Bartolomeo Colleoni, and the composer, Donizetti, were natives of Bergamo, and they still preside in spirit over their unspoiled city. There is nothing in Italy quite like Bergamo's Cathedral Square dominated by the Colleoni Chapel and the church of Santa Maria Maggiore. Grandeur on so perfectly proportioned a scale is rare, as is the gilded modesty of the interior of Amadeo's mausoleum for Colleoni and his daughter, Medea. Sweetness and naturalness, allied to perfect decorum, mark Donizetti's music, and, looking about Bergamo, it is easy to think that the great composer derived his personality from the city itself.

In the fifteenth century, Mantua, surrounded on three sides by the waters of the river Mincio, was a paradise to the eye but a haunt of fever to its denizens. Its

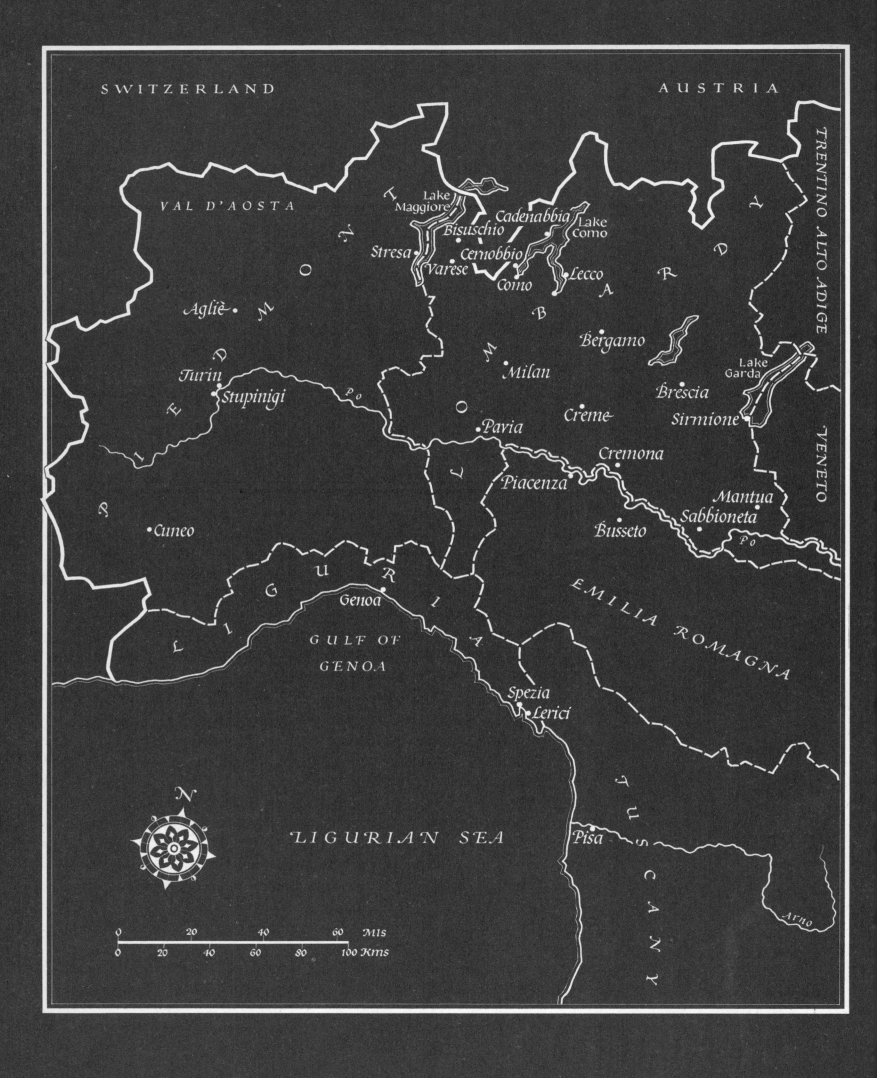

216 Early eighteenth-century Baroque staircase and vestibule by Filippo Juvarra (1676–1736), Palazzo Madama, Turin.

217 The main dome and the dome over the presbytery, church of S. Lorenzo, Turin, by Guarino Guarini, late seventeenth century.

218 Dome of the Chapel of the Holy Shroud, Turin Cathedral, by Guarino Guarini, built between 1668 and 1694 to house one of the holiest relics in Christendom.

219 The oval saloon, Palace of Stupinigi, Piedmontese Baroque by Filippo Juvarra, pointing forward to the Rococo.

220 The eighteenth-century Palace of Stupinigi behind its magnificent gates.

221 Violin in the Palazzo del Comune, Cremona, made in 1658 by Nicolo Amati under whom Stradivarius served his apprenticeship; in the background the façade of Cremona Cathedral.

222 The diminutive nineteenth-century Teatro Verdi, at Busseto (near Verdi's home), province of Parma.

223 King Arthur, Charlemagne, Godfrey of Bouillon and three of the Nine Heroines: part of a fresco cycle painted 1418–30 by Giacomo Jaquerio and assistants; they illustrate a chivalresque epic poem in French written by Tommaso III, Marquess of Saluzzo; Castle of Manta, province of Cuneo.

224 Detail of the tomb effigy of Count Gaston de Foix left unfinished in 1525, by the sculptor Bambaia (1483–1548); Castello Sforzesco, Milan.

225 Recumbent marble figure of Beatrice d'Este, 1498, from the tomb of Lodovico Sforza and his wife by Cristoforo Solari, Certosa of Pavia.

226–27 Two views of the marble *Rondanini Pietà*, Michelangelo's last sculptural work, left unfinished at his death in 1564; Castello Sforzesco, Milan.

228–32 Monumental nineteenth-century tombs in the cemetery of Staglieno, Genoa; the prosperous bourgeoisie immortalized in stone.

233 Detail of a mid-nineteenth-century stained-glass window by Giuseppe Bertini, 1851, in the Saletta di Dante, a room dedicated to Dante's works; Poldi-Pezzoli Museum, Milan.

234 Coat-of-arms of the powerful Brignole-Sale family in silk appliqué; Palazzo Rosso, Genoa.

235 Detail of the main fountain, 1599, in the gardens of Palazzo Doria Pamphili, Genoa, with the central figure of Neptune in a chariot drawn by horses; all the work of the Carlone brothers.

236 The Sala dei Giganti, Palazzo Doria Pamphili, Genoa; chimney-piece by Silvio Cosini (1495–1547), frescoes by Pietro Buonaccorsi, called Perino del Vaga, (1501–47) and stucco work by Luzio Romano.

237 Main reception room of Palazzo Clerici, Milan, with marvellous ceiling frescoes, 1740, by Giambattista Tiepolo (1696–1770).

238 Mirrored banquet table, Palazzo Carrega-Cataldi, Genoa.

239 The Cathedral, Milan; begun in 1386 and not finished until 1887 – an Italian interpretation of Flamboyant Gothic. We are looking along the roof of the nave towards the cupola over the crossing.

240 The Redeemer surrounded by the Apostles and symbols of the Evangelists; detail of gem-encrusted Carolingian golden altar frontal, AD 835, Basilica of S. Ambrogio, Milan.

241 Poplars in the Plain of Lombardy.

242 Sirmione, Lake Garda – a favoured beauty spot since Roman times.

243 The Wedding of the Virgin; detail of a gilded and painted Venetian marriage coffer, sixteenth century, Poldi-Pezzoli Museum, Milan.

244 Detail of Baroque confessional, early eighteenth century, by Andrea Fantoni (1659–1734), church of S. Maria Maggiore, Bergamo.

245 The Baroque parish church of S. Marta at Agliè, province of Turin, 1760 – in the process of restoration.

246 Eighteenth-century frescoed ballroom with *trompe-l'œil* scenes by Giacomo Lecchi and Carlo Carloni, Villa Lechi, Montirone, province of Brescia.

247 Eighteenth-century stables for twenty-four horses, with elegant decoration and a frescoed ceiling, Villa Lechi, Montirone.

248 Sixteenth-century frescoed loggia of the Villa Cicogna-Mozzoni, Bisuschio, province of Varese.

249 Maidservants and cherubs looking down from a circular balcony; frescoed ceiling, Camera degli Sposi, Ducal Palace, Mantua, painted by Andrea Mantegna between 1465 and 1474.

250 Sala dei Giganti, Palazzo del Tè, Mantua, painted by Rinaldo Mantovano and assistants after cartoons by Giulio Romano (1492–1546).

251 Cupid and Psyche, marble by Antonio Canova (1757–1822); in the background the marble frieze of Alexander's Triumph at Babylon by Bertel Thorvaldsen (1770–1844), Villa Carlotta, Cadenabbia, province of Como.

252 Sala dei Fiumi, Ducal Palace, Mantua, painted by Giorgio Anselmi, 1776.

253 The 'Theatre' on the penultimate terrace of the seventeenth-century gardens, Isola Bella.

254 View over the Lago Maggiore from a terrace in the garden of Isola Bella.

255 Main altar, twelfth-century Basilica of S. Michele, Pavia.

256 Façade of the Cathedral of Crema, fourteenth century, in the Lombard-Gothic style.

Gonzaga lords beautified the city and celebrated their own immortality in a fashion unequalled by any of their neighbours. The rooms in the Ducal Palace decorated by Mantegna surpass all other royal chambers: this is how the idealized prince would live, if he had read Castiglione or Machiavelli. The family is the nucleus of Mantegna's ideal vision, and around it flows, like the celestial galaxies, the magnificence of the created world. A hundred years after Mantegna, Monteverdi worked at the Mantuan court, staging *Orfeo* there in 1607.

The malarial waters have drained away and so, alas, has Mantua's glory. But greater Lombardy remains the most prosperous part of Italy. A millennium has passed since the Long-Beards descended on the plains of the Po, which were already exhausted by the ravages of Attila and Totila. These practical and determined men fostered art with the same determination as they did industry and trade. The past and the present live together here more harmoniously than in most areas of the world. The one would be merely academic or would lack savour without the other. Beauty lies in the attitude of men to the world about them, and in Lombardy that attitude has always been active and life-enriching.

Dr Burney on Turin

Turin is a very beautiful city, though inferior perhaps to many others of Italy in antiquities, natural curiosities, and in the number of its artists. The streets are straight, regular, and well built, mostly of white brick, which, at a distance, has the appearance of stone. The grand place or square, with the King's palace, which entirely occupies one side, and the palace of Madame in the middle, both of white stone, are built after designs of Vignola, as some say, but others affirm that Guarino Guarini was the architect.

Dr Charles Burney, 'The Present State of Music in France and Italy', 1771

Boswell's first Italian miracle

At the Bernardines' is a little place railed in like a particular burying-place, on the floor of which is recorded a miracle, which, as it is the first I have met with in Italy, I shall here relate. Some sacrilegious villain had broken into a church and stolen away the sacred calix with the Body of Jesus Christ. As he was driving his beast laden with his impious spoils, it fell down of a sudden, and the holy transub-stantiated wafer rose into the air and hovered there in the sight of thousands. The Archbishop of Turin came out with a train of his clergy and kneeled in solemn adoration holding the calix in his hands, when lo! the host gently descended into the calix. In commemoration of this miracle an annual feast is observed in Turin in this church which was erected on the spot.

James Boswell, Journal on the Grand Tour, 1765

FOLD OUT ▷

228

229

230

231

G. MORENO
SCUL. GENOVA 1891

232

233

Milan, fourth century AD

At Milan also are all things remarkable, and wealth abundant.

Ausonius (AD 310–95), 'Ordo nobilium urbium'

Leonardo among the Milanese

The Duomo, work of artists from beyond the Alps, so fantastic to the eye of a Florentine used to the mellow, unbroken surfaces of Giotto and Arnolfo, was then in all its freshness; and below, in the streets of Milan, moved a people as fantastic, changeful and dreamlike. To Leonardo least of all men could there be anything poisonous in the exotic flowers of sentiment which grew there. It was a life of brilliant sins and exquisite amusements: Leonardo became a celebrated designer of pageants; and it suited the quality of his genius, composed in almost equal parts, of curiosity and the desire of beauty, to take things as they came.

Walter Pater, 'Leonardo da Vinci', 1878

Dorothy Wordsworth views Milan

I cannot describe our astonishment at the first view of the Cathedral of Milan; yet even then, while a sentiment of awe mingles with other sensations, I felt as if that splendid pile might have been raised more for the glory of temporal Princes than for the worship of the Creator. It is immensely large – all of polished marble – which one might call white, were it not for the spotless purity of the hundreds of statues that, even when seen from below, appear as large as life, each upon its pinnacle above the balustrades of every division of the roof . . . There is, at the *first* bursting of the view, an enchanting power in the building to conjure up and even to realise those imaginations that stir the youthful mind in reading Fairy Tales or the Arabian Nights Entertainments, or histories of the glory of antient Cities decayed or overthrown. Such romantic pleasure could not be recalled at will.

Dorothy Wordsworth, Journal, 1820

The Bay of Lerici

I sat and saw the vessels glide
Over the ocean bright and wide,
Like spirit-wingèd chariots sent
O'er some serenest element
For ministrations strange and far;
As if to some Elysian star
Sailed for drink to medicine
Such sweet and bitter pain as mine. . . .
And the fisher with his lamp
And spear about the low rocks damp
Crept, and struck the fish which came
To worship the delusive flame.

Shelley, from 'Lines Written in the Bay of Lerici', 1822

From Genoa to San Remo

I walked five miles to Finale (the first post, which a punster would say should be the last). Here I saw a sort of Genoese triumphal arch erected on I don't know what occasion. There was a Latin inscription upon it, as how thunder had set the sand on fire, which did not pass the arch, and this happened during the magistracy of Signor somebody.

Nothing is more agreeable in travelling up the river of Genoa than to find oneself gradually transported from a cold air to an agreeable warmth. By the time I got to San Remo I had entirely changed climate. At Genoa we were shivering over large fires, and at San Remo I sat with the windows open in a room without fire and basked in the rays of a benign sun. The town is remarkable for the immense quantity of oranges and lemons which grow in its territories. I went with the postmaster to his garden and had the pleasure of pulling in December sweet oranges to eat and lemons to squeeze in my wine.

James Boswell, Journal on the Grand Tour, 1765

234

240

241

247

249

The pleasures of Bergamo

Bergamo is a large fine city, divided into upper and lower. It is built on a hill, and the country in its vicinage abounds in beautiful Villas and prospects. While the horses and Chaise were changed, I walked about the Town a little, and found the houses very high; but there seems in Italian Architecture as much the taste and harmony of proportion as in their Music: every pillar we see, every gateway, portico, and colonnade, has something light and graceful in it.

Dr Charles Burney, 'The Present State of Music in France and Italy', 1771

Thomas Coryate on Mantua

Truely the view of this most sweet Paradise did even so ravish my senses with such inward delight, that I said unto myselfe, this is the Citie which of all other places in the world, I would wish to make my habitation in, and spend the remainder of my dayes in divine Meditations amongst the sacred Muses.

Thomas Coryate, 'Crudities', 1611

'Battaglia'

In one of the Borromean isles (the Isola Bella), there is a large laurel – the largest known – on which Buonaparte, staying there just before the battle of Marengo, carved with his knife the word 'Battaglia'. I saw the letters, now half worn out and partly erased.

Byron, in a letter to Thomas Moore, 1816

'Armida's gardens'

There is an almost forced gaiety about the landscape of the lakes, a fixed smile of perennial loveliness. And it is as a complement to this attitude that the Borromean gardens justify themselves. Are they real? No; but neither is the landscape about them. Are they like any other gardens on earth? No; but neither are the mountains and shores about them like earthly shores and mountains. They are Armida's gardens anchored in a lake of dreams and they should be compared, not with this or that actual piece of planted ground, but with a page of Ariosto or Boiardo.

Edith Wharton, 'Italian Villas', 1904

Catullus at home

In all the lakes and plains of Neptune's sway
   No eye shines forth so brightly as yours, Sirmio,
Peninsula of pleasure: how happily I return,
   Scarcely daring to believe my fortune, from dusty
Thynia and the Bythinian plains. What is more blessed
   Than to lay aside all cares and unburden the mind
In one's own and dearly trusted home, to rest after
   Long and painful travel in the place one knows?
Welcome, beautiful Sirmio, rejoice with Catullus,
   Let all your waters laugh with him, and let
Our southern lakes take up the sound till earth
   Becomes the home of love and playful laughter.

Gaius Valerius Catullus (c. 85–54 BC), 'Veronensis Liber', XXXI,
translated by Peter Porter

250

BOOK SIX

VENICE
THE VENETO
FRIULI

Beneath is spread like a green sea
The waveless plain of Lombardy,
Bounded by the vaporous air,
Islanded by cities fair;
Underneath Day's azure eyes
Ocean's nursling, Venice lies,
A peopled labyrinth of walls,
Amphitrite's destined halls,
Which her hoary sire now paves
With his blue and beaming waves . . .
Sun-girt City, thou hast been
Ocean's child, and then his queen.

Shelley, 'Lines written among the Eugenean Hills', 1818

257 Sixteenth-century frescoes in the Villa Chiericati, now Villa Lambert, Longa di Schiavon,
province of Vicenza. The page with the hound
is in the style of Paolo Veronese.

Venice, the Veneto, Friuli

GEOGRAPHY AND HISTORY have worked together to make the whole area to the east of Lombardy into a compact and easily understood unit. Geography in the shape of the natural features that bound it – the Dolomites in the north, Lake Garda in the west, the Adriatic Sea and the peninsula of Istria in the east and the mouths of the Po in the south. History in the shape of Venice. By the fifteenth century the great maritime republic was in decline: she no longer held the monopoly of trade with the East and she was forced to turn inwards, to involve herself with Italian politics in a way which she would have disdained to do a century earlier. Her new empire stretched westwards as far as Bergamo in the immediate vicinity of Milan, and eastwards down the Adriatic to the Illyrian coast. And the citizens of Bergamo, Verona, Vicenza, Padua and the thousands of towns and villages which owed allegiance to Venice were satisfied enough with the Serene Republic's rule. Venice during the seventeenth and eighteenth century became a byword for decadence, luxury and idle pleasure, and we tend to forget her still considerable claims to respect – the millions of people who lived securely and prosperously in the Venetian empire. Yet the most cursory walk through any place which was a Venetian administrative centre will reveal the insignia of the winged lion. In St Mark's Square, he proudly displays his book, inscribed *Pax tibi Marce, Evangelista Meus*. His paw rests lightly on the book, but the book cannot get away.

Verona is the ideal city to appreciate that layered or laminated sense of history which is so peculiarly an Italian experience. The layers of history did not build up steadily but were added by the whims of tyrants and just as quixotically destroyed. What has survived is not the ideal cross-section of some historian but the out-wearing of power by time and chance, and the juxtapositions can have a surrealist logic which outstrips history: in the Roman amphitheatre today Verdi's ancient Egypt is recreated with as much care as the ruins themselves are preserved.

Walking round Verona and noting the parts which have survived from the past, you build up a mosaic of history in your own mind. Besides the arena, which could be from the first century AD or could date from Diocletian's reign, there is a section of an older Roman gate in the Porta dei Borsari; the city walls date from the time of the Emperor Gallienus. If little remains contemporary with Theodoric the Ostrogoth, at least his name survives in the city, while the fourth century

Roman forum, Aquileia

353

Bishop of Verona, St Zeno, presides in the beautiful church named for him, in the form of a multi-coloured marble statue of the fourteenth century, smiling and blessing his people. Few Italian cities are as rich in medieval and early Renaissance buildings and works of art. The bronze panels of the main door of San Zeno Maggiore are rare in their combination of the primitive and the sophisticated, while the church itself is perhaps the ideal of Romanesque art in North Italy. But San Zeno has to compete with Santa Anastasia and San Fermo, both begun in the thirteenth century, the end of which saw the rise of the della Scala family, whose hundred years of rule has marked Verona to this day. The very names of this Scaliger dynasty suggest a medieval absolutism entirely unconcerned whether it was benign or evil. Only city bosses assured of immortality through art as well as power would have adopted nicknames like Cangrande (Big Dog) and Cansignorio (Top Dog).

During the first half of the fifteenth century, Verona came under Venetian hegemony. When you look at the Venetian lion in the Piazza delle Erbe in Verona, you feel a different and more casual warmth than you get from the surrounding swallow-tailed Ghibelline crenellations or the amazing medieval fantasies of the Scaliger tombs. If Verona declined, it was a comfortable decline. And it was a gradual and almost imperceptible process. Such magnificent examples of late medieval art as Pisanello's frescoes – St George and the Princess of Trebizond in Santa Anastasia and the Annunciation in San Fermo – date from this time. Then comes Mantegna and finally Paolo Caliari, called Veronese, whose best work is not in his home town but in his adopted Venice. Intarsia of the strangest sort by Fra Giovanni da Verona fills the church of Santa Maria da Organo. All this, which is the merest shadow of the past preserved at Verona, now fits into a modern, prosperous city. The old and the new, the old restored, and the new imitating the old, lie folded into each other.

From Verona to Trieste, the traveller should keep in mind that almost everything he sees has been lovingly shaped by the most passionately inventive intelligences of Europe. The intellect does not predominate, as it does in Florence and the Tuscan domains, but nor does the opulence and love of good living shown in the many villas of Venetia and the Trento mean that the makers of this landscape were escapists: rather it suggests a calm and an order from which experiment and excitement have departed.

Only during the years of Roman expansion, during the first millennium BC, did the north of Italy suffer invasion from the south. Thereafter, each new wave of invaders and settlers came over the Alps and dispersed on the plains of Lombardy and the north east. The visitor from northern Europe does the same today. Before him lies marvellous scenery in the jutting mountains and steep valleys that fan out behind the Venetian plain – the peaks and plateau country which formed the bloody front line of the Italian army's struggle during the First World War; the great Alpine valley of the Adige; the warm oases of Arco, Bolzano and Merano, and the sports centre of Cortina d'Ampezzo. At the eastern end of the plain is Friuli and Venetia Julia. This strip between the mountains and the sea contains some small cities whose ancient heritage and present charm are not well enough known by the tourist who may be content with Alpine skiing or the innumerable delights of Venice. Aquileia was once a Roman capital and the seat of the Patriarch of Byzantium; sacked by the Huns, it had its own renaissance in the early Middle Ages, the witness of which is its fine basilica, and inside it an astonishing fifth century mosaic floor stands as a mark of its early grandeur. Cividale, to which the Patriarch of Aquileia fled, combines Lombard and Frankish influences in a way that characterizes the whole of this disputed region, while Udine, elegant with its Piazza della Libertà, is equally outstanding for its Tiepolo frescoes and pictures. Mountain and plain, Teuton and Latin, have merged and blended through geological and historical time to create in this Venetian hinterland a conjunction of landscape and atmosphere that is unique.

The surroundings of the Alto Adige and the half-German names of Spilimbergo and Bolzano (Bozen, where both Mozart and Goethe stopped on their journeys into Italy) point to a long cycle of interrelation between the civilized plain-dwellers and the 'unshaven horsemen of the horizon'. Venice itself (or perhaps more properly Torcello) was founded by remnants of the Roman Imperium and the Byzantine Pale fleeing from Attila the Hun, Europe's most celebrated scourge. They never lost their unique sense of survival, and in the middle of the nineteenth century Verdi offered them a memorial in his opera, *Attila*, given its first performance at Venice's La Fenice theatre.

Along the banks of the Brenta canal, in and around Vicenza and scattered along the roads to such towns as Bassano and Treviso, lie the villas of the Venetian patricians. They can be very grand or they can be idealized farm houses, but, whatever their style, they came into being as much for the convenience and pleasure of their owners as to impress people by their magnificence. This is true even of such famous Palladian villas as the Villa Barbaro at Maser, the Villa Malcontenta and the Rotonda. Behind Palladio's austere reflection of classical façades are practical country houses, meant to be lived in and not to cost too much to run. Few of these villas have kept their original gardens but much of their decoration is intact, such as the Tiepolo frescoes at Villa Valmarana and the Veroneses at Villa Barbaro. The finest procession of country houses and rural palaces is by the rather muddy Brenta canal, down which the quaint passenger launch, the *burchiello*, passes each day on route to Padua. Lord Byron lived by the Brenta, as did Voltaire's Senator Pococurante. This last, with his superiority to all enthusiasm, was a very un-Venetian figure, since affectation in Venice rarely led to an indifference to pleasure.

In Vicenza itself the Roman setting is more authentic, the *gravitas* more sustained. Tutored and subsidized by his humanist patron Trissino (who gave the unpretending Andrea della Gondola his epic and immortal nickname), Palladio reclothed the old town-hall in classical stone, lined the streets with palaces, and recreated the theatre of Plautus and Terence for the learned Vicentine Academy. Later his pupil Scamozzi built his own Teatro Olimpico nearby at Sabbioneta.

Both Vicenza and Padua are cities with a stronger humanist bias than Venice herself. The University at Padua is one of the oldest in Europe; its extraordinary anatomy theatre would have been in use when William Harvey, the discoverer of the circulation of the blood, studied there. The Botanical Gardens were also the first in Italy, and later were much admired by Goethe, the classic traveller in search of culture.

Padua is also the city of St Antony, with St Francis and St Catherine of Siena, the most loved of medieval saints. The great church dedicated to him unites traditional Italian basilica design with an Eastern fantasy of cupolas and towers that recalls St Basil's in Moscow or a mosque at Acre. It contains fine reliefs by Donatello as well as offering a site to his statue of Gattamelata. Anyone who has been in Padua on the feast day of St Antony will have experienced that extraordinary sense of the continuity of past and present which is so striking a feature of Italian life. Balloon sellers, religious bodies with banners and floats, children, dogs, the pious and the merely curious, tourists, pilgrims and persons too singular to categorize, throng the square and file continuously into the church. St Antony is one of the genuinely popular saints: he is the property of ordinary people and the fact that his shrine is surrounded by art treasures and administered by great dignitaries of the church does not daunt his followers. According to legend, his preaching was so eloquent it caused the fish to leap from rivers to listen to him. The piety of those who flock to his church is independent of dogmas and authorities, and the liturgy being impervious to vulgarity, the devout come and go in the great church's chapels to take part in the continuous services and prayers. In such manifestations of faith as this, modern Italy becomes briefly what she was in medieval times.

Not far from San Antonio is the Prato della Valle, half miniature park and half open-air market, and one of the most agreeable places of public assembly in Italy. Indeed, despite its rather sombre tone, Padua is a great and characterful city. Like so many cities not particularly well sited on a plain (Florence is another), Padua gives one the sense that it has created all its excellences for itself.

Coming to Venice is like coming to a new world, being born into a wonderland that miraculously was saved from being vulgar. But Venice is best experienced close up. All great cities are agglomerations of villages, but none more effectively than Venice. Its districts (*sestieri*) are easily traced on the map. What cannot be shown is the marvellous naturalness of Venetian life, the quick change from (say) the western limits of the Dorsoduro by the Accademia Museum to San Paolo and the utterly different milieu of Campo Santa Margherita, a spacious and relaxed working-class district, which itself abutts on the grandeur of the Scuola di San Rocco and the Church of the Frari. The imposing sights of Venice are magnificent, but they are rooted on the common sense of a practical people, on the judgment of engineers who drove wooden piles into islands of mud. Even Venetian Gothic can be austere and uncompromising: the great church of San Zanipolo (Santi Giovanni e Paolo) is gloomier than most of its Gothic brothers in northern Europe. The fantasy of the Doge's Palace, with its decorative façade resembling a Moorish screen, disappears on closer acquaintance to be replaced by a stern arrangement in stone that would deter the most convinced malefactor. It was a prison as well, and close-up it looks it. Venice was the Serene Republic; it defied excommunication, the League of Cambrai and the French and Spanish invasions, but it was never a participatory democracy as Florence was. Walking down a *fondamenta*, a *calle*, or even ducking under a *sottoportego*, watching the lithe Venetian cats scuttling away into the mossy shadows, the visitor finds it all too easy to romanticize Venice.

Every lover of Venice has his own special view of the city. Wagner wrote Act Two of *Tristan und Isolde* in Venice and returned to the Palazzo Vendramin-Calergi to die. Why has Venice so often been associated with death? Thomas Mann's youthful story of the writer Aschenbach's last days on the Lido made the imaginative link. Diaghilev was told he would die on water and now he is buried on San Michele, with his greatest discovery, Stravinsky, nearby. Stravinsky's magnificent *Canticum Sacrum* is dedicated to the city of St Mark. The great parade of Venetian music starts with the Netherlander Willaert, goes on to the Gabrielis, Monteverdi, Cavalli, Vivaldi, Marcello, Albinoni and the rest, right up to the present day and Luigi Nono.

The Venice that is evoked in literature is Venice in old age, Venice in decline, and the black of the gondolas and gondoliers can easily take on funereal overtones. Yet Venice still lives. It has come to terms with its great past, as no other city has done so that today it stands for the prior rights of civilization, for the deeds of men over the needs of machines. This isn't wide-eyed idealism: the same principle motivated the expansionist policies of the Doges of the early Renaissance. They wanted wealth so that their city could be still more beautiful and pleasant to live in. It was for these men that the great Venetian painters created Europe's most magnificent heritage of worldly paintings. Bellini is suffused with the sweetest strength; Carpaccio elevates the surface of life to a mystical vision; Titian and Tintoretto can both convey the culminating pleasures of this world – and then effortlessly assert values that make them valueless; Veronese shows that magnificence is more than mere vanity.

The gondola is so archetypical an image of Venice, that one ignores the fact that it is primarily a city to walk through. It cannot grow any bigger, since the sea acts as the most intractable city wall. In one week, a visitor can walk down every Venetian alleyway, thoroughfare and public place. He will visit and re-visit favourite parts, such as the old ghetto district, five minutes walk from the railway station, and come to the peaceful prospect of Santa Maria dell'Orto facing away from Venice's north shore. No Venetian church is as mysterious as San Francesco della Vigna, which marks the spot where the angel first pronounced the words *Pax tibi Marce*, which became the Serenissima's device. When in St Mark's, he will rejoice in the mosaics, go up to the horses and creep around forty feet above the floor to admire the superb designs in the paving. He will cross the Piazza to the Correr Museum, which records life in the city through the ages. The lover of Tintoretto will find himself propelled from one Venetian church to another. The musician scrambling after the *ad hoc* groups of performers of modern and Baroque music who give concerts around Venice will penetrate to districts far from the luxury hotels. But a man with an obsession will enjoy Venice more than an ordinary visitor. Ruskin imposed his own vision of a noble Gothic city on the

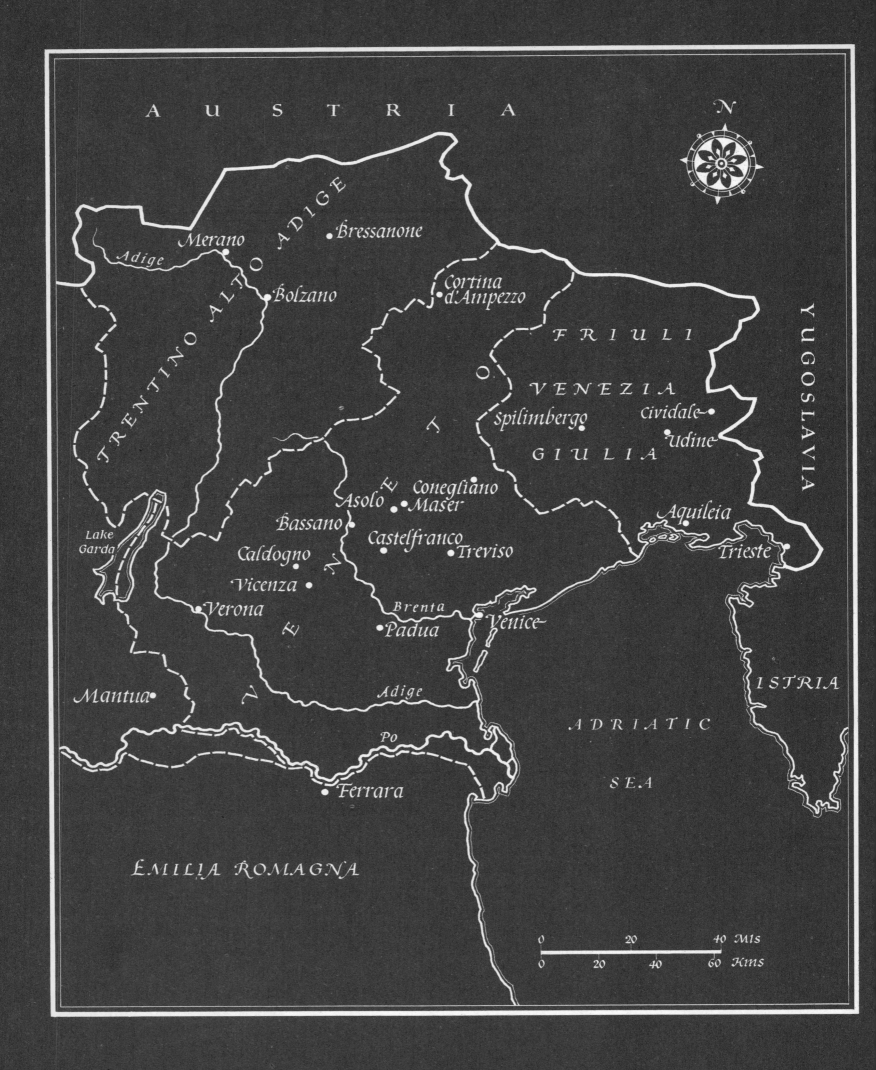

258 Lake Lungo, Giogaia di Tessa, Province of Merano, originally part of a glacier.

259 Interior of the eleventh-century Basilica at Aquileia, built on the site of an earlier church and once the centre of a powerful see.

260 The bridge over the Brenta canal at Bassano del Grappa erected in 1948. A replica of the nineteenth-century bridge destroyed in World War II.

261 Lower panels of one of the bronze doors of S. Zeno, Verona, the work of twelfth-century German craftsmen.

262 Façade of S. Zeno, Verona, built in the twelfth century, with marble relief panels round the doors.

263 The Palace of the Loggia, Udine, a fine example of the Venetian-Gothic style. The frescoes are late nineteenth-century copies by Giuseppe Ghedina of originals by Il Pordenone.

264 Rachel hiding the images; fresco by Giambattista Tiepolo, one of a series of scenes from Genesis in the gallery of the Archiepiscopal Palace, Udine. Tiepolo painted his self-portrait in the centre next to Rachel's father Laban.

265 The Teatro Olimpico, Vicenza, begun in 1580, Palladio's most famous work, completed after his death by Vincenzo Scamozzi.

266 Gallery of the Theatre, Sabbioneta, built by Scamozzi for the Duke whose beautiful and ambitious city-state was called 'The Athens of the Gonzagas'.

267 Scale model of Palladio's most famous villa, the Villa Capra, or Rotonda.

268 *Trompe l'œil* frescoes by Veronese in the Villa Barbaro at Maser which was built by Palladio for a rich Venetian humanist.

269 Villa Manin, Passariano, province of Udine, the most ostentatious of the country villas of the Veneto and the residence of the last Doge.

270 Scala dei Giganti, the ceremonial staircase of the Palace of the Doges at Venice.

271 Detail of the bronze equestrian statue of the

Condottiere Bartolomeo Colleoni by Andrea Verrocchio (1435–1488).

272 The Lion of St Mark, the symbol of Venice; detail of the eighteenth-century gate of the Loggetta.

273 The church of S. Maria della Salute, designed in 1633 by Baldassare Longhena, seen from one of the last private gondolas in Venice.

274 Marble lions in front of the Arsenal, Venice, once the pivot of the Venetian Republic's great maritime power.

275 Eighteenth-century ceiling, Palazzo Albrizzi, Venice; twenty-four putti hold up the billowing stucco drapery, the work of the Swiss stuccoists Abbondio Stazio (1675–1757) and Carpoforo Mazzetti-Tencala (1684–1748) from Lugano.

276 View from the Palazzo Venier dei Leoni, Venice; a gondola, caparisoned for the annual regatta, glides along the Grand Canal.

277 One of the loveliest of Venice's many lovely vistas, S. Giorgio Maggiore seen across the Lagoon from the Piazzetta.

278 Fireworks celebrating the Feast of the Redentore, Venice, a festival held annually since the days of the Republic.

279 The multi-coloured marble-fronted Palazzo Dario, Venice, built in 1487 in the characteristic style of the Lombardi; on one side the tall Palazzo Barbaro, on the other a low building where Lorenzo Boschetti's ambitious Palazzo Venier dei Leoni, 1749, should have extended but was never completed.

280 Portico of Palladio's Villa Cornaro at Piombino Dese, province of Padua.

281 Detail of sixteenth-century frescoes, part of a vast pictorial cycle in Palladio's Villa Caldogno at Caldogno, province of Vicenza.

282 Palladio's Villa Emo, Fanzolo di Vedelago, province of Treviso. The farm buildings and offices are masked by the long arcaded wings on either side of the temple-fronted residential quarters.

283 Asolo.

284 Partially dismantled set for *Aida*, performed in the Roman arena at Verona.

285 Basilica of St Anthony, begun in 1232, the heart of 'many domèd Padua' and the shrine of one of Christianity's most popular saints.

286 An old water-mill in the Stringa ceramic factory at Nove, province of Vicenza, in use for centuries for grinding stones used in glazing maiolica.

287 The first anatomical theatre in Europe, in the University of Padua, built in 1544.

288 Allegorical frescoes on houses in the Piazza delle Erbe, Verona.

289 Detail of an old frescoed patrician mansion at Spilimbergo, province of Udine, now fallen into decay.

290 Detail of the Altar of Ratchis, Cividale del Friuli, eighth century.

291 Lively biblical scenes – signed frescoes by Jakob Sunter, late fifteenth century, on the ceiling of the arcade, cloister of the Duomo, Bressanone.

292 Crucifix near the Well of the Seven Wond in the courtyard of the Convent of Novac near Bressanone in the Italian Tyrol.

293 The Baroque church of Our Lady, of Novacella, near Bressanone, a la semble of painted and gilded stucc frescoes, ostentatious polychrome ubiquitous putti.

294 Ruined castle strategically placed on a top near Bolzano, in a region contested for centuries by the Counts of Tyrol and the Hapsburgs, and where the constantly changing allegiances of the feudal barons and counts created a need for fortified strongholds.

295 Autostrada. Italy's imposing network of modern motorways, nearly all constructed in the last twenty years, link the Northern Alps to the extremities of Calabria and the Ligurian coast and cross from the Tyrrhenian to the Adriatic.

Venetian reality, but by so doing he found more in Venice than even its own inhabitants could see.

No sight, however famous, can sum up Venice – not St Mark's, the Bridge of Sighs, the view across to San Giorgio Maggiore, the Riva Schiavoni, the Grand Canal looking down to the Accademia Bridge. The first and last view of the city is perhaps the most evocative – an unbelievable vision hanging in the mist of the lagoon, poised on water like the Ancient Mariner's, burning green and blue and white. We all come to Venice to surprise some part of ourselves, some dormant reflex of beauty which we have never properly indulged. We who come to it from outside all misunderstand the city, from Coryate in the sixteenth century, via the English Palladians, Goethe, Byron, Shelley, Browning, Wagner, Corvo, Thomas Mann, Werfel, Hemingway, down to the makers of romantic films and the writers of travel books. But the city is still there, still the most spectacular in the world, the jewel of Italy, the reality that surpasses every hyperbole.

Hannibal enters the Promised Land

On the ninth day the army reached the summit. Most of the climb had been over trackless mountain sides; frequently a wrong route was taken – sometimes through the deliberate deception of the guides, or again when some likely-looking valley would be entered by guess-work, without knowledge of whither it led. There was a two days' halt on the summit, to rest the men after the exhausting climb and the fighting ... Seeing their despair, Hannibal rode ahead and at a point of vantage which afforded a prospect of a vast extent of country, he gave the order to halt, pointing to Italy far below, and the Po valley beyond the foothills of the Alps. 'My men,' he said, 'you are at this moment passing the protective barrier of Italy – more, you are walking over the very walls of Rome. Henceforward all will be easy going – no more hills to climb. After a fight or two you will have the capital of Italy, the citadel of Rome, in the hollow of your hands.'

Livy (59 BC–AD 17), 'The History of Rome', Book XXI, translated by Aubrey de Sélincourt

The Villa Capra

The sumptuous Palace of the ... Earle Odoricus Capra ... is a little mile distant from the City. It is built upon a pretty eminent hillocke, and is round (in which respect it is called in the Italian Rotonda) having foure very beautiful fronts, which doe answere the foure parts of the world ... Every front hath six most stately great pillars, and two pairs of stairs to ascend to the same, each contayning eighteene faire greeses. The roofe of the house is round, and very pretily adorned partly with curious pictures, and partly with statues.

Thomas Coryate, 'Crudities', 1611

FOLD OUT ▷

261

271

Byron in Venice: the poet

I stood in Venice, on the Bridge of Sighs;
A palace and a prison on each hand:
I saw from out the wave her structures rise
As from the stroke of the enchanter's wand:
A thousand years their cloudy wings expand
Around me, and a dying Glory smiles
O'er the far times, when many a subject land
Look'd to the winged Lion's marble piles,
Where Venice sate in state, throned on her hundred isles.

Byron, 'Childe Harold's Pilgrimage', 1818, Canto IV, stanza 1

Byron in Venice: the man

In going, about an hour and a half ago, to a rendezvous with a Venetian girl (unmarried and the daughter of one of their nobles), I tumbled into the Grand Canal, . . . my foot slipped getting into my Gondola to set out (owing to the cursed slippery steps of their palaces), and in I flounced like a Carp, and went dripping like a Triton to my Sea nymph and had to scramble up to a grated window: –
    Fenced with iron within and without
    Lest the lover get in or the Lady get out.

Byron, in a letter to John Murray, 1819

Thomas Coryate takes a gondola

None of them are open above, but fairly covered, first with some fiteene or sixteene little round peeces of timber that reach from one end to the other, and make a pretty kinde of Arch or vault in the Gondola; then with faire blacke cloth which is turned up at both ends of the boate, to the end that if the passanger meaneth to be private, he may draw downe the same, and after row so secretly that no man can see him: in the inside the Benches are finely covered with blacke leather, and the bottomes of many of them together with the sides under the benches are very neatly garnished with fine linen cloth, the edge whereof is laced with bonelace. The ends are beautified with two pretty and ingenuous devices . . . in the forme of a Dolphins tayle, with the fins very artificially represented, and it seemeth to be tinned over. Of these Gondolas they say there are ten thousand aboute the citie, whereof sixe thousand are private, serving for the Gentlemen and others, and foure thousand for mercenary men, which get their living by the trade of rowing.

Thomas Coryate, 'Crudities', 1611

Dante remembers the Arsenal

For as at Venice in the Arsenal
  In winter-time they boil the gummy pitch
  To caulk such ships as need an overhaul,
Now that they cannot sail – instead of which
  One builds him a new boat, one toils to plug
  Seams strained by many a voyage, others stitch
Canvas to patch a tattered jib or lug,
  Hammer at the prow, hammer at the stern, or twine
  Ropes or shave oars, refit and make all snug –
So, not by fire, but by the art divine,
  A thick pitch boiled down there, spattering the brink
  With viscous glue.

Dante, 'Inferno', Book XXI,
translated by Dorothy L. Sayers

'Afloat'

Afloat; we move. Delicious! ah,
What else is like the gondola?
This level floor of liquid glass
Begins beneath it swift to pass.
It goes as if it went alone
By some impulsion of its own.
How light it moves, how softly! Ah,
Were all things like the gondola!

Arthur Hugh Clough, 'Dipsychus', 1850

Villas on the Brenta

A few miles from Padua, at Ponte di Brenta, begins the long line of villas which follows the course of the river to its outlet at Fusina. Dante speaks in the *Inferno* of the villas and castles on the Brenta, and it continued to be the favourite *villegiatura* of the Venetian nobility till the middle of the nineteenth century ... The Villa Pisani is a palace. Its majestic façade, with pillared central *corps de bâtiment* and far-reaching wings stands on the highway bordering the Brenta; ... the palace is built about two inner courts, and its innumerable rooms are frescoed by the principal Italian decorative painters of the day, while the great central saloon has one of Tiepolo's most riotously splendid ceilings.

Edith Wharton, 'Italian Villas', 1904

Petruchio comes to Padua

Lucentio : Tranio, since for the great desire I had
    To see fair Padua, nursery of arts,
    I am arriv'd for fruitful Lombardy,
    The pleasant garden of great Italy ...
Petruchio : I come to wive it wealthily in Padua.

Shakespeare, 'The Taming of the Shrew', Act I, c. 1595

Paduan countryside

By the skirts of that grey cloud
Many-domèd Padua proud
Stands, a peopled solitude,
'Mid the harvest-shining plain,
Where the peasant heaps his grain
In the garner of his foe,
And the milk-white oxen slow
With the purple vintage strain,
Heaped upon the creaking wain.

Shelley, 'Lines Written among the Eugenean Hills', 1818

Around Verona, 1611 and 1787

I observed great abundance of vineyards on both sides of the way, and exceeding fertile Champaines, goodly meadows, pastures, corne fieldes, and arable groundes both betwixt Padua and Vicenza, and also betwixt Vicenza and Verona.

Thomas Coryate, 'Crudities', 1611

The road from Verona to Vicenza runs in a north-easterly direction parallel to the mountains. To the left one sees a continuous range of foothills, composed of sandstone, limestone, clay and marl, dotted with villages, castles and isolated houses. A vast plain stretches to the right, across which we drove on a wide, straight and well-kept road through fertile fields. There trees are planted in long rows upon which the vines are trained to their tops. The gently swaying tendrils hung down under the weight of the grapes, which ripen early here. This is what a festoon ought to look like.

September 19th, 1786: Goethe, 'Italian Journey',
translated by W. H. Auden and Elizabeth Mayer

Goethe at Padua University

The anatomical theatre, in particular, is an example of how to squeeze as many students together as possible. The listeners sit in tiers one above the other in a kind of high funnel. They look down from their precipice on to the narrow platform where the dissecting table stands. This gets no daylight, so that the professor has to demonstrate by the light of a lamp.

September 27th, 1786: Goethe, 'Italian Journey',
translated by W. H. Auden and Elizabeth Mayer

The Ruskins at Verona

John says there is work for him here for at least six months and we intend returning here after we leave Venice for another week which will enable us to see three important towns, Mantua, Modena and Parma . . . John is engaged in some very elaborate and beautiful drawings from the Monuments of the Scaliger family, formerly Lords of Verona in the Middle Ages. They are very splendid and stand in a little court in the middle of the town beside their former Palace . . .

Effie Ruskin, in a letter to her parents from Verona in 1849

Shelley on Venice

If I had been an unconnected man
I, from this moment, should have formed some plan
Never to leave sweet Venice, – for to me
It was delight to ride by the lone sea;
And then, the town is silent – one may write
Or read in gondolas by day or night,
Having the little brazen lamp alight,
Unseen, uninterrupted; books are there,
Pictures, and casts from all those statues fair
Which were twin-born with poetry

Shelley, from 'Julian and Maddalo', 1819

A cure for melancholy

To take a boat in a pleasant evening, and with music to row upon the waters, which Plutarch so much applauds, Elian admires upon the river Pineus in those Thessalian fields, beset with green bays, where birds so sweetly sing that passengers, enchanted as it were with their heavenly music, *omnium laborum et curarum obliviscantur*, forget forthwith all labours, care and grief – or in a *Gundilo* through the grand *Canale* in Venice, to see those goodly palaces, must needs refresh and give content to a melancholy, dull spirit.

Robert Burton, 'The Anatomy of Melancholy', 1621

Torcello and Venice

Beyond the widening branches of the lagoon, and rising out of the bright lake into which they gather, there are a multitude of towers, dark and scattered among square-set shapes of clustered palaces, a long and irregular line fretting in the southern sky.

Mother and daughter, you behold them both in their widowhood – TORCELLO and VENICE.

Thirteen hundred years ago, the grey moorland looked as it does this day, and the purple mountains stood as radiantly in the deep distances of evening; but on the line of the horizon, there were strange fires mixed with the light of sunset, and the lament of many human voices mixed with the fretting of the waves on their ridges of sand. The flames rose from the ruins of Altinum; the lament from the multitude of its people, seeking, like Israel of old, a refuge from the sword in the paths of the sea.

John Ruskin, 'The Stones of Venice', 1853

The cemetery island of San Michele

He slowly paced along cypress-avenues, between the graves of little children with blue or white standards and the graves of adults marked by more sombre memorials. All around him were patricians bringing sheaves of painted candles and gorgeous garlands of orchids and everlastings, or plebeians on their knees grubbing up weeds and tracing pathetic designs with cheap chrysanthemums and farthing night-lights. Here, were a baker's boy and a telegraph messenger, repainting their father's grave-post with a tin of black and a bottle of gold. There, were half a dozen ribald and dishonest licentious young gondolieri, quiet and alone on their wicked knees round the grave of a comrade.

Frederick Rolfe, Baron Corvo, in 'The Desire and Pursuit of the Whole', 1909

Thomas Coryate on his first view of Venice

The most glorious and heavenly show upon the water that ever any mortal eye beheld.

Thomas Coryate, 'Crudities', 1611

Then all things being ready, that were to be carried in their journey, Tobias bade his father and his mother farewell, and they set out both together.

And Tobias went forward, and the dog followed him, and he lodged the first night by the river of Tigris.

And he went out to wash his feet, and behold a monstrous fish came up to devour him.

And Tobias being afraid of him, cried out with a loud voice, saying : Sir, he cometh upon me.

And the angel said to him : Take him by the gill, and draw him to thee. And when he had done so, he drew him out upon the land, and he began to pant before his feet.

Then the angel said to him : Take out the entrails of this fish, and lay up his heart, and his gall, and his liver for thee : for these are necessary for useful medicines.

And when he had done so, he roasted the flesh thereof, and they took it with them in the way : the rest they salted as much as might serve them, till they came to Rages the city of the Medes.

Then Tobias asked the angel, and said to him : I beseech thee, brother Azarias, tell me what remedies are these things for, which thou hast bid me keep of the fish ?

And the angel, answering, said to him : If thou put a little piece of its heart upon coals, the smoke thereof driveth away all kind of devils, either from man or from woman, so that they come no more to them.

And the gall is good for anointing the eyes, in which there is a white speck, and they shall be cured.

And Raphael said to Tobias : As soon as thou shalt come into thy house, forthwith adore the Lord thy God : and giving thanks to him, go to thy father, and kiss him.

And immediately anoint his eyes with this gall of the fish, which thou carriest with thee.

For be assured that his eyes shall be presently opened, and thy father shall see the light of heaven, and shall rejoice in the sight of thee.

Then the dog, which had been with them in the way, ran before, and coming as if he had brought the news, shewed his joy by his fawning and wagging his tail.

And his father that was blind, rising up, began to run stumbling with his feet : and giving a servant his hand, went to meet his son.

Then Tobias taking of the gall of the fish, anointed his father's eyes.

And he stayed about half an hour : and a white skin began to come out of his eyes, like the skin of an egg.

And Tobias took hold of it, and drew it from his eyes, and immediately he recovered his sight.

And they glorified God, both he and his wife and all that knew him.

296 *Tobias and the Archangel Raphael*, by the brothers Piero (1443–1496) and Antonio (about 1432–1498) Pollaiuolo. Galleria Sabauda, Palazzo dell'Accademia delle Scienze, Turin.

TOBIAS V 22; VI 1–9; XI 7–16

Epilogue by Gore Vidal

'Gorino, why you live in Rome?'

I sit at a table, staring into a dozen powerful lights and a camera. Off to one side is Federico Fellini. He wears a heavy overcoat, a long woolen scarf, a dramatic black hat. He is under the impression that Gore was the name of an obscure Celtic saint and so suitable for diminuizing.

'Gorino, why you live in Rome?' I was asked the question a dozen times between midnight and five in the morning. In the film *Fellini Roma*, I am seated at an outdoor trattoria in Trastevere during the August festival of *De' noi antri*. In reality, I was shivering in a small piazza off the Via dei Coronari in late November. Fellini had already asked the same question of the actors Mastroianni, Sordi and Anna Magnani. According to Fellini (in a press interview – not to me!), I was added to the film 'as a typical Anglo-Saxon gone native'. Well.

My answer varied with each take but the theme was always the same. The artist deals in illusions. Modern Rome has only three industries: the government, the Church and the movies; each a dream-dispenser. I waffled about the world's end through over-population and pollution (a subject the Italians still find amusingly exotic), and concluded that a city which calls itself 'eternal' is obviously the best place to watch eternity go down the drain.

Two years have passed since that cold November night and things are a lot worse for all of us. Certainly Rome is a mess – not at all like the quiet (fairly quiet) city I first visited in 1939. Yet I have lived in Italy for the last decade. Why? Italophiles tend to cliché when asked to defend their *philia*. There is the human scale. And the joy in living. And the . . . uh, the *light*! That Italian light which the romantics went on and on about for two centuries can still be observed whenever the wind is from the Alps and the fumes from thirty million Fiats float toward Africa.

Actually most of the romantic clichés about Italy are as true as they ever were; that is to say, they are half-truths as perceived by Northern puritans. But I doubt if a modern-day wet like E. M. Forster would very much want to tread, fearfully or not, among the life-enhancing peasants of today. For one thing, the Italians have grown a bit sullen with prosperity and their good manners are apt to fray under stress. Even so, they are still delightful to be with, particularly the Romans (what does SPQR mean? goes the Roman joke: *sempre puttane questi Romani* – always whores these Romans). It is true that Anglo-Saxons (I use the term in de Gaulle's lordly imprecise sense) are often distressed to find that Italians are not *sincere*. Thank God. They are better than that: they are delicate in human relations

408

yet openly selfish; above all, they want for you to make them laugh, preferably without meaning to. Like the thousands of cats that fill the ruins of Rome, they are neutral, self contained. . . . Now I am drifting into purest cliché. But then Rome does that to everyone after a while. It was Henry James who said that Rome was the perfect place in which to lose all earthly vanity. After this splendid – even original – *aperçu*, the Master wisely moved on to London.

But Rome is not Italy. Rome was not built in a day. All roads lead to Rome. How the cornucopia of old saws flows when one starts to describe my adopted land (land of my ancestors, too: the Vidals are Romanisch, from Friuli in the Cadore alps)! So I shall try to relate my platitudes to Mr Roloff Beny's fine gallery of pictures.

Right off, the uniqueness of Italy is its diversity; the tragedy its unification. Milan has nothing to do with Naples, Naples has nothing to do with Palermo (could this have been said before?). I have visited every Italian city (excepting Enna) and found each to be entirely itself and unlike the others because, once upon a time, each was its own independent world. Now all are united by Fiat and by television (that is to say, by soccer and popular song contests). But once the traveller penetrates each city's periphery of cement-block high-rises in their setting of trash, it is still possible to see what Mr Beny shows us: a thousand worlds caught at various moments in history – a palimpsest (curious, I *knew* this word was going to surface despite all efforts at suppression) of a dozen civilizations. Dare I mention the fly in amber? No.

But I would advise those who have not had the luck to visit Italy to come fairly soon and see the countryside before it is all covered over with cement. Everywhere farms are abandoned while suburbs pullulate around the ancient cities whose monuments and museums deteriorate because the state has not the money or the will to keep them up. The ruins are being ruined while Venice sinks and in the remaining woods, songbirds are slaughtered by hunters. Even so . . . even so, Italy is still the most beautiful of this world's countries and the Italians are still the most agreeable of our earth's fellow travelers.

Certainly, in the altogether too likely demise of our race, I highly recommend Mr Beny's photographs to the visiting android. Although your galaxy is far-removed from ours and you breathe purest methane through those curious nozzles, do study these pictures and see what we were, what we built, and through those multi-facetted lenses of yours note for the universal record what a lovely earth we had.

409

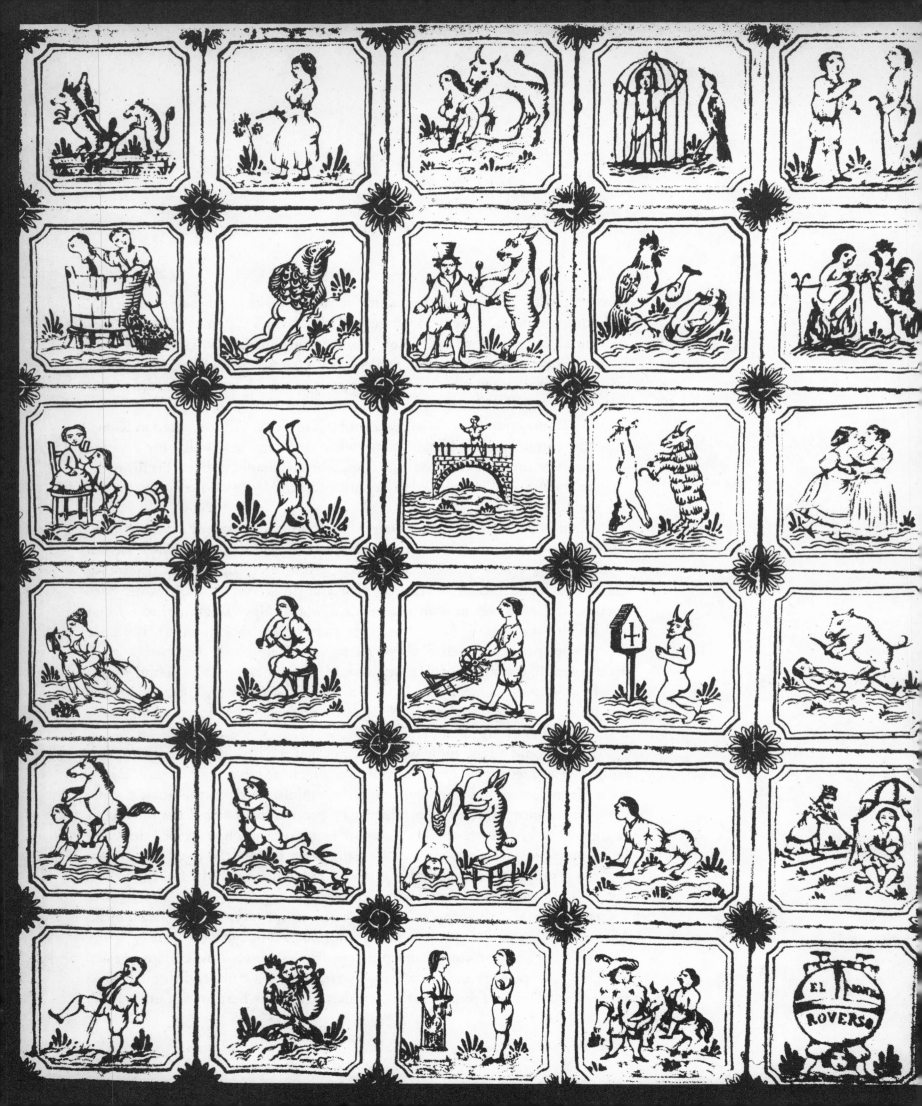

Historical notes on the plates
by Brian de Breffny

9   THE STRAIT OF MESSINA

The Strait of Messina, called Fretulum Siculum by the Romans, separates Sicily from the Calabrian mainland, overshadowed on the Sicilian side by the peaks of the Peloritani Mountains. A dialect of Greek origin is still spoken in some of the fishing villages on the Calabrian coast between Cape Spartivento and Pellaro.

0   GREEK THEATRE, TAORMINA

Refugees from Naxos founded the Greek city of Tauromenion in 358 BC on the site of an earlier Siculian settlement. Built on a natural terrace of Mount Tauro from which it takes its name and suspended between mountain and sea, its position is unparalleled. Taormina was reduced to a Roman colony when its inhabitants sided unsuccessfully with Sixtus Pompey against Octavian.

Of the Greek remains the most impressive is the theatre over 700 feet above the sea, which was built in the third century BC but enlarged and renovated by the Romans a century later who used it for gladiatorial spectacles. The floor of the *orchestra* has been partly excavated to show the underground passages, and a few of the forty-five columns of the *scenae frons* re-erected. This was originally faced with marble and adorned with statues.

The view from the *cavea*, cut in a natural cavity of the mountain-side, is one of the most beautiful in Sicily, embracing Mount Etna, the sea, and the town of Taormina far below at sea-level.

2,   AGRIGENTO, TEMPLES OF ZEUS, HERCULES AND CONCORD
3

Settlers from Rhodes founded the Greek city of Akragas in 581 BC. It grew rapidly in size and importance and at its zenith was described by Pindar as 'incredibly opulent' and 'the most beautiful city of man'. Diogenes Laertius asserted that its population reached 800,000: 20,000 citizens, 180,000 free settlers and 600,000 slaves. While these figures must be taken with great reserve there is no doubt that prior to falling to the Carthaginian Hannibal who sacked and burned it in 406 BC it was a phenomenon of prosperity and included among its inhabitants poets, athletes, doctors and philosophers such as Empedocles. The city was reconquered by Timoleon in 340 BC but fell to the Romans eighty years later, then again to the Carthaginians and once again to the Romans in 210 BC under whose rule it enjoyed a further period of splendour.

The Temple of Hercules, the earliest of those in the temple area, was built at the end of the sixth century BC. It was famous in antiquity for the beautiful bronze statue of the demi-god which it housed and which Verres (among others) tried to steal.

The colossal Temple of Olympian Zeus, the third largest in the Greek world, was built in 480–479 BC by Carthaginian prisoners taken at the Greek victory of Imera. Ancient writings imply that it was never finished and earthquakes have ensured that not one of its thirty-eight immense columns still stands.

The Temple of Hera has twenty-five of its original thirty-four columns

standing. In the best position of the temple area at its extreme eastern end, it embodies the Greek genius for fusing architecture and landscape.

The Temple of Concord built in the middle of the fifth century BC is the best preserved of all Greek temples save the Theseion at Athens. Its tawny-gold colour, the grace and serene majesty of its proportions and its magnificent setting make it one of the most impressive and memorable works of Greek civilization that have survived. Like all the temples at Agrigento, it uses the Doric order – sturdy fluted columns without bases, simple capitals and an entablature of alternating triglyphs (the stones with multiple vertical grooves) and metopes (the blank squares in-between).

46   NISIDA, CAPE MISENO AND THE ISLES OF PROCIDA AND ISCHIA

On the west side of the Bay of Naples rises the island of Nisida, the Nesis of the ancients, now joined to the mainland by a causeway. It has a rich classical history; it once belonged to Lucullus; here Cicero visited Marcus Brutus and Brutus and Cassius hatched their plot against Caesar. In the last century the castle was a grim penitentiary where the patriot Carlo Poerio was imprisoned. To the right is the tip of Cape Miseno; next in the centre is the island of Procida also overshadowed by the castle which is also a prison. Beyond that, in the distance to the left, is Ischia, the Pithecusa of the Greeks and Aenaria of the Romans; it is the largest of the islands in the Bay of Naples; hot mineral springs famed for their curative waters gush from the rocks and the lush lower slopes of the volcanic Mount Epomeo nourish excellent vines.

47   SEGESTA THEATRE

The theatre at Segesta is carved out of the live rock and has as a natural backdrop a sublime vista of hills and sea. This row of seats next to one of the semi-circular aisles is, unusually, furnished with backs, which have now weathered so that they seem like sculptures by Henry Moore, gazing out in timeless reflection.

48   STATUE OF VENUS ANADYOMENE, National Museum, Syracuse

This Hellenistic statue is a 2nd century BC Roman work based on a Praxitelean model. The goddess is represented emerging from her bath.

49   PAPYRUS NEAR THE FOUNTAIN OF CYANE

The little river Cyane joins the Anapus to flow into the sea outside Syracuse. According to Greek mythology Hades abducted Persephone and took her to the infernal regions, one of her nymphs Cyane attempted to oppose the ravisher and the god changed her into the spring which bears her name. Around the source the ancient Syracuseans held an annual festival immersing bulls as public sacrifices in its waters in memory of Hercules who is supposed to have passed here with the cattle of Geryon. The papyrus, which is not found elsewhere in Europe, grows around the source and along the banks bending gracefully with its tufted head of delicate filaments over the imperceptibly flowing stream. Its existence here was discovered by an English naturalist in the eighteenth century. In

411

recent years vandals have grievously reduced the growth but fortunately the Department of Civil Engineering has undertaken a programme of preservation and re-planting.

50 SEGESTA, TEMPLE

The city of Segesta, once the traditional enemy of Selinuntum, has all but disappeared leaving only the grand and solitary temple and theatre (pl. 47). The temple is one of the most notable remaining examples of the Doric style but also one of the most mysterious. It is certainly unfinished, the columns not being fluted, but not even the foundations of a cella have been traced. It dates from the fifth century BC.

52, ROMAN MOSAICS, PIAZZA ARMERINA
53 The luxurious Roman villa at Piazza Armerina was the country house of an unidentified magnate, possibly the Emperor Maximian, and has superb mosaics. These photographs show part of the famed hunting scenes depicting the capture of wild beasts for use in the Roman amphitheatres. In Plate 52 the hunters have cornered a wild boar with spears and fierce dogs – one of the men has a large rock with which to stun the animal while others look on tired by the struggle. In Plate 53 the weary hunters carry off the netted boar on a pole while a dog continues to bark and harry it.

54 PORTA NUOVA, PALERMO

This city gate, originally called the Porta d'Austria, was erected in 1535 to celebrate the passage of the Emperor Charles V returning victorious from Tunis where he had expelled Barbarossa and freed 10,000 Christian slaves. The four gigantic telamones, the work of the local sculptor Gaspare Lo Guercio and representing Tunisian prisoners, were added in 1668.

55 PALERMO CATHEDRAL

Like many buildings in the Sicilian capital the Cathedral is a palimpsest of Norman, Arab, Gothic, Renaissance and Baroque styles. It was begun in 1169, added to throughout the Middle Ages and partially transformed into a Baroque church by the eighteenth-century Florentine architect Ferdinando Fuga. The plate shows part of the south-east flank with a clock tower of 1840 designed to harmonize with the rest. The interior contains the tombs of Frederick II and his wife.

56 RUINS OF PALAZZO BONAGIA, PALERMO

This Baroque palace of a Palermitan noble family was destroyed by Allied bombs in the Second World War. Like many of the Baroque palaces of Palermo, it had a sumptuous staircase. Only the façade now remains, standing in a builder's yard.

57 FOUNTAIN, PIAZZA PRETORIA, PALERMO

This enormous fountain built about 1555, the work of the Florentine sculptor Francesco Camilliani, was commissioned for his villa in Florence by Don Pietro de Toledo but sold to the city of Palermo in 1573 by his son. The plate shows some of the animal heads which together with statues of pagan divinities, allegories and herms combine to make an exuberant monument reminiscent of a carousel.

58 CAPRI AND PUNTO CAMPANELLA FROM THE SLOPES OF MOUNT COSTANZO

The island of Capri in the Gulf of Naples has long been a playground of rich sybarites and eccentrics. Following his visit to Capri in 29 BC the Emperor Augustus caused roads, aqueducts and villas to be built. Many wild tales of profligacy are connected with the residence of Tiberius sixty years later. He was the first of a long line of famous residents which includes Jacques de Fersen, Axel Munthe, Friedrich Krupp and Norman Douglas. Kaiser Wilhelm II and the Queen of Sweden were frequent visitors early in this century and here too Maxim Gorky lived for six years prior to the First World War and conducted a school for revolutionaries which attracted Lenin and Stalin. Capri is still a tourist Mecca; thousands of visitors cross from the mainland every day throughout the summer to admire the luxuriant vegetation, the remarkable views and the celebrated Blue Grotto.

61 STROMBOLI

Stromboli is one of the seven Lipari, or Aeolian, Islands, which lie between Sicily and Italy, and which were believed by the ancients to be the seat of the winds. Aeolus, the king of storms (and the inventor of the sail) gave Odysseus a bag containing all the winds, which was inadvertently opened by his companions. Stromboli, one of Italy's three active volcanoes, is about a mile wide, completely dominated by the crater mountain. Yet three small villages – Stromboli (formerly called S. Vincenzo), S. Bartolomeo and La Ginostra – manage to eke out an existence and sixty years ago the population was over 2,000. This has now shrunk to a few hundred by emigration to America and Australia. The people live mainly by fishing, with a little agriculture.

62 LEMON-PICKERS IN ISCHIA

On Ischia, often called the Green Isle, the English composer Sir William Walton and his wife have created an exotic garden out of the mountainside.
    These two brothers, the gardeners, tend the traditional Ischian lemon trees which grow in happy co-existence with rare shrubs and trees from all parts of the world.

63 WALL OF THE NURAGHE SANT'ANTINE near Torralba, Sardinia

There are several thousand of these early stone dwellings in Sardinia, conical shapes built of blocks of unmortared stone and going back as far as early fourteenth century BC. Sometimes found in clusters like the early Irish beehive-dwellings or the French *bories*, they usually contain one room on the ground with a stone stair to a room above. The Nuraghe Sant'Antine, unusually, has three storeys and is the largest of these constructions on the island. Its complexity shows it to be a late example, possibly built after the Carthaginian occupation of Sardinia in the sixth century BC.

64, YOUNG MAN AND WOMAN IN THE CAVALCATA SARDA,
65 Ascension Day, Sassari

Sassari, the second largest town in Sardinia after the capital, Cagliari, has two great annual festivals of which the Sardinian Cavalcade on Ascension Day is the most brilliant. From all over the island people come in colourful and beautiful local costumes to participate in the parade. The boy holding the orange is dressed in black velvet and rode in the cavalcade. The girl has an impressive array of gold jewellery and hand-worked lace, all heir-looms passed down in her family for generations.

67, MONREALE CATHEDRAL
69,
70 The splendid Cathedral of Monreale in the centre of the town was begun by the third Norman King of Sicily, William II, in 1174, two years after his accession. Soon after he ordered the construction of the adjacent monastery for the newly founded 'Ordo Cavensis' which was closely modelled on the Cluniacs.
    This was the last of the Norman cathedrals in Sicily and surpasses everything that they had previously built, especially in the splendour of its decoration. The nave has an arcade of pointed arches using a variety of columns, some antique Corinthian, others Byzantine.
    The mosaics, row upon row along the sides of the nave and aisles, show scenes from the Old and New Testaments. In the upper level of the clerestory in the section shown here can be seen Adam and Eve tempted by the serpent, God sentencing them, the Angel expelling them from Eden and scenes from the story of Cain and Abel. In the lower layer is Abraham sacrificing Isaac and other Old Testament stories. In the aisle, beyond the arcade, are some of the healing miracles of Christ. In the apse (Plate 71) the powerful figure of Christ Pantocrator seems to bless and embrace the entire church. Below is the enthroned Madonna (with Greek motto 'Panagia') with Child, assisted by angels and apostles. In the lower part are saints including the then recently martyred Thomas Becket. The founder of the cathedral, King William II of Sicily, had married in 1177 the child-Princess Joan, a daughter of King Henry II of England, who

three years previously had done penance for his complicity in the Arch-bishop's murder.

The ceiling of the nave was replaced in 1811 after its destruction by fire, but that of the crossing is original and shows marked Arab influence with its stalactite-like projections which can be seen in Plate 70, with the mosaic figures of the Eastern soldier-saints, St Mercury and St George.

The cathedral is a favourite marrying place for couples not only from Monreale and the surrounding villages but also from nearby Palermo.

68 MOSAIC, LA MARTORANA, PALERMO

This lovely Norman church was built in 1143 at the wish of George of Antioch, an Admiral of King Roger II, and its real name is S. Maria dell'Ammiraglio (St Mary of the Admiral). Its popular name comes from Eloisa Martorana, the foundress of a nearby monastery to which this church was given in 1433.

The decorative scheme of the mosaics in the cupola follows the strict rules of the mid-Byzantine period: in the centre Christ Pantocrator sur-rounded by angels, below the window prophets, and in the corners evangelists.

71 THE SANTISSIMA TRINITÀ, DELIA

This late twelfth-century church was successfully restored in the last century by the Saporito family on whose land it stands. Like most of the medieval churches of Sicily, it reflects the three cultures that ruled the island between the seventh and twelfth centuries. The Arabs succeeded the Byzantines in Sicily in 827 and were in turn supplanted by the Normans in 1072. At the Santissima Trinità the plan (a Greek cross) is Byzantine, the dome Saracenic.

72 BALLROOM, VILLA PALAGONIA, BAGHERIA

This villa a few miles from Palermo is an architectural caprice. It was built originally as a country villa for Ferdinando Francesco Gravina, Prince of Palagonia, at the beginning of the eighteenth century when it was fashion-able for the Palermitan nobles to have a residence outside the city. About 1746 Ferdinando Francesco III Gravina, Prince of Palagonia, added to and altered the villa transforming it into a vast folly. In the mirrored and painted ballroom with marble busts of his own ancestors and monarchs in medallions around the walls the eccentric prince is said to have danced alone, imagining in the myriad reflections that the room was crowded with dancers.

The villa was approached by a long balustraded gallery flanked like the garden walls by grotesque statues, dwarves, clowns, weird monsters, musicians, parodies of mythologies, devils and surrealist animals who might be at home in the world of Lewis Carroll. This astonishing place, the wonder of many travellers of the Age of Enlightenment, was visited by Goethe in 1787.

73 ORATORY OF S. ZITA

Giacomo Serpotta (1656–1732) spent his life in Palermo where he worked in stucco with a beguiling virtuosity. His most important works were commissioned by the aristocratic confraternities of the capital for their exclusive oratories. This plate shows the altar of one of these with a painting above it of Our Lady of the Rosary by Carlo Maratta (1625–1713). Around the altar are Serpotta's elegant and ebullient plaster figures of angels, precious allegorical statues and lively putti. His decoration here also included a large bas-relief of the Battle of Lepanto on the opposite wall. In the long lofty rectangular chapel the stuccoist has achieved a sceno-graphic masterpiece, frothy and dazzling white in its overall effect.

74 BAPTISMAL FONT, CHIESA MADRE, CASTELVETRANO, SICILY

The Church of the Assumption or Chiesa Madre in this provincial town was built in the sixteenth century but the finely carved wooden cover to the baptismal font is the work of a local craftsman, Pietro di Giato, and was executed in 1610.

THE CHINESE PALAZZINA, PALERMO

This residence of the Bourbon monarchs of Naples and Sicily was destined for use as a hunting lodge, but became the favourite home of King Ferdinand III and Queen Caroline when they were evacuated to Sicily during the Napoleonic wars, and here Admiral Nelson and Lady Hamilton were their guests.

It is a delightful conceit born of the taste for *Chinoiseries* at the end of the eighteenth century. It was designed by Venanzio Marvuglia of Palermo (1729–1814) and built in 1799. On the ground floor are a ballroom and audience chamber. The King's bedchamber, with its gaily painted ceiling of peacocks, pagodas and mandarins, is on the first floor, together with the dining-room, which has a novel contraption for removing the plates without the appearance of servants, and the Chinese drawing-room. On the second floor are reception rooms in Turkish and in Pompeian styles.

77 INLAID MARBLE ALTAR FRONTAL, Church of St Agata, Caltanis-setta, Sicily

The collegiate church of St Agata in the hill-town of Caltanissetta in central Sicily was built by the Jesuits in the seventeenth century. This beautiful inlaid altar-slab is the work of the Sicilian sculptor Ignazio Marabitti (1719–97). It features birds from all parts of the world, their names inscribed on swirls, amid a maze of stylized foliage and exotic flowers. In this detail one can see the magpie, the pelican, the parrot, the 'Chinese ostrich', the Mexican cardinal and the flamingo.

78 SIDE ALTAR, S. GIUSEPPE DEI TEATINI, PALERMO

This church, on one corner of the Quattro Canti in the centre of the capital, begun in 1612 by the Genoese architect Giacomo Besio, has a simple exterior which contrasts sharply with the richness of its Baroque interior executed in the latter part of the seventeenth century. The altar with the statue of the Madonna and Child leaves no square inch undecorated, the sculptor's skill making the marble look like lace.

80 CASTEL DEL MONTE

There is a persistent but unproved tradition that Frederick II himself designed his castle built about 1240 near Andria in the heart of Apulia. Its perfect symmetry and regularity of form make it one of the most perfect and at the same time unusual secular buildings of the Middle Ages. Despite its severe exterior this was a pleasure house; its interior walls were panelled with pink marble and there were Arab-style mosaics and graceful columns probably inspired by the castles which Frederick had seen in Syria. In the photograph the great octagonal castle crowning the hill is seen from the yard of a neighbouring farm with dry-stone walls and buildings in the form of trulli (see plate 117).

81 SERAPEUM, POZZUOLI

When the first excavations of this site were made in the eighteenth century, the archaeologists named it the 'Serapeum', thinking it was a Temple of Serapis whose statue they found in the ruins. It was, in fact, a Roman public market, built in the first century AD and one of the best preserved of its kind. Around a square courtyard under a pillared gallery were booth-type shops which probably sold fish and meat, and at two of the corners, sumptuous marble latrines with perforated marble bench-seats and sewers. In the centre of the courtyard was a raised circular podium under a dome supported by sixteen columns. Three of the four taller columns of the portico to the cella still stand. These have been eaten away by shell-fish starting at 12 feet above the ground and up to 18 feet, which seems to indicate that they were once buried 12 feet under ground and then submerged in sea-water for a further six. It is possible that they were raised again to sea-level by the earthquake of 1538. A conduit joins the market to the sea.

82 VENOSA

Venosa, at the foot of the Apennines, was the ancient Venusia, the birth-place of the poet Horace. Early in the eleventh century the Benedictines founded their church here on the site of a paleo-Christian church, itself

413

built on the site of a Roman temple. When the building of the grandiose Abbey complex began in 1063 a great deal of material was taken from the adjacent Roman amphitheatre and the temples. The stones of the Abbey abound with Roman inscriptions. The plate shows the apse of the old church and the columns of the nave of an ambitious new church on the Cluniac plan, which was to have been joined to the old one, but was never completed.

84 S. LEONARDO DI SIPONTI
Originally, in the twelfth century, an Augustinian Abbey, restored and modified by the Teutonic Knights to whom it passed in the thirteenth century, subsequently a Consistorial Abbey in the fifteenth century, the buildings finally passed to the Franciscans who held it until the last century, when it was abandoned, only to be restored and re-opened as a church in 1950. A richly decorated twelfth-century portal is its most important feature. The part on the right (shown here) depicts the Three Magi bringing their gifts. Its companion on the left shows a pilgrim, and in the lunette above the portal is a bas-relief of Christ in a mandorla upheld by two angels.

85, THE CATTOLICA, STILO
86 Basilian monks, refugees who fled from Byzantium, settled at Stilo on the flank of Mount Consolino in southern Calabria. The celebrated and singularly interesting brick-built tenth-century church called the Cattolica is directly due to their taste and influence. Not only has it kept the Greek name for a parish church of the Byzantine era, it is in fact a replica of the classic type of ninth-century church in Georgia, Armenia and Asia Minor. The plan is a square divided by four columns into nine equal squares, and with three apses projecting at the east. Four cylindrical domes top the corners of the church and a fifth, taller one, the centre. The four columns of the church are re-used classical columns from some monument or temple. The very name of the town, Stilo, is from the Greek 'stylos' – a column.

87 TROIA
The superb Cathedral at Troia, begun in 1093, is one of the major Romanesque monuments of southern Italy. Here Byzantine and Arab themes met and fused with the current of Romanesque ideas coming from Pisa. The compartmented bronze doors are the work of Oderisio da Benevento. The main doors on the west were made in 1119 – they have a delightful variety of motifs in high-relief. The detail shown here is from the south doors, which consist of twenty-four compartments with figures and insignia of saints and bishops and lion masks, and date from 1127.

88 TROIA
This splendid twelfth-century window in the richly sculpted upper part of the façade is divided into eleven sections by slender columns which radiate to trefoiled arches. The lights, instead of being glazed, are filled with thin stone perforated with a variety of intricate designs.

89 SANSEVERINO TOMB, Charterhouse of S. Lorenzo, Padula
Tommaso Sanseverino, Count of Marsico, founded this great Carthusian house in 1306. His tomb was erected in the sixteenth century, but the name of the sculptor is unknown. The Madonna and Child group above the reclining figure of the Count is a replica of one in the church of Santa Maria a Mare at Mairoi attributed to the Spanish sculptor Diego de Siloe (1495–1563).

90 CHARTERHOUSE OF S. LORENZO, PADULA
The church was begun in the fourteenth century but building work continued for five centuries and the interior is predominantly Baroque of the late seventeenth and early eighteenth centuries. The choir stalls, however, dating from about 1503 are remarkable, with marquetry scenes of landscapes, architecture, events from the New Testament and lives of the saints. The Baroque main altar, on the right, is of polished stucco encrusted with mother-of-pearl.

91– STATUES, ROYAL PALACE, NAPLES
94 These are four of the eight statues of the most illustrious sovereigns of Naples, executed and placed in niches outside the Royal Palace in 1888 on the instructions of King Umberto I of Italy. The statue of Charles I of Anjou, the first monarch of the Angevin dynasty, is by the Neapolitan sculptor Tommaso Solari (1820–97). That of the Emperor Charles V, who also ruled Naples, is based on a model by Vincenzo Gemito of Naples (1852–1929). The figure of King Charles III of the Bourbon dynasty who abdicated in favour of his younger son in order to take the throne of Spain is by Raffaele Belliazzi of Naples (1835–1917). The statue of Napoleon's brother-in-law Murat, who was given the Neapolitan throne, is by Giovanni Battista Amendola (1848–87).

95 CASERTA
The Bourbon Royal Palace at Caserta with its beautiful three hundred acre park, fountains and statuary, was designed in the middle of the eighteenth century, by the Neapolitan architect Luigi Vanvitelli (1700–73) and the park was completed, with modifications, after his death, by his son Carlo (1739–1821). Its central feature is a long cascade, at the bottom of which are two sculptural groups, executed by the Florentine Angelo Brunelli (1740–1806), Paolo Persico (c. 1729–80) from Sorrento, and a local craftsman Pietro Solari. One, shown here, depicts Actaeon transformed into a stag, being assailed by his own hounds. The other shows Actaeon being chased off by Diana surrounded by her nymphs.

96 THE DEAD CHRIST, SANSEVERO CHAPEL, NAPLES
The tomb-chapel of the Sangro family, Princes of Sansevero, formerly joined by a foot-bridge to their (now demolished) palace across the street, was built in 1590 but owes its extraordinary interior decoration of frescoes, marbles and statuary to the enterprising and eccentric Prince Raimondo who commissioned the work in 1749. One of the most notable statues is the corpse of Christ covered by a shroud (1753), gruesome in its skilful but macabre realism, the work of the prolific Neapolitan Baroque sculptor Giuseppe Sammartino (1720–1793).

97 PAESTUM
Paestum was the Poseidonia of the Greeks, the City of Poseidon (Neptune) founded by settlers from Sybaris in the sixth century BC. The ruins remained hidden in a malarial swamp for generations and were only brought back to public notice in the eighteenth century when a new road was being built. Its discovery gave impetus to the Neo-classical movement, attracting many of the leading artists and intellectuals of Europe. The earliest temple, dedicated to Hera, was mistakenly called the 'Basilica' when the ruins were found, and has retained this name. Three of its columns, showing the extreme entasis and flat capitals of the archaic Doric style, are in the foreground of the photograph. Behind it is the Temple of Neptune, a majestic building of the fifth century BC comparable in style and degree of preservation with the Parthenon, the Theseion at Athens and the Temple of Concord at Agrigento (see plate 43). Built of travertine which has a golden glow in the sunlight, magnificently sited on the shore beside a glittering sea and backed by the mountains, it ranks as one of the most impressive monuments of antiquity.

98 THE CAMPANIAN AMPHITHEATRE, S. MARIA CAPUA VETERE
In this Roman amphitheatre of ancient Capua, once the most flourishing town of southern Italy, Spartacus led the revolt of the gladiators in 73 BC. It was adorned with statues including the Venus of Capua now in the National Archaeological Museum in Naples but through the centuries it was pillaged and quarried for other constructions such as the Cathedral of S. Maria Capua Vetere, and the Campanile and Church of the Addolorata at Capua. In the photograph some of the extensive sub-structure, similar to that of the Flavian amphitheatre at Pozzuoli (plate 99), can be seen. Seven marble busts of divinities once the keystones above the arches of the amphitheatre are set in the façade of the sixteenth-century town hall at Capua.

99 FLAVIAN AMPHITHEATRE, POZZUOLI

Constructed during the reign of Vespasian in the first century AD, this is the third largest Roman amphitheatre in Italy, ranking after the Colosseum in Rome (plate 127) and the Campanian amphitheatre (plate 98); it seated 40,000 spectators. Beneath the theatre are subterranean corridors, dens for the wild animals with apertures through which their cages were hoisted into the arena, and rooms for the scaffolding and stage machinery. It was possible to flood the arena for grandiose water spectacles, by means of a conduit linking the theatre to an aqueduct.

00 ROMAN MOSAIC

This mosaic which comes from the Roman Temple of Diana at Sant'Angelo in Formis depicts choristers from a *scola cantorum* who would have sung in the Temple.

02 THE SIBYL'S CAVE, CUMAE

The ten sibyls were wise women who were reputed to live in various cities of the Roman Empire. As with most oracular traditions, the site and the legend are of Greek origin. Cumae was one of the earliest Greek colonies in Italy and the trapezoidal corridor of the Sibyl's cave, over 100 metres in length, is reminiscent of the Minoan style. This corridor, lit by six galleries, leads to the rectangular secret chamber of the Sibyl where she pronounced her oracles. The sanctuary, one of the most venerated and famous of the ancient world, was only uncovered in the course of excavations in 1932.

03 PISCINA MIRABILE

This great subterranean Roman reservoir, fed by an aqueduct, and capable of containing 12,000 cubic metres of water, was built to serve the Tyrrhenian fleet in the nearby harbour of Misenum. Its long lofty pillared aisles give it an almost cathedral-like effect.

04 THE DIVER

The five panels which formed the sides and cover of a painted sarcophagus, the work of a Greek artist of 480 BC, were only discovered at Paestum in 1968. The cover depicts a naked youth diving into the sea (perhaps a symbol of the soul's journey beyond death), and the side panels show scenes at a funeral banquet where the guests played music, sang and made love, in order to make the dead man's journey beyond the tomb more cheerful. The realism, purity and sensuality of the paintings make them works of the utmost interest and importance.

05 CLOISTER, S. CHIARA

The Neapolitan architect Domenico Antonio Vaccaro (1680–1750) designed a lavish Baroque interior for the austere Gothic church of Santa Chiara in 1742. This was destroyed by incendiary bombs in 1943 but Vaccaro's transformation of the fourteenth-century cloister of the adjoining Clarist convent, done at the same time, has survived thanks to restoration work in 1939 and again after the bombings of World War II. The colourful maiolica tiles, so popular in Naples in the eighteenth century, with landscapes, rustic scenes, masquerades and allegories, are the work of the Neapolitan ceramists Giuseppe and Donato Massa.

06, OLD PHARMACY, NAPLES
07

The Hospital of the Holy House of the Incurables was founded by a Spanish noblewoman Maria Longo in 1519. A bequest from the governor of the hospital, Antonio Maggiocca, who died in 1747, paid for the building, decoration and furnishing of the amazing pharmacy which was completed in 1750 and has remained intact and unspoiled.

In the elegantly panelled workroom next-door the apothecaries prepared their potions. The pharmacy proper has a maiolica floor and walnut *boiseries* with gilded pediments to the cabinets and gilded capitals on the pilasters between the rows of shelves. The collection of eighteenth-century glass and maiolica pharmaceutical jars and vases, decorated by the Massas (see plate 105) and other noted eighteenth-century Neapolitan ceramists, is unique.

108 SANT'ANGELO IN FORMIS

This basilica was built in the eleventh century on the site of an earlier church which incorporated the pavement of a Temple of Diana (see pl. 100), an inscription of 74 BC and some of the ancient columns.

Abbot Desiderius of Montecassino, the founder, is known to have imported painters and mosaicists from Constantinople to decorate his monastery. Artists of the Montecassino school working under this direct Byzantine influence no doubt executed these frescoes at Sant'Angelo in Formis during the lifetime of the Abbot who died in 1087. The photograph shows part of the apse with figures of the archangels Michael and Raphael. Above them are part of the figure of the Enthroned Christ and the symbol of St Luke the Evangelist. The side apses and the nave are painted with cycles of prophets and New Testament scenes of the same school.

109 PRESEPE

This elaborate Nativity scene is called after its donor, the nineteenth-century Neapolitan architect Ciro Cuciniello, who arranged it according to the design of Filippo Palizzi (1818–99) a painter of the Posillipo school. It contains hundreds of statuettes, many of them dating from the eighteenth century.

110 TRANI

This cathedral standing on the edge of the sea, near the harbour, was begun in 1096 and dedicated to St Nicholas the Pilgrim who died here in 1094. Built of pale pink stone, it is amongst the finest of the many beautiful Romanesque churches of Apulia. Barisano, the twelfth-century sculptor, was born at Trani and the splendid bronze doors of the west portal are his work; he also made the doors of the cathedrals of Monreale in Sicily and Ravello. The plate shows the back of the church with the walls of the three tall apses projecting from the lofty transept and the graceful thirteenth-century campanile which was successfully re-built in 1954 entirely with the original material.

111 MATERA

The old town of Matera is perched on the edge of a deep ravine, on two massive rock formations, the Sasso Caveoso and the Sasso Barisano. Until a few years ago several thousand families still lived in a labyrinth of quaint dwellings in caves in the rock, like troglodytes, and often with only the façade built in masonry. Other houses were built up against the face of the rock. Under the auspices of a governmental programme most of the inhabitants have been moved from these dark, dank, unhygienic places to new housing developments a few miles away.

114 SERRA S. BRUNO

This monastery, the most ancient Carthusian establishment in Italy, was founded by St Bruno himself in 1094; he is buried in it. The early twelfth-century buildings having fallen into decay, the monastery was rebuilt early in the seventeenth century and the cloister was still later. Then in 1783 an earthquake destroyed the whole monastery in a few minutes and its former magnificence has all but vanished. The present monastery dates from 1900.

115 ALTAR, ADDOLORATA, SERRA S. BRUNO

The elaborate ciborium was assembled in 1810 from pieces of polychrome marble and bronze, rescued from the ruins of the Charterhouse after the earthquake. The fine gilded bronze statues of saints and angels were formerly parts of an even more grandiose ciborium designed by Cosimo Fanzago (1593–1678).

117 TRULLI AT NIGHT

There are thousands of these curious and picturesque dwellings in the region called the 'Murgia dei Trulli' between Bari and Brindisi, where they are the natural homes of the local population – either scattered singly or in groups through the countryside or in streets of towns such as Alberobello or Locorotondo, with 8–10,000 inhabitants. Conical in shape (but square inside), the *trulli* are constructed of spiralling concentric rows of rough unmortared limestone, usually crowned with a finial, and often whitewashed. For centuries these practical and economical houses have been made of the readily available stone gathered from the fields and although those to be seen today are rarely more than 150 years old, the form may have existed since very ancient, even prehistoric times.

118 BOHEMOND'S TOMB

Bohemond, Prince of Antioch, son of the intrepid crusader, Robert Guiscard, Duke of Apulia, was buried at Canosa at his own request when he died in 1111. The chapel over his tomb, built in the form of a cube topped by a Moslem dome, is in a small courtyard off the Cathedral, against the wall of the transept. The singularly interesting and beautiful bronze door is a marriage of Byzantine and Arab art, with delicately chased Byzantine figures and plaques in high relief with Arab decoration. The name of the artist 'Rogerius Melfie' can be seen in the Latin inscription at the bottom right in the plate.

119 SANTA CROCE, LECCE

The city of Lecce is a riot of exuberant Baroque architecture. Perhaps the most impressive of its many superb buildings is the Basilica of Santa Croce begun in 1548. A century later, the local sculptor Cesare Penna executed the astonishing upper part of the façade to the design of another local prodigy, Giuseppe Zimbalo. Beneath the central rose window with its profusely decorated frame, a balustrade stretches across the façade and on this stand thirteen cheeky little putti carrying a variety of crowns or impudently trying them on.

120 ARCH OF CONSTANTINE

This majestic triple triumphant arch, which served as the model for the arches of the Neo-classicists throughout the world, was erected by the Senate and people of Rome in 315 to celebrate Constantine's victory over Maxentius. Many elements of the arch, however, are taken from earlier monuments, such as the beautiful bas-reliefs of the triumphs of Marcus Aurelius, the four medallions on each side with hunting and sacrificial scenes from the time of Hadrian and the columns which came from the Temple of Domitian. The Colosseum can be seen in the distance.

121 APPIAN WAY

The Appian Way, partly open in 312 BC, earned the name 'Regina Viarum', Queen of Roads, on account of its great length and because of the sumptuous tombs built along the first ten miles. Along it the insurgent slaves of Spartacus' rebellion were crucified and here too the early Christians took refuge in the catacombs which penetrate the surrounding area. After centuries of disuse this historic road was opened again at the end of the eighteenth century by Pope Pius VI. Now carefully nurtured pines and cypresses shade the ancient tombs, the catacombs and both ruined and modern Roman villas.

122 HEAD OF TREBONIANUS GALLUS

Gaius Vibius Trebonianus Gallus was Emperor of Rome AD 251–253 but having concluded a pact with the Goths, considered by many dishonourable, he was overthrown and killed and succeeded by Aemilianus who had defeated the Barbarian invaders, and was supported by the Army. Realistic portraiture was one of the arts which Rome made her own, and this head is an expressive example.

123 CHIMERA

The Chimera was a monster of Greek mythology with the head of a lion, the body of a goat and the hindquarters of a dragon. It could spout flames from its three mouths, and was slain by Bellerophon who flew over it on his steed Pegasus and threw lead into its mouth. The lead melted in the intense heat and, bursting out of its veins, killed the beast. This famous Etruscan bronze of the fifth century BC was discovered at Arezzo in 1555 and together with many of the finest works of Etruscan craftsmanship is housed in the Archaeological Museum in Florence.

124 VESTAL VIRGINS' POOL

The Temple of Vesta and the adjacent residence of the Vestal Virgins, who were the consecrated custodians of the sacred fire of the goddess, were the most important religious buildings in the Forum. They took vows for thirty years, ten as novices, ten as officiators and ten as novice-mistresses and if during this time one lost her virginity she was buried alive. The fire, the symbol of the perpetuity of the state, was kept constantly alight; the priestesses in charge of it wielded considerable power. The atrium of their residence adjoining the circular temple was planted with a symbolic wood and had ornamental pools.

125 ARCH OF SEPTIMIUS SEVERUS

This great triumphal arch, one of the largest in existence, was erected in AD 203 to celebrate the tenth anniversary of the reign of Septimius Severus and owes its good state of preservation to the fact that during the Middle Ages it was incorporated in other buildings. The inscriptions record the victories of the Romans over the Parthians, Arabs and Assyrians under Septimius Severus and his sons Caracalla and Gela. The sculptures in panels depict triumphal feats of the Emperor in war, and in a panel on the plinth, seen in the plate, a group of barbarian prisoners. In the background rises the Palatine Hill.

126 PIAZZA OF ST PETER'S

The Piazza of St Peter's, designed and built in 1656–57, is the masterpiece of Gian Lorenzo Bernini (1598–1680). A vast oval is formed by two arms of an imposing Doric colonnade, open at one side in the direction of the Tiber and at the other in the direction of St Peter's, to which it is joined by straight wings. Along the balustrade stand statues of 140 saints overlooking the two grandiose fountains and the central obelisk. The fountain on the right is the work of Carlo Maderno (1556–1629), erected in 1613 for Pope Paul V; Bernini made another to match it on the left in 1675. The obelisk which Bernini used as the centre of his arrangement was erected here in 1586, borne on the backs of four bronze lions, by Domenico Fontana (1543–1607), on the instructions of Pope Sixtus V. It was brought by Caligula from Heliopolis in AD 37 and now contains a relic of the Holy Cross.

127 COLOSSEUM

Begun in AD 72 by the Emperor Vespasian and completed by his son Titus in the year 80. No less than 5,000 beasts and many gladiators perished during the inaugural celebrations, which lasted for 100 days. In 249 to celebrate the thousandth anniversary of the founding of Rome vast and splendid spectacles were organized, including a battle between one thousand pairs of gladiators, and elephants, lions, tigers, hyenas, giraffes, zebras and hippopotami were slain in considerable numbers. It is probable too that many Christians perished here. In the eighteenth century Pope Benedict XIV consecrated the Colosseum to the Passion of Jesus, and fourteen stations of the Cross were erected around the arena, but these were demolished in the last century. In recent years the big wooden cross was erected for use in the Easter ceremonies when the Pope leads the 'Via Crucis'.

128 PIAZZA NAVONA, ROME

The original fountain in front of the Renaissance church of Our Lady of the Sacred Heart was by the architect Giacomo della Porta (c. 1540–1602) and executed in 1574. In 1655, Pope Innocent X, who had built the Pamphili Palace opposite the church for his sister-in-law, engaged the sculptor Giovanni Antonio Mari to embellish the fountain and he sculpted the Ethiopian struggling with a dolphin to a design by Bernini. The four tritons and other ornamental sculpture on the fountain are the work of Luigi Amici (1817–1897), copies made in 1874 to replace the original statuary which was removed to the gardens of the Villa Borghese.

129 PIAZZA NAVONA, ROME

The church is built on the spot where, according to tradition, the adolescent St Agnes' long hair miraculously loosed itself and fell to cover her when she was exposed naked on the pillory in the fourth century. The Roman architects Girolamo Rainaldi (1570–1655) and Carlo Rainaldi (1611–1691) began the building in 1652 but Francesco Borromini (1599–1667) took over the work in the following year and considerably modified their plan, completing the church in 1657. The Fountain of Neptune, originally a plain work without decoration was executed by Giacomo della Porta in 1574. In 1873, the winners of a competition for the best decoration to balance the fountain with the one at the other end of the square in front of the Pamphili Palace were Gregorio Zappalà, a Sicilian (1833–1908), the sculptor of the water-nymphs, putti and sea-horses and Antonio della Bitta (born 1807), the sculptor of the central figure of Neptune fighting with an octopus.

PIAZZA MATTEI, ROME

Four lithe young men in bronze, standing on marble scrolls, hold dolphins beneath the basin of this lovely fountain designed by Giacomo della Porta and executed in 1581–84 by Taddeo Landini. A century later the tortoises were added to the rim of the basin so that they appear to be being pushed to drink by the youths. The joyous harmony of the composition makes this one of the most successful Mannerist monuments in the city.

THE RAPE OF PERSEPHONE

The twenty-four-year-old Gian Lorenzo Bernini (born 1598) was already the supreme master of dramatic realism. A detail like the hand of Pluto pressing down the flesh of Persephone's thigh as he carries her forcibly down to the underworld, is both technically and imaginatively a stroke of genius.

CASTEL SANT'ANGELO

The Castel Sant'Angelo was probably planned by the Emperor Hadrian himself as a burial place for his family and descendants. Begun in 135 it was completed by Antoninus Pius in 139. Frequent demolitions and alterations have radically changed its original appearance. It was walled round and made into a fortress in the third century because it held a key position at the head of a bridge. During the Middle Ages, it served as a stronghold for the popes in times of violence and changed hands many times, but is perhaps best remembered as a prison. First put to this use by Theodoric, it continued to serve as a prison until 1901 and over the centuries was the scene of many gruesome murders. Illustrious prisoners from all walks of life were incarcerated in it, popes, princes, patriots, cardinals, artists and philosophers. It now houses the Artistic and Military Museum. The three central arches of the bridge over the Tiber are those of the Roman bridge built by the architect Demetrian in 136 for the Emperor Hadrian to give access to his mausoleum. The ten statues of angels holding symbols of the Passion along the parapets of the bridge were designed by Bernini and executed by his followers.

HADRIAN'S VILLA, near TIVOLI

The Emperor Hadrian (65–138) built a magnificent villa near Tivoli in which he copied and re-assembled on an intimate scale the places throughout his Empire that had impressed him most during his travels.

At the ancient city of Canopus in Egypt the dilettante Emperor had been struck by the canal leading to the Temple of Serapis and bordered by the elegant villas of the Alexandrian aristocracy. At Tivoli, therefore, he made use of a natural valley, deepening it and creating a shallow pond 380 feet in length. This was closed at the northern end by a marble pergola of Corinthian columns supporting alternating arched and flat architraves. Statues decorated the sides of this pool – the crocodile symbolizes the Nile whence the canal at Canopus derived. The statues in the colonnade are modern copies of the originals which are kept in the nearby Museum.

ORVIETO CATHEDRAL

In 1263 occurred the Miracle at Bolsena, a town near Orvieto, when the consecrated host began dripping real blood – thus disposing of a current heresy concerning the sacrament. Next year, 1264, at Orvieto, Pope Urban IV proclaimed the feast of Corpus Christi. A special office was composed for the feast by St Thomas Aquinas, who was teaching in Orvieto, and by the end of the century funds were being solicited throughout the Christian world and artists invited to contribute their talents in building a church of unparalleled magnificence to commemorate the miracle. The first director of works, Fra Bevignate, a Franciscan friar, began in the Romanesque

style but his successor the Orvietan Giovanni di Uguccione switched to Gothic. About 1305 the Sienese architect Lorenzo Maitani was called in for advice and he strengthened the transept with elegant flying buttresses, one of which appears in the plate. Altogether the cathedral is a harmonious meeting of Romanesque-inspired and Gothic-inspired impulses. The external walls are built of parallel bands of pale travertine and dark basalt.

The lower part of the façade is covered with bas-reliefs by Maitani and his school showing sacred history from the Creation to the Last Judgment. Part of the latter is shown in plate 136.

BOMARZO

The unusual *Parco dei Mostri* in a valley below the town of Bomarzo which belonged to the Orsini princes is sparsely documented. Its mysterious grotesque figures carved out of the living rock and their eccentric creator Prince Vicino Orsini remain subjects of rumour and supposition.

It is thought that Turkish soldiers captured when retreating from Vienna were used for the arduous task of sculpting the rock; certainly the workmanship is clumsy. Scattered through the park are a domed classical temple (traditionally dedicated to Prince Vicino Orsini's wife Giulia Farnese); an enormous open-mouthed mask with a little room carved in the mouth and containing a stone table and benches; a dragon attacked by dogs, an elephant attired for battle (presumably a reference to Hannibal), a gigantic tortoise surmounted by a statue of fortune, a tipsy fountain, a trick house with sloping floors and a giant dismembering a man. Until recent years the park was overgrown and hardly visited by tourists.

SPOLETO FESTIVAL

The lovely medieval town of Spoleto in Umbria has taken on a new life since 1959 as the home of a very successful annual international festival of the arts. The Festival of The Two Worlds, as it is called, begun in 1959 by the Italo-American composer Gian Carlo Menotti, takes place at the end of June. Ballet, opera, chamber music, concerts, plays and art exhibitions are all included in the programme. The display of modern sculpture against the medieval settings arranged in 1960 achieved a most unusual and striking effect and the idea has been repeated.

QUIRINAL

Pope Gregory XIII commissioned the building of the Quirinal in 1574 as a papal summer residence. The first architect was Ottaviano Mascherino (1524–1606) who designed the splendid spiral stair. He was followed successively by Domenico Fontana (1543–1607), Flaminio Ponzio (c. 1560–1613), Carlo Maderno (1556–1629), Gian Lorenzo Bernini (1598–1680) and lastly Ferdinando Fuga (1699–1781) who all worked on the palace. It remained a papal residence until 1870 when it became the Royal Palace. Following the abdication of the last monarch, King Umberto II, in 1947, it became the official residence of the President of the Republic but its magnificent rooms are open to the public every Thursday afternoon.

VATICAN LIBRARY

The *Salone Sistino* was the grandiose conception of Domenico Fontana (1543–1607) executed between 1587–1589. The richly frescoed walls and ceilings are the work of several artists, among them Paul Brill (1554–1626), Giovanni Battista Ricci (1537–1627) and Orazio Gentileschi (c. 1563–1638). Among the treasures exhibited are the famous Vatican B Codex (a fourth-century Greek Bible) and fragments of a sixth-century Gospel according to St Matthew, written in gold and silver on purple parchment.

PALAZZO BORGHESE

The city palace of the Borghese family, probably designed by Vignola, was begun about 1560 and completed between 1605 and 1614 for Pope Paul V Borghese who had acquired it. Still the property of the Borghese family, it is now divided into a number of residential apartments, a shop and an exclusive club. Perhaps its best remembered resident was the beautiful and extravagant Pauline, Princess Borghese, sister of Napoleon, and its most virtuous the beautiful and charitable English Gwendaline, Princess Borghese (née Talbot).

148 VILLA LANTE

The Villa Lante, a pair of symmetrical pavilions in a formal late-Renaissance garden, was designed by the architect Jacopo Barozzi (1507–73), better known as Vignola, for a Bishop of the diocese who was the Pope's nephew. It was a later owner, Cardinal Gambara, who supervized the laying-out of the gardens and the building of the first pavilion (which is decorated with his punning arms, a crayfish) between 1566 and 1578. The second pavilion was built by the next owner, also a cardinal and nephew. It was a later owner, Cardinal Gambara, who supervised the family who have owned it since 1656. The gardens are ornamented with grottoes of Venus and Neptune, Fountains of the Giants, of the Dolphins, of the Rain, a water-chain, *jeux d'eaux* in the stairs and the Cardinal's table for al fresco meals. Outside the garden walls in the park is the great oval fountain of Pegasus.

149 CAPRAROLA

The Palace was built between 1559 and 1575 for Cardinal Alessandro Farnese to designs by Vignola; it is considered one of the masterpieces of the Mannerist movement. From the Farnesi it passed by marriage to the Spanish and eventually Neapolitan Bourbons and now belongs to the state. The casino in the park, once a rustic escape from grandeur for a cardinal, is the official summer residence of the President of Italy. Before it is the Place of the Caryatids, with fountains. Lower in the terraced gardens are other fountains and a lovely water-chain formed of dolphins who splash the water on to shells.

150 PIAZZA DEL CAMPIDOGLIO, ROME

The Piazza del Campidoglio on the summit of the Capitoline hill is the first example of town planning in Renaissance Rome, designed by Michelangelo and carried out by Giacomo della Porta (1540–1602) and Girolamo Rainaldi (1570–1655). On the suggestion of Michelangelo the gilded bronze equestrian statue of Marcus Aurelius was set in the centre – it had only been saved from the melting pot because for centuries it had been thought to be of the Christian Emperor Constantine. The Palazzo Senatorio overlooks the square and in a niche beneath its fine double stair is a Roman statue of Minerva flanked by colossal allegorical figures of the Nile with a sphinx and the Tiber with a wolf (formerly the Tigris with a tiger), brought from the ruined Baths of Constantine on the Quirinal.

151 NINFA

The medieval town of Ninfa, a fief of the Caetani family, was abandoned by its inhabitants in the seventeenth century because of the scourge of mosquitoes. Today the ruined city walls, castle, mansions, churches and towers half covered with lush creepers are part of the unusual gardens of Donna Lelia Caetani (Hon. Mrs Hugo Howard) who has a villa on her lands there. They are open to the public once a month during the summer. Mountain springs feed a lake from which the River Ninfa winds among the clematis-clad ruins and a variety of beautiful trees. High above, in the background of the photograph the walls of the ancient town of Norba, dating from the fourth century, can be seen near the present town of Norma.

152 CIVITA DI BAGNOREGIO

This picturesque medieval town has been called 'The Dying City' because the volcanic rock on which it is perched is slowly crumbling away through erosion and when the bridge across the kilometre-wide ravine which joined it to Bagnoregio and the rest of the world collapsed its inhabitants remained isolated in their eyrie. All but a very few families left but now a new bridge has been built and actors, painters, poets and their friends have bought houses there, giving a new if rather unreal life to the place.

155 BRIDGE AT L'ABBADIA

This bridge, one of the oldest in the world, dates from two periods. The sandstone piers were put up by the Etruscans to support a primitive wooden bridge. The Romans reinforced the piers and using stones from the Etruscan necropolis nearby built the bridge with one major and two minor arches. The bridge adjoins a medieval castle, now an archaeological museum, which was once a customs post of the Papal States at their border with Tuscany.

156 TODI

The cathedral of the ancient hill-city of Todi stands at the head of a great broad stair; its Gothic façade dominates one of the most beautiful medieval city squares of Italy. Building began in the twelfth century. The nave and transept date from the thirteenth century; the capitals of the alternating columns and piers are the product of the blending of late Romanesque and early Gothic forms. The magnificent rose-window was inserted about 1520. The enormous fresco of the Last Judgment on the inner wall of the entrance is by Ferrau da Faenza, Il Faenzone (1562–1645), who was clearly inspired by Michelangelo.

158 ASSISI

This view of Assisi from the west is dominated by the great convent and basilica of the city's most famous son, St Francis (1182–1226), whose life and deeds have been immortalized by a host of painters from Giotto onwards. The monastery built upon a massive arcaded sub-structure was begun soon after the death of the Saint. The campanile was erected in 1239; behind it the town spreads out in the shadow of the Rocca Maggiore, its pink and white stone houses with gaily flowered balconies on winding medieval cobbled streets and a plethora of lovely churches.

159 MADONNA WITH A POMEGRANATE

This is perhaps the earliest surviving work of Jacopo della Quercia, who was born in 1374 at Siena, and took part in the competition for the Florence Baptistery doors in 1401. In 1407 he was working in Lucca and in collaboration with Francesco da Valdambrino carved the superb tomb statue of Ilaria del Carretto. The Madonna at Ferrara, executed just before or just after the tomb at Lucca, reveals the same combination of naturalism and classical dignity.

160 PINETA, RAVENNA

The vast pine forest which covered the region between Ravenna and the Adriatic sea is now divided into three parts, all dwindling rapidly owing to pollution from the industrial zone. The pines of Ravenna once furnished the timber for the ships of the Roman and Venetian fleets, and the forest has been celebrated in literature by Dante, Boccaccio and especially Byron, who loved to ride here when he lived at Ravenna.

161, POMPOSA
162

The Abbey of Pomposa was founded by the Benedictines in the ninth century on the site of an earlier church. It was raised to the dignity of a Royal Abbey by the Emperor Otto III and acquired colossal wealth (and consequently power) from the donations of princely patrons. In the eleventh and twelfth centuries the Abbot of Pomposa exercised civil and ecclesiastical authority over a vast area and his Abbey was an important cultural centre. The musical theoretician Guido d'Arezzo, who was responsible for the modern note-names Ut, Re, Mi, etc., of the tonic Sol-Fa, passed his early years as a monk here. Here too the reformer and arch-critic of clerical misconduct St Peter Damian wrote part of his 'The Gomorrah Book'. The great complex of abbey buildings includes a Romanesque church, a magnificent campanile, and monastery and an impressive Abbatial Court of Justice. As the marshy location was propitious to the spread of malaria, by the fifteenth century the Abbey was entirely deserted. Restoration was begun at the end of the last century and is still under way. The façade of the atrium contains fragments of Byzantine carving and Islamic pottery.

163 PISA, BAPTISTERY

The original Romanesque baptistery was built at the same time as the Cathedral and finished in 1278. Of this only the two lower storeys, with their arcades of round arches, one large, the other miniature, are still visible from the exterior. The upper part added in a more lacy Gothic style, in the next century. As seen today, therefore, the exterior is the creation of the thirteenth-century masters Nicola and Giovanni Pisano, father and son, and the fourteenth-century masters Cellino di Nese and Zebellino da Bologna who completed the drum below the dome in 1365. Inside the Baptistery on a column is an inscription recording the name of the first mason, Master Diotisalvi, and the date August 1153. The delicate proportions and graceful decoration of this building lend it a daintiness which belies its actual size – it is 179 feet high and 117 feet wide at the base.

164 S. MINIATO AL MONTE, FLORENCE
The church of S. Miniato crowns a hill which dominates Florence from across the Arno. Its façade is a particularly fine example of the twelfth- and thirteenth-century Florentine fashion for covering wall surfaces in a veneer of coloured marble (the Cathedral and Baptistery follow the same style). In front of it, on the steep slope, is a cemetery where many famous Italians, including Leoncavallo the composer of *Pagliacci* and the writer Giovanni Papini, are buried. The group in the foreground belongs to a modern monument.

165 PALAZZO PITTI
The immense Pitti Palace with its distinctive all-over rustication was begun about 1440 to designs of Filippo Brunelleschi (1377–1446). Luca Pitti, first a friend, then a rival of the Medici, never saw his palace completed for lack of funds brought the work to a halt. Eleanora of Toledo purchased the property in 1549 and commissioned Bartolomeo Ammanati (1511–92) to complete the building according to Brunelleschi's designs and enlarge it. The photograph shows an arcade of the courtyard at the back; the heavy rustication applied to the exterior can just be glimpsed on the pier on the left. This palace now houses a wealth of works of art in its Museum of Modern Art, Pitti Gallery, Royal Apartments and Silver Museum. Behind it are the Boboli Gardens, a formal layout with elements dating from the seventeenth and eighteenth centuries, and combining architecture, statuary, water and horticulture.

166 BOBOLI GARDENS
See note to plate 213.

167 FLORENCE, VIEW FROM PALAZZO GONDI
The Palazzo Gondi, a perfect example of a lordly palace, designed by Giuliano da Sangallo (1445–1516), is situated in the centre of the city and its windows and balconies afford some stupendous views. Here in the left-hand window is the dome of Florence Cathedral – the most felicitous element in the varied and attractive Florentine skyline. Designed by Filippo Brunelleschi (1377–1446), it soars to a height of 350 feet. On the right is the crenellated Palace of the Podestà, the civil authority in medieval times, now known as the Bargello. It houses the most important collection of sculpture in Italy.

168 PALAZZO VECCHIO
The Palazzo Vecchio was the seat of government in medieval and Renaissance Florence. It was begun in 1298, probably to the plans of Arnolfo di Cambio, and the façade facing the Piazza della Signoria is still basically as he left it. It was as much a fortress as a palace, with crenellations and widely projecting machicolated gallery. The bell-tower rises daringly from the *outer* edge of the gallery, and the whole building directly underneath it is solid masonry. The great rusticated stone blocks, which give it such a grim and unyielding appearance, are characteristic of Florentine secular architecture. It was successively added to by Il Cronaca, Vasari and Buontalenti.

170 MARQUETRY PANELS, MODENA
Cristoforo Canozzi, better known as Cristoforo da Lendinara, and his brothers were painters and marquetry workers who were associated with Piero della Francesca. The brothers are responsible for the splendid marquetry work in the choir stalls of Modena Cathedral with landscapes, fruit, musical instruments and abstract designs. The marquetry portraits of the four evangelists in the sacristy are the work of Cristoforo, possibly to designs of Piero della Francesca.

171 STUDIOLO, URBINO
Federigo da Montefeltro, Duke of Urbino, a powerful and enlightened condottiere prince, made his capital, Urbino, one of the most remarkable cities in Italy in the late fifteenth century. Under his energetic leadership Urbino rivalled more important states and became a brilliant intellectual and artistic centre withva fine library, schools of art, poetry, mathematics and humanism while the vast ducal palace built of creamy Dalmatian limestone dominated the city. Here the famous painter Raphael (Raffaele Sanzio, 1483–1520) was born and the distinguished painter and architect Bramante (1444–1514) was trained. The study, the smallest but the most beautiful room in the palace, where the Duke read and studied the classics and humanists, is panelled with an astonishing variety of marquetry scenes – *trompe l'œil* statues in niches, half-open cupboards, musical instruments, portraits of philosophers and poets, arms, books and loggia with a view of the landscape. These are the work of Baccio Pontelli of Florence and his assistants, 1475, based on designs by Botticelli and Francesco di Giorgio.

172 MARQUETRY, S. QUIRICO D'ORCIA
The fine marquetry panels in the apse of the twelfth-century Collegiate church of Saints Quirico and Giulitta at San Quirico d'Orcia are the work of the Sienese architect and artisan Antonio Barili (1443–1516). He made them in 1500 for the Cathedral at Siena where they were placed in the choir of St John's Chapel before being removed to their present home. These panels are a good example of the best marquetry work at the end of the fifteenth century, revealing an absolute mastery of perspective together with a poetic quality which was lacking in earlier intarsia compositions.

173 PALAZZO BONCOMPAGNI, VIGNOLA
The famous architect Jacopo Barozzi (1507–73), better known as Il Vignola – he took the name of his birthplace – may have been the designer of the Palazzo Boncompagni in his native town. The skilfully cantilevered oval stair was added by Bartolomeo Tristano in the last quarter of the sixteenth century.

174 S. GIOVANNI EVANGELISTA, PARMA
The luminous nave of the church of S. Giovanni Evangelista at Parma is a perfect preparation for the ecstatic *Vision of St John the Evangelist* painted in the cupola by Correggio (1489–1534).

This church was built between 1498 and 1510 by Bernardino Zaccagni and as well as the famed Correggio contains works by Parmigianino (1503–40).

The frescoes of candelabra and of alternating Hebrew and pagan sacrificial rites on the ceiling of the nave were painted by Francesco Maria Rondani (*c.* 1490–1550) after cartoons by Correggio who died before they were executed.

175, 176 TEMPIO MALATESTIANO
Sigismondo Malatesta, tyrant of Rimini, transformed a Franciscan church into one of the most famous monuments of the Italian Renaissance with the help of the Veronese architect, sculptor and painter, Matteo de'Pasti. The work began in 1447, reached its zenith in the 1450s but stopped in 1460 because of a reversal in Sigismondo's fortunes; he died in 1468. Throughout the church one sees Sigismondo's initial entwined with that of his mistress and finally third wife Isotta degli Atti, his emblem, and medallions with his portrait (plate 176). There is also a marvellous fresco by Piero della Francesca of Sigismondo kneeling before his patron saint. As the name implies, the whole church reflects the glory of its builder and his family. Sigismondo's own sarcophagus by Agostino di Duccio is placed high on the wall of a chapel. On each side of a dedicatory inscription are fine bas-reliefs. In the one on the left Sigismondo himself appears, with Scipio from whom he claimed descent, among the heroes surrounding Minerva; that on the right depicts a military triumph of Scipio. In the niches are statues of sibyls and prophets and beneath them profiles of Sigismondo wreathed in laurel. The putti on the balustrade are nineteenth-century replacements repeating the form of the other chapels.

S. PETRONIO, BOLOGNA

The church of S. Petronio is the largest in Bologna, dedicated to the patron saint of the city. Work on it began in 1390 but the façade was never completed. Jacopo della Quercia's reliefs round the central door show how much his style had changed at the end of his life from the Madonna at Ferrara (plate 159). On a small scale and in very shallow relief he creates massive and muscular forms that look forward unmistakably to Michelangelo.

179, S. DOMENICO, BOLOGNA
180

The shrine of St Dominic in the grandiose church dedicated to him at Bologna is a fascinating and highly successful amalgam of styles carried out over a period of more than 200 years between 1265 and 1494. The central portion, highly reminiscent of a Roman sarcophagus, has a Madonna and Child in the centre and miracles of St Dominic at the sides – this was all carved between 1265 and 1267 by Nicola Pisano and his pupils, Arnolfo di Cambio, Lapo and Fra Guglielmo. In 1469, one Niccolò, an itinerant Apulian sculptor, was commissioned to execute an upper structure for the shrine. Such was his success that he is known as Niccolò dell'Arca. He designed the wonderful top for Pisano's base, rising gracefully to an elaborate pinnacle with a strong figure of God the Father. On the four corners below the pinnacle are the Evangelists, and on the same level angels adoring Christ of the Pietà. On the lid of the reliquary eight saints stand on scrolls and below it on each side kneel candle-bearing angels. Niccolò died in 1494, leaving three figures on the shrine unfinished. Opportunely the young Michelangelo was in Bologna, having fled there from Florence for political and personal reasons. He was commissioned to finish the shrine and carved the kneeling angel on the right (Plate 179), finished the statue of St Petronius and executed the one of St Proculus which is believed to be a self-portrait.

181 DONATELLO'S MAGDALEN

After his return to Florence from Northern Italy in 1453 Donatello, then a man of seventy, was one of the major exponents of the wave of intense penitential emotion that swept the city in the early 1450s. His lonely penitent Magdalen, specially commissioned for the Baptistery, where it still stands, is a powerful expression of the highly-charged emotional climate of that decade.

182 ANGEL, S. CROCE, FLORENCE

This charming marble boy-angel holding an heraldic shield on the right of Chancellor Marsuppini's monument in the Church of Santa Croce resembles other works in the early style of Antonio Rossellino (1427–79) who worked in the studio of Desiderio da Settignano, the principal sculptor of the monument, and could be by his hand.

183 GUIDARELLO GUIDARELLI

This statue by the elderly Tullio Lombardo of the disquietingly handsome warrior Guidarello Guidarelli, who served the Duke of Ravenna and was killed in 1501, was executed in 1525 and originally placed in the Basilica of St Francesco. Women through the centuries have admired, touched and even kissed the inviting marble lips of the figure who thus became a sort of local idol around whom a cloying cult grew up. In the minds of the simple people he was even confused with the saints, thought capable of intercession, and loved, in a way that was not always purely spiritual.

184 BUST BY DESIDERIO DA SETTIGNANO

Desiderio da Settignano died in his early thirties in 1464. During his short lifetime he had achieved a small but extraordinarily fine output. The amazing lightness of his modelling seems to give the cold marble a haunting feeling of life.

185 DONATELLO'S DAVID

This is one of Donatello's earliest works, carved when he was in his early twenties, before he had properly freed himself from the style of his masters,

Ghiberti and Nanni di Banco. David is represented with Gothic elegance, triumphing by moral superiority rather than strength or stratagem.

186 VERROCCHIO'S DAVID

This bronze statue was made in the 1460s for the Medici villa at Careggi and sold to the Florentine Signoria in 1476. It still stands on its original granite base. Verrocchio learned much from Donatello, but could not acquire his tragic and emotional power. David, tranquil and elegant, seems ready to accept the applause of the populace for his courage in slaying Goliath.

187 VERROCCHIO'S *Lady with Primroses*

Andrea di Cione, known to the world as Verrocchio (1435–88), a Florentine, led an important workshop in his native city whose influence was far-reaching, profoundly effecting Italian art in general. He excelled not only as a sculptor in marble, bronze and terracotta, but also as a painter and goldsmith. Among his pupils were Perugino and Leonardo da Vinci who particularly admired the sensitive *Lady with Primroses* who seems on the brink of making a pondered 'Thank you' as she clutches her flowers with her elegant hand.

189, GIULIANO AND LORENZO II DE'MEDICI
190

These are two of three funerary monuments planned by Michelangelo in the unfinished chapel. Duke Giuliano is portrayed seated and in classical armour, representing Active Life; below on the sarcophagus recline allegorical figures of Day and Night – the latter, the sculptor's last work before leaving Florence. The young Duke Lorenzo, who died at the age of twenty-seven, is portrayed seated, absorbed in thought, representing Contemplative Life, and the allegorical figures beneath on his tomb are of Dawn and Dusk. The whole project was to have included other statuary and frescoes representing the whole cycle of death and the resurrection of the soul. It is related that when it was pointed out to Michelangelo that the statues did not at all resemble the late Medici Dukes he retorted that in a thousand years no one would know or care.

191 S. VITALE, RAVENNA

The marvellous church of S. Vitale at Ravenna is contemporary with the great St Sophia at Constantinople, built and lavishly decorated at the zenith of the flourishing art of Byzantium. The consecration took place in 547 while the Emperor Justinian, who had defeated the successor of Theodoric the Ostrogoth, held Ravenna. The Emperor himself is portrayed with his general and soldiers in a panel on the left of the apse opposite the one in the plate depicting his wife the Empress Theodora, bejewelled, with a glittering halo and rich purple robe embroidered with figures of the three Magi, surrounded by ladies of her court and ministers. In the ceiling of the apse the brilliant mosaic portrays a beardless Christ seated on a blue universe between archangels, St Vitale and Bishop Ecclesius. In the lunette below the upper loggia are represented the offerings of Abel and Melchisedek, types of the Eucharistic sacrament. Around them in the arch is part of the story of Moses. Exquisitely carved capitals and veined marble veneers make it a brilliant animated panoply in the Byzantine tradition, swirling acanthus leaves, floral garlands, and vivid scenes.

192 FIDENZA

The Cathedral was begun in the Romanesque style but finished in the thirteenth century with a transition to the Gothic. The statues of Ezekiel and David on the façade are the work of Antelami or of a close follower, and in the frieze above the niche are sculpted scenes from the life of S. Donnino. Works by this early virtuoso are known from 1178 when he signed the Deposition in the Cathedral at Parma (where he also worked on the Baptistery), and his energetic influence and robust style spread quickly through Lombardy and Emilia Romagna.

193 THE ANGEL OF THE ANNUNCIATION BY BALDOVINETTI

This painting was specially commissioned for this burial chapel of the Cardinal Archbishop of Lisbon, a nephew of the King of Portugal, who died in 1459. The Latin inscription under the painting refers to the coats-of-arms of the thirty families connected with the Portuguese royal house which decorate the frieze around the chapel. Alessio Baldovinetti (1425–99), a native Florentine who preserved the serene style of Domenico Veneziano, is renowned for his delicate tranquil colour and a certain monumentality of composition that reminds one of his contemporary (also influenced by Domenico) Piero della Francesca.

DETAIL OF BAPTISTERY DOORS, FLORENCE

The bronze Renaissance east doors of the Baptistery at Florence, called by Michelangelo 'the doors of Paradise', are the masterpiece of Lorenzo Ghiberti (1378–1455). Begun in 1425, they were not finally placed in position until 1452. They comprise ten exquisitely chiselled bas-relief panels depicting scenes from the Old Testament framed by niches containing little statues of prophets, sibyls and Biblical characters, among heads of contemporary artists. This panel comes at the bottom of the right-hand door and shows the Queen of Sheba visiting Solomon. Within the depth of the bronze panel Ghiberti manages to convey a strong sense of recession, by combining variation of modelling with linear perspective.

ILLUMINATED MANUSCRIPT, FERRARA

The Biblioteca Comunale Ariostea in the fourteenth-century Palazzo Paradiso at Ferrara was founded by the municipality in 1729 and thanks to numerous bequests now possesses about 150,000 volumes as well as 1,600 incunabula, 3,400 prints and engravings and 2,500 manuscripts. Among the latter are some writings of Tasso, a MS of Orlando Furioso and the Astrological Tables of Blanchinius illuminated by an anonymous artist.

LIBRARY, PALAZZO GUICCIARDINI

The Palazzo Guicciardini, in the Via Guicciardini which runs from the Ponte Vecchio to the square in front of the Palazzo Pitti, dates from the beginning of the fifteenth century. Alterations were made to the original building in the late sixteenth century by the Pisan Ludovico Cardi, called Il Cigoli (1559–1613) and in the seventeenth century by the Florentine architect Gherardo Silvani (1579–1675). The historian Francesco Guicciardini was born in this palace in 1482 and its library contains many old and valuable works. The palace is still owned by the Guicciardini family.

TREASURE CHAMBER, FERRARA

The Palace, called that of Lodovico il Moro, was in fact built about 1500 by Biagio Rossetti (1447–1516) for Antonio Costabili an ambassador of Duke Ercole I. The bold decoration of the Treasure Chamber is attributed to the painter Benevento Tisi, Il Garofalo (1481–1559).

CASTELLO ESTENSE, FERRARA

The impressive castle of the Este Dukes who ruled Ferrara from the twelfth to the sixteenth centuries when the Duchy fell under the sovereignty of the Church, stands in the centre of the city. Duke Niccolò II began the building in 1385 with the architect Bartolino da Novara. The fortified medieval military aspect of the castle is still evident from the massive flanking towers, the ravelins and the deep moat. Inside there are rooms decorated with fine sixteenth-century frescoes, a small Protestant chapel of Renée of France, wife of Duke Ercole II (she was a Protestant and a protectress of Calvin while he was in Ferrara), reception rooms, and the Throne Room. In the subterranean dungeons under the castle the wife of Duke Niccolò III and her lover were imprisoned and later beheaded.

FONT, S. FREDIANO, LUCCA

This church, dedicated to the sixth-century Bishop of Lucca, Frediano, who may have been the Irish St Finnian of Moville, was built between 1112 and 1147 on the site of an important earlier basilica. The nave of the church follows the same principles as that of the Cathedral of Pisa. The arches are supported by antique columns and a variety of re-used capitals. The elaborate decoration of the twelfth-century font is enhanced by the simplicity of the church. Around the circular base, in the style of a Roman

sarcophagus, are sculpted Biblical scenes: here we see the Israelites crossing the Red Sea and Moses receiving the tablets from God in the burning bush. Under the basin, which stands on a single pillar, are little devils – perhaps symbols of Hell – while the cover is decorated with figures of the Apostles and symbols of the months.

200 FARNESE THEATRE, PARMA

In its heyday in the seventeenth century this was the finest theatre in Europe, inaugurated in 1628 during the wedding celebrations of Odoardo Farnese and Margherita de' Medici. It was built on the second floor of the Ducal Palace in 1618, and designed by Giovanni Battista Aleotti. The elaborate proscenium arch was no doubt inspired by Palladio's Teatro Olimpico at Vicenza, but the stage space, instead of being filled with permanent perspectives, is left open for movable scenery. Aleotti was one of the pioneers of sliding scenery, or 'wings', essential for the development of the Baroque theatre. The *parterre* in front of the stage was left free for ballets and spectacles. Round it are banks of seats ending in a two-tier arcade based on Palladio's Basilica at Vicenza. After some decades of disuse, Marie-Louise, the wife of Napoleon, refurbished the theatre during her reign in Parma in the last century. Bombs devastated this precious monument in 1944 but it has been rebuilt and restored to its original grandeur.

201 CASTLE OF LA ROCCA

This imposing fortified castle was built for Uguccione Contrari between 1400 and 1435. In 1577 it became part of the fief of Prince Jacopo Boncompagni whose descendants held it for many years. It is now the property of the local Savings Bank who have undertaken repairs and restoration work. Inside, the castle has interesting fifteenth-century decoration, both secular and religious, of the Lombard school.

202 PARMA BAPTISTERY

Work began on the Baptistery at Parma at least as early as 1196 when the great Lombard sculptor Benedetto Antelami incised his name and the date on an architrave of the building. Built during the transition from the Romanesque to the Gothic style it was finished in 1260. The balustrade and eight pinnacles were added about fifty years later. The interior has rich sculptural decoration and important thirteenth- and fourteenth-century frescoes. The baptismal registers in the archives of the Baptistery are the oldest in Italy, dating from 1459.

203 ST GEORGE AND THE DRAGON

Bologna boasted a brilliant school of painters in the fourteenth century of whom Vitale was the most accomplished. In this vigorous painting of St George, Vitale displayed his forcefulness, abandoning the restraint exercised in his earlier fresco work. The style is that known as International Gothic, centred on Bohemia, but practised all over Europe.

204 LAST JUDGMENT

This representation of the Last Judgment by a Bolognese painter is a contemporary derivative of the magnificent frescoes painted by Giovanni da Modena and assistants, 1410–15, in the Bolognini Chapel of the church of S. Petronio, Bologna. The iconography is unusual: where we should expect Christ as Judge comes the Coronation of the Virgin. Otherwise the scheme is traditional, with St Michael weighing souls in the centre, Satan and the infernal regions beneath.

205, DELLA ROBBIA ANGELS, DELLA ROBBIA HOLY CHILD
206

St Francis of Assisi spent some years at La Verna and it was here in 1224 that he received the stigmata. In consequence La Verna became an important Franciscan centre with a flourishing monastery which attracted many pilgrims.

Both the small church of S. Maria degli Angeli and the fourteenth-century Chiesa Maggiore have many glazed polychrome terracottas by the Florentine sculptor Andrea della Robbia (1435–1528), his son Giovanni and artisans from his workshop. The technique of glazing and colouring terracotta had been perfected and popularized by Luca della Robbia

(1400–1482), uncle of Andrea, famous for his mild blue-mantled Madonnas encircled in floral garlands. Andrea's work is more sophisticated and showy.

208 CANOSSA

An immense castle was founded here in 940 by Azzo Adalberto, son of Sigifredo of Lucca, and originally included within its triple walls a small town, a church and a monastery. In 1077, when it was in the hands of the powerful Countess Matilda of Tuscany, great grand-daughter of Azzo Adalberto, it was the scene of the famous interview between Pope Gregory VII and the Emperor Henry IV. After a series of bitter disputes, Gregory had excommunicated the Emperor, a step which encouraged his enemies in Germany and led to a movement for his deposition. In order to retrieve the situation Henry came barefoot in the snow, garbed in rough clothing, to implore the Pontiff to revoke his excommunication; he was only admitted to the papal presence on the third day of his humiliation and pardoned. The castle of that time was razed to its foundations in the thirteenth century.

209, S. NICOLA DA TOLENTINO
210 The St Nicholas who lived at Tolentino was an Augustinian friar who died there in 1305; he was a most effective preacher but also achieved fame and veneration through the numerous miracles attributed to him – from one of which comes his symbol, the sun. The Basilica dedicated to him was once one of the most important and frequented sanctuaries of Central Italy. It incorporates the large chapel of St Nicholas with a glorious cycle of frescoes of the school of Rimini, fourteenth century, depicting scenes from the life of the saint and episodes from the New Testament.

211 VILLA TORRIGIANI

The formal gardens of the Villa Torrigiani were laid out in the seventeenth century by the Santini family who then owned the property. The sunken garden is connected to a higher garden (with a pool and fringed with lemon trees in pots) by the grand double staircase in which is fitted a system of *giochi d'acqua*. This Italian practical joke dates from Roman times. The host could turn on the concealed jets of water, dowsing his guests, driving them into other hidden showers, or imprisoning them behind a screen of water.

212 VILLA GARZONI

The garden of the Villa Garzoni at Collodi, built on a hillside, is one of the most impressive in Italy, with a green theatre, shady terraces, showy parterres, shimmering fountains, and a great water staircase. Throughout the garden there is terracotta statuary including a troupe of monkeys playing bowls. The garden which is open to the public now belongs to the municipality of Pescia.

213 BOBOLI GARDENS

The Boboli Gardens, most famous of the many gardens laid out for the Medici family, still largely preserve their original plan despite some minor changes. The gardens were commissioned by Eleanor of Toledo, wife of Cosimo I, and designed in 1549 by Nicolò Pericoli called Il Tribolo (1500–50) as a suitable backdrop for her recently acquired Pitti Palace. The gardens were extremely lavish and contained grottoes such as the one in the plate (with its ceiling painted with trellis, flowers, vines and little birds) executed between 1583 and 1588. There were cypress and ilex avenues; an amphitheatre modelled on a Roman hippodrome, in which seventeenth-century pageants were staged; formal lakes with animated sculptural groups and many antique statues in shady niches.

214 LORETO

The house in which the Holy Family dwelt in Nazareth is said to have been saved from the infidels by being miraculously transported first to Yugoslavia then to Recanati and other spots in the Marches finally landing at its present site in Loreto on 10 May 1291. Over it has been built a magnificent church, rich in works of art, the gifts of visitors to this famous sanctuary. Early in the seventeenth century the elegant fountain, seen in this photograph, was designed by Carlo Maderno (1556–1629) and Giovanni Fontana (1540–1614) with bronze figures of tritons astride dolphins, winged dragons and heraldic devices by Tarquinio and Pietro Paolo Iacometti.

215 ROYAL PALACE, TURIN

The eighteenth-century apartments of Queen Maria Teresa are among the most sumptuous in the Royal Palace of the Kings of Sardinia who became Kings of Italy. The painted ceilings, Sèvres vases, Gobelin tapestries, mirrors and gilded *boiseries* vie with the precious furniture by Pietro Piffetti, inlaid with tortoise-shell and mother-of-pearl, of which a prie-dieu is in this oratory.

216 PALAZZO MADAMA, TURIN

The Palazzo Madama takes its name from Madama Reale Maria Cristina, widow of Victor Amadeus I, Duke of Savoy, regent of the realm 1638–40, and Madama Reale Giovanna Battista, widow of Charles Emanuel II, who commissioned Filippo Juvarra to reconstruct it and who died in the Palace in 1724. Only Juvarra's Baroque front was actually carried out, with the monumental scenographic staircase and upper vestibule, built about 1720. The entrance side is on the left in the photograph. Flights of steps lead off to left and right (we are standing on the right-hand landing) and then double back to meet in the centre of the first floor.

217 S. LORENZO, TURIN

Guarino Guarini (1624–83) spent the last seventeen years of his life at the service of the Court of Savoy in Turin; his S. Lorenzo and his Chapel of the Holy Shroud are among the finest products of seventeenth-century architecture in Italy. His style is characterized by daring novelties and complicated geometrical experiments. The dome of S. Lorenzo is reduced to a star-pattern of ribs, through which light penetrates at unexpected angles. There is something here of the ingenuity of late Gothic, but expressed with all the energy of Baroque.

218 CHAPEL OF THE HOLY SHROUD

The chapel behind the apse of Turin Cathedral was designed by Guarino Guarini (see note to Plate 217) to house the Holy Shroud, the sheet in which Christ was wound after his deposition from the Cross, and which miraculously bears the imprints of His body. This holy relic belonged to the Savoy family since 1452. Over the circular ground-plan Guarini built three arches, which form a triangular base for a circular dome. This dome is itself vaulted by a series of shallow segmental arches resting on each other and diminishing in size until they end in a transparent umbrella of ribs – perhaps the most astonishing of all Baroque inventions.

219, STUPINIGI
220 This royal hunting box a few miles from Turin was begun in 1729 for King Victor Amadeus II of Sardinia, a ruler anxious to keep up with his fellow monarchs, but he died soon afterwards and his son King Charles Emmanuel, being more interested in enlarging his territories than in architecture, curtailed his father's original plans. The work dragged on for years and several architects were involved, but the main features go back to the original design by Filippo Juvarra. The palace was first used by the next king, Victor Amadeus III, who gave sumptuous wedding receptions at Stupinigi for his sons in 1773 and 1781.

The palace is approached by a long drive between stables and barns laid out in a formal pattern, ending at wrought iron gates enclosing a garden. On the other side a splendid deer park stretches for miles. The high oval saloon is the centre of the building, the other rooms leading off it in four lower wings. This saloon, lavishly decorated with stucco work and frescoes by the brothers Valeriani, epitomizes the change from Baroque to Rococo in eighteenth-century Italy. In 1926 the Italian royal family presented the property to the Order of St Maurice and St Lazarus on whose land it stood.

AMATI VIOLIN

In the seventeenth century Cremona was a centre of musical instrument makers; the famous Nicolas Amati (1596–1684) and his even more famous pupil Antonio Stradivari (1644–1737) lived and worked in the town, which proudly conserves examples of their craft in the Town Hall, opposite the cathedral. Through the window the cathedral façade appears, a mixture of Romanesque and Gothic.

TEATRO VERDI

Giuseppe Verdi (1813–1901) was born a peasant near Busseto. After his rise to fame and wealth he bought a country house near the town. A new opera house was inaugurated at Busseto in 1868 with a performance of *Rigoletto* but the composer's box, the place of honour in the centre, was conspicuously empty. Verdi had quarrelled with the municipality about the theatre both because they wished to give it his name, which he thought in bad taste, and because they had solicited a large contribution from him towards the construction. He returned to Busseto two days after the first opera season ended.

FRESCOES, CASTLE OF MANTA

The Castle of Manta, originally a fortified stronghold of the Marquesses of Saluzzo, was transformed into a residence by Valerano, Count of La Manta, bastard son of Marquess Tommaso III, who inherited it in 1416. The cycle of frescoes in the International Gothic manner is an outstanding and unique product of the early Piedmontese Renaissance. Valerano ordered the painter Giacomo Jaquerio and his assistants to portray scenes from 'Le Chevalier Errant', a chivalresque epic poem written by his late father at the French court. In this detail are three of the Nine Worthies – King Arthur, Charlemagne and Godfrey of Bouillon – and three of the Nine Heroines – Delphine, Sinope, and Hyppolita, all in fourteenth-century dress.

MONUMENT OF GASTON OF FOIX IN THE CASTELLO SFORZESCO, MILAN

At his death in 1391 Gaston, Count of Foix, bequeathed his state, now the French department of Ariège, to the Kings of France. In recognition of this, over a century later, King Francis I of France, who was also an admirer of the enlightened Gaston, commissioned Agostini Busti, Il Bambaia (1483–1548), to sculpt an elaborate tomb for him. It was left unfinished and abandoned in 1525 due to the French King's defeat at Pavia, but fragments of it are in the Ambrosiana Museum, Milan.

MONUMENT OF BEATRICE D'ESTE

Solari's effigy of Beatrice d'Este, the young wife of Lodovico Sforza, Duke of Milan, who died in 1497, shows the same elegance and precise attention to detail which characterized sculpture all over Europe at this period. Lodovico was a cunning politician who usurped the powerful Duchy from his nephew but he was also a great patron of the arts, a fact of importance in the cultural history of Italy.

RONDANINI PIETÀ

Michelangelo was working on this Pietà until a few days before his death in 1564, but had so radically changed his conception of it that it could never have been satisfactorily finished. Its fascination for us lies in the fact that it shows him actually in the process of creation. The body of Christ was originally larger and further away from the Virgin. Of this scheme the legs and right arm remain. But he then decided to bring the two bodies closer together, almost to merge them in one form, and began carving the two heads out of what had previously been the upper part of the Virgin. The result is confused but strangely powerful and haunting.

STAGLIENO

The cemetery at Staglieno to the north of the city of Genoa was built between 1844 and 1851 by the local architect Giovanni Battista Resasco (1799–1872) based on a plan by Carlo Barabino (1768–1835). At that time Genoa had a prosperous, mercantile, middle-class, and many a family laid its loved ones to rest in monumental chapels or tombs more impressive than the rooms they had occupied when living. Sculpture too reached a high degree of naturalism and technical skill. Much of it is pompous or sentimental, and the incongruity of medieval angels confronting stout nineteenth-century businessmen in frock coats today strikes the onlooker as slightly comic. But the cemetery remains a unique collection of funerary art; the agony of death and the pathos of bereavement are often presented with genuine feeling.

233   SALETTA DI DANTE

When the rich Milanese nobleman Gian Giacomo Poldi-Pezzoli built a town mansion to house his collection of art treasures, he decorated some of the interiors in the prevailing Neo-Gothic fashion, and dedicated one room to Dante, with a stained-glass window by the painter Giuseppe Bertini. It is a smaller version of Bertini's great Dante window in the Ambrosiana. The Palazzo Poldi-Pezzoli has been a museum since the death of its builder.

234   BRIGNOLE-SALE ARMS

Palazzo Rosso – the Red Palace, so named for the colour of its façade – was built in 1671–77 for the powerful and rich Brignole-Sale family by Matteo Lagomaggiore an architect who was active in Genoa. It now houses an important museum incorporating the family pictures and furniture which were left to the city in 1874. Appliqué work such as this with heraldic devices is still done in Italy today.

235,   PALAZZO DORIA PAMPHILI, GENOA
236

The Palace of the Doria princes in Genoa was formed from two earlier palaces purchased by their ancestor Admiral Andrea Doria in 1521. The Sala dei Giganti and other beautiful rooms were painted by Perino del Vaga about 1530. The giants, not seen in the photograph, represent the great rivers and fables connected with the sea. The great chimney piece is by the sculptor Silvio Cosini. The gardens of the palace stretch over a wide area of the steep hillside and have fountains decorated with Neptune and eagles, the Doria emblems.

237   PALAZZO CLERICI

Marshal Giorgio Antonio Clerici bought the palace that still bears his name from the Visconti family and began re-decorating it in 1736. He was a favourite of the Empress Maria Theresa, had considerable means and used them to employ the best artists. Giambattista Tiepolo (1696–1770) decorated the main reception room with a magnificent fresco of Apollo in the Chariot of the Sun passing across the continents of the world. A sumptuous Murano glass candelabra lights the room, reflected again and again in the richly gilded mirrors. The building is now the Court of Appeal of Milan.

238   PALAZZO CARREGA-CATALDI

The Palazzo Carrega-Cataldi, now the Chamber of Commerce of Genoa, was built by Tobia Pallavicino in the middle of the sixteenth century. The Carrega family bought it in 1704 making many additions to the building. In 1820 it was sold to the Cataldi family. The rooms have lavish gilded stucco decoration, much of it by Lorenzo de Ferrari (1680–1744) who painted the Feats of Aeneas in the gallery. The mirrored banquet table is thirty feet long.

239   CATHEDRAL, MILAN

The Cathedral of Milan was founded in 1386 but the building was only completed five centuries later in 1887. The plan is a long broad nave with double aisles, a large transept and a polygonal apse. The work began with the Campione masters, sculptors who were at the same time stonemasons, influenced by Gothic forms from France and Germany and under the sporadic direction of imported French, Flemish and German architects. Work on the cathedral continued in the fifteenth century under the architects Filippino degli Organi, Giovanni Solari and his son, his grandson and his grandson-in-law Giovanni Antonio Amadeo. Much of the façade was accomplished between 1616 and 1645 by Carlo Rozzi to earlier plans of the painter Pellegrino Tibaldi (1527–96); but it was completed in a further spate of work 1805–13. Externally the whole cathedral is faced with pearly pinkish-white marble, and covered with a wealth of tall pinnacles crowned by statues. Over the crossing rises the highest pinnacle of all, which supports the Madonnina, a gilt copper statue of the Madonna made in 1773.

240 ALTAR, S. AMBROGIO
The precious altar casing, of sheet gold in front and gilded silver at the back, was the gift of the Archbishop Angilbert II to the new basilica of Milan's patron saint in 835. It is exquisitely worked in panels with enamel and gem-set surrounds, masterpieces of Carolingian art by a goldsmith named Vuolvinus. Christ the Redeemer in the central oval is surrounded by the symbols of the Evangelists in the arms of the Cross and the twelve Apostles in groups of three in the corners.

243 MARRIAGE COFFER
Girls of all walks of life in Italy had marriage coffers in which to store the trousseau, patiently collected often from birth, for their marriage. Those of the peasants were simple chests, those of the rich, handsomely carved and gilded such as this splendid gilded and painted Venetian one of the sixteenth century, depicting the wedding of the Virgin. It is now in the Poldi-Pezzoli Museum.

244 CONFESSIONAL, S. MARIA MAGGIORE, BERGAMO
This ornate confessional in the twelfth-century church of S. Maria Maggiore, Bergamo, was originally made for the parish church of Zandobbio in 1704–05. It is the work of Andrea Fantoni (1659–1734), a member of a prolific family of skilled woodworkers from Rovetta, province of Bergamo, who excelled in late Baroque wood sculpture and marquetry.

245 AGLIE
This richly stuccoed church, now in the process of restoration, was designed in 1760 by the little-known architect Costanzo Michela, who had also worked on another parish church in the Canavese region, that of Valperga, in 1749. He may have been a pupil of Filippo Juvarra, whose work has already been illustrated, but was also influenced by Vittone. The undulating plan and idiosyncratic style of decoration at Agliè make it an interesting example of Piedmontese Baroque just before the advent of Neo-classicism.

246, VILLA LECHI
247 The Villa Lechi is still in the possession of the Lechi family for whom it was built by Antonio Turbino in 1741–45. The whole is more like a Venetian than a Lombard country house and the delightful frescoed ballroom begun in 1745 with architectural settings by Giacomo Lecchi and figures by Carlo Carloni (1686–1775) is particularly reminiscent of the Tiepolo salon in the Palazzo Labia at Venice of about the same date. Among the famous guests at Villa Lechi were Mozart and Napoleon.

The extraordinary stables for twenty-four horses are among the most magnificent in the country. The ceiling is frescoed with a sun chariot and the horses fed between columns topped by elegant urn-finials or statues of antique gods.

248 VILLA CICOGNA-MOZZONI
The Villa Cicogna built as a hunting box in the fifteenth century is still owned by the Cicogna-Mozzonis who descend from the original owner, and who have opened this lovely house to the public. It is a perfect example of a Renaissance villa in Lombardy, with delightful frescoed rooms. Most of this decoration dates from the sixteenth century when the house was drastically renovated and decorated by Antonio and Bernardino Campi of Cremona on the marriage of the heiress Angela Mozzoni to Ascanio Cicogna.

249 DUCAL PALACE, MANTUA
The vast Gonzaga Ducal Palace in Mantua is a treasury of Italian art, in spite of major losses by sale and pillage. Generations of Gonzagas from 1290 to 1707, followed by their Austrian successors, added to it, employing the leading artists and architects of their day. The frescoes by Andrea Mantegna (c. 1431–1506) in the Camera degli Sposi are the most important works of art in the palace. On the walls are scenes of Gonzaga family life with portraits of the leading members. On the ceiling Mantegna painted the first example in Italian art of sotto in sù perspective. We seem to look up through an opening in the vault to the blue sky. Women lean over the balustrade; a bowl containing a shrub balances on a rod over our heads; three putti cling precariously to the inner rim of the opening.

250 PALAZZO DEL TÈ, MANTUA
Federigo Gonzaga, First Duke of Mantua, entrusted the design and execution of a pleasure palace to Giulio Romano (1492–1546) a pupil of Raphael. The actual building was completed within eighteen months in 1524, then a veritable army of painters, gilders, sculptors and stuccoists worked on the lavish decoration for ten years. Romano was an imaginative extrovert and in the decoration of the Sala dei Giganti he gave full reign to his grandiose ideas. The colossal giants of the Fall of the Gods, painted by Rinaldo Mantovano and others after his cartoons, expand luxuriously over the walls. On the ceiling is the victorious realm of Jupiter, with another sotto in sù perspective comparable to that painted by Mantegna fifty years earlier.

251 CUPID AND PSYCHE
The Villa Carlotta, originally built by the rich and extravagant Marshal Clerici in 1745, takes its name from Princess Carlotta of Prussia to whom it was given as a wedding present in 1847. The Cupid and Psyche is by the foremost Italian Neo-classical sculptor Antonio Canova (1757–1822). The marble frieze in the background of the photograph, depicting Alexander's Triumph at Babylon, was sculpted 1817–28 for the then owner of the Villa, Count Giovanni Battista Sommariva, by the Danish sculptor Bertel Thorvaldsen (1770–1844); it is a copy of the one he had done in 1811–12 for Napoleon for the throne room of the Quirinal. Besides its sculpture gallery the Villa boasts a world-famous garden.

252 DUCAL PALACE, MANTUA
See note to plate 249.

253, ISOLA BELLA
254 Count Carlo III Borromeo, nephew of St Charles Borromeo, conceived the idea of a palatial residence and garden on an island which he owned in the Lago Maggiore, and named it Isola Bella in honour of his wife Isabella. The Count and his architect, Crivelli, died before the work was much advanced and it was the Count's son Vitaliano who proceeded with the ambitious project with the help of Carlo Fontana (1634–1714) and other architects. An army of builders and sculptors were employed to erect the great Baroque palace and lay out the gardens but the project was so grandiose that it was only completed almost three hundred years later by the Borromeo family who still own the island, with the proceeds of entrance-money paid at the gate by visitors.

The whole was designed to give the effect of a great galleon – the garden extending like a prow suspended above the water. White peacocks strut in the ornate gardens which consist of ten terraces, the lowest on piles over the lake, a riot of mimosa, camellias, azaleas and exotic plants amid obelisks, statues and cascading fountains which have been commemorated in painting by Turner and Corot. Here the Borromeos gave a fête champêtre for Napoleon and Josephine, engaging the leading diva of the Scala to sing his favourite arias.

255 S. MICHELE, PAVIA
The Basilica of S. Michele at Pavia was the scene of many solemn royal and imperial coronations. It is a plain Romanesque building, the chancel raised up on steps above an open crypt. The main altar has a magnificent gilded wood tabernacle. Above it a fresco in the ceiling of the apse depicting the Coronation of the Virgin was painted in 1491 by Agostino di Montebello.

256 DUOMO, CREMA

This church in the Lombard-Gothic style was built between 1284 and 1341. The façade, in brick, with an attractive blind loggia crowned by pinnacles, is divided into three arcades. A fine marble rose-window marks the central arcade and smaller ones in the side arcade beneath the windows maintain the symmetry.

257 VILLA CHIERICATI, NOW LAMBERT

The ante-chamber of the villa, now a dining-room, has an interesting cycle of landscape frescoes of the four seasons, attributed to Lodovico Pozzoserrato (c. 1550–c. 1603), a Flemish artist who worked in the Veneto. The page with a hound is attributed to a student of Paolo Veronese and is certainly in his style. The villa was built in 1590 and the frescoes were undoubtedly executed shortly after that date.

259 BASILICA, AQUILEIA

Aquileia, once the capital of a Roman region and a flourishing city under the Emperor Augustus, was sacked successively by Alaric the Goth, Attila the Hun, Theodoric the Ostrogoth and the Lombards. According to tradition it was proselytized by St Mark and it grew again in importance under the Patriarchate. This was the rule of the bishops and later archbishops who had spiritual jurisdiction over seventeen dioceses and temporal jurisdiction over a wide area, exercising both civil and ecclesiastical authority.

On the site of the edifice where St Ambrose attended the Council of 381 and of a later basilica which had been endowed by Charlemagne, the powerful Patriarch Poppo consecrated the present church early in the eleventh century. The brilliantly coloured mosaic pavement, uncovered in the nave in 1909, belonged to the fourth-century building. The Basilica as it stands today is still principally the eleventh-century church and in the apse are original frescoes including one of the Patriarch Poppo presenting a model of the Basilica to the Madonna.

260 BRIDGE OVER THE BRENTA, BASSANO DEL GRAPPA

Through the centuries many wooden bridges have spanned the River Brenta at this spot. The beautiful one designed by Palladio in 1569 replaced a medieval bridge but it was destroyed by fierce Alpine floods and replaced by another in the eighteenth century. This, in turn, was burned by the retreating troops of the Viceroy Beauharnais. The next bridge built by Angelo Casarotto in 1821 was destroyed in the Second World War and the present one, a replica of it, was erected in 1948.

261 DOOR, S. ZENO, VERONA

The bronze doors of S. Zeno are the work of twelfth-century German craftsmen and have affinities with work in Germany at Hildesheim. They consist of separate bronze plaques nailed to a wooden backing. Still naive in many respects, they have a directness and simple power that make them among the most expressive works of Romanesque art. The photograph shows the six lower panels of the right-hand door including a lion mask, miracles of St Zeno, and Noah's ark. The bronze doors by Bonanno at Pisa and Monreale derive from the work at S. Zeno.

262 FACADE, S. ZENO, VERONA

The porch and surrounds of the bronze doors are equally notable. Like most north Italian Romanesque porches, its columns rest on crouching lions. The marble reliefs on either side, however, are highly unusual. They are the work of sculptors named Niccolò and Guglielmo. Guglielmo's on the left depict New Testament scenes while Niccolò's on the right are from the Old.

263 PALACE OF THE LOGGIA, UDINE

The old municipal palace at Udine was designed by a local goldsmith, Nicola Lionello, and built between 1448 and 1456 but the exterior was not decorated until a hundred years later. This fine building in the Venetian-Gothic style of architecture was badly damaged by fire in 1876 and subsequently restored in the original style. The fresco depicting the three angel musicians is a late nineteenth-century reproduction by Giuseppe Ghedina (1825–96) of the original by Il Pordenone which was damaged in the fire. Reflected in the screen on the loggia which protects the frescoes can be seen two huge stone statues of Hercules and Cacus and the slender columns and elegant renaissance arches of the Porticato of S. Giovanni built in 1533.

264 RACHEL HIDING THE IMAGES, FRESCO BY GIAMBATTISTA TIEPOLO, Archiepiscopal Palace, Udine

Chapter 31 of Genesis tells how Jacob fled with his wives Leah and Rachel from his father-in-law Laban. Unknown to him, Rachel had stolen her father's household images. Laban pursued them and searched for the images, but Rachel had hidden them underneath her and refused to stand up. There is a tradition that Tiepolo painted his self-portrait as Jacob, standing next to the bearded figure of Laban. The Udine frescoes were his first major commission. In 1725, when they were begun, he was only twenty-nine, but the characteristic bravura quality of his composition and light, festive colour range were already present.

265 THE TEATRO OLIMPICO, VICENZA

This theatre and the Villa Rotonda are Palladio's best known works. It was begun in February 1580 but Andrea Palladio (1508–80) died in August of the same year and the work continued under the direction of Vincenzo Scamozzi (1552–1616) who completed it in 1584. The theatre was inaugurated in the following year with a performance of *Oedipo Tiranno* with choral music composed by Andrea Gabrieli, then the organist at St Mark's in Venice.

Palladio's scheme is based on a Roman theatre with *Cavea*, *Orchestra*, *Proscenium* and *Scena* but he was forced to make the cavea more elliptical than in antique examples because the municipality restricted the space available – and thus it seems rather flattened. The photograph shows part of the proscenium which is peopled by gesticulating statues who seem to be both actors and spectators. Through the central arch and at the sides the artfully deceptive perspectives of the streets of Thebes can be seen, a scenographic trick which has no classical precedent, but derives from Renaissance attempts to recreate descriptions by Vitruvius.

266 GALLERY OF THE THEATRE, SABBIONETA

Though geographically out of place in this section, this theatre has been included here because it is the work of Vincenzo Scamozzi built four years after he completed the Teatro Olimpico at Vicenza. The same unity is achieved by a colonnaded gallery topped by statues and which joined the middle tier of the proscenium. The stage was originally filled with a permanent perspective set like those at Vicenza but this was soon dismantled to make way for movable scenery. Sabbioneta, called 'The Athens of the Gonzagas', has a number of beautiful buildings – it was built to realize the dream of a Renaissance prince as the capital of his little state.

267 ARCHITECTURAL MODEL OF THE VILLA CAPRA OR ROTONDA

This scale model (1:33) in wood was made by the firm of Pietro Ballico of Schio for the Palladio Exhibition held at Vicenza in 1973.

The Villa Almerico Capra, better known as 'La Rotonda', was not finished in the lifetime of its designer Andrea Palladio (1508–80) and, like the theatre at Vicenza, was completed by Vincenzo Scamozzi (1552–1616). Its fame is great for it is the prototype of many buildings in other countries. Burlington's Chiswick House and Campbell's Mereworth are the best known of the four English versions; in the United States is Jefferson's Monticello; and in Poland the Villa Lubostron near Poznan.

268 FRESCOES BY VERONESE, VILLA BARBARO, MASER

This lovely villa, still a private residence, is the result of a felicitous partnership between two great artists of the sixteenth century, the architect Andrea Palladio (1508–80) and the painter Paolo Veronese (1528–88). Although Palladio usually enthused about his collaborators, he has left no mention of Veronese and it is possible that he resented the painter's daring *trompe-l'œil* innovations. Here the interior decoration may have been directed by the owner Daniele Barbaro, a learned humanist. Besides landscapes and seascapes, Olympian gods peer over the cornice above members of the Barbaro family and their pets on a balcony. In the photograph the Barbaro's little maidservant cautiously opens a door – all in masterful *trompe-l'œil*.

269 VILLA MANIN

This, the most ostentatious of the Venetian country villas with extensive outbuildings, was built early in the eighteenth century for the Manin family. Later it was the residence of the last Doge Lodovico Manin and here Napoleon stayed in 1797 during the talks preceding the Treaty of Campoformio.

The vast forecourt of the villa is flanked by the wings which have lofty colonnades and handsome wrought-iron gates.

270 SCALA DEI GIGANTI, PALAZZO DUCALE, VENICE

The impressive ceremonial staircase at the Palace of the Doges was made after the fire of 1483 and is the work of the prolific Antonio Rizzo. Flanking it at the bottom stand the two giant statues of Mars and Neptune by Jacopo Sansovino (1486–1570) completed in 1567.

271 DETAIL OF EQUESTRIAN STATUE OF BARTOLOMEO COLLEONI

Bartolomeo Colleoni was one of the leading mercenary generals, or *condottieri*, who conducted war on behalf of the Italian states during the fourteenth and fifteenth centuries. He first entered the service of Venice in 1429, left it in 1443 for Milan, but returned again in 1455. He died twenty years later, leaving a large fortune to the city of Venice on condition that they erected a statue to him. It has secured him an immortality which his feats of arms alone would hardly have won. Designed by Verrocchio in 1480, it expresses the fierceness of his profession rather than his actual features.

272 GATE OF THE LOGGETTA, VENICE

One of Jacopo Sansovino's most charming enrichments to the city is the Loggetta at the base of the Campanile in St Mark's Square. The Loggetta was closed off in 1737 by this elegant bronze gate, the work of the Venetian sculptor Antonio Gai (1686–1769). The Lion of St Mark is the symbol of the city; behind it is the façade of St Mark's cathedral, where the body of the saint, according to medieval belief, rests.

273 S. MARIA DELLA SALUTE, FROM THE GRAND CANAL

The church of S. Maria della Salute, designed by Baldassare Longhena in 1633, was erected as a thank offering after the recovery of Venice from a visitation of the plague. To build the foundations 1,106,650 oak piles, each 12 feet long, were driven into the mud. The gondola belongs to Mrs Peggy Guggenheim.

274 MARBLE LIONS IN FRONT OF THE ARSENAL, VENICE

In the seventeenth century the drawbridge at the entrance of the Arsenal was enclosed by railings and beside these were placed two colossal lions, war trophies, brought back from Greece in 1692 by Francesco Morosini. The lion on the left, lying down, came from the road between Athens and Eleusis. The one with the sad expression came from Delos and is thought to date from the sixth century BC. Behind the lions can be seen the Baroque allegorical figures on the pilasters of the imposing railings.

Sixteen thousand workers were once employed in the Arsenal building and repairing the ships of the powerful Venetian fleet and manufacturing explosives and armaments.

277 S. GIORGIO MAGGIORE SEEN ACROSS THE LAGOON, VENICE

Across the water lies the monastery of S. Giorgio Maggiore, with its superb church by Palladio. In the foreground, at the end of the Piazzetta, are the two oriental granite columns looted from Constantinople. One of these holds aloft a statue of the first patron of the city, St Theodore on his crocodile, while the other bears a fourth-century winged beast transformed into the Lion of St Mark, who replaced St Theodore as the protector of Venice. This space was once used for executions – hence the Venetian proverb 'Between Mark and Theodore', meaning 'to be in a tight spot'.

278 FIREWORKS ON THE FEAST OF THE REDENTORE, VENICE

Annually on the third Sunday of July the Venetians celebrate this festival which is one of the few to survive from the days of the Republic. A bridge of gondolas forms from the Zattere to the Church of the Redentore (the Redeemer), over which the Doge and the Signoria used to pass in state, and on the evening of the festival most of the city is afloat to watch the fireworks. The church itself was built to Palladio's designs between 1577 and 1592 as a votive offering for the abatement of a terrible plague.

280 PORTICO, VILLA CORNARO, PIOMBINO DESE

'The following fabrick', says Palladio in his *I Quattro Libri dell'Architettura*, 'belongs to the magnificent Signor Giorgio Cornaro, at Piombino. The first order of the loggia is Ionic. The hall is placed in the most inward part of the house, that it may be far from the heat and cold . . . The loggias above are of the Corinthian order. The columns are one fifth less than those underneath.' These great columned porticoes, which Palladio's example made so popular in later architecture, were believed by him to be features of Roman villas. This is now known to be quite mistaken.

281 FRESCOED ROOM, VILLA CALDOGNO

The interior of this Palladian villa, which was built about 1565, is decorated with a vast pictorial series attributed to the Brescian painter Giovanni Antonio Fasolo (c. 1530–1572) and the painters Giovanni Battista Zelotti (1526–1578) and Domenico Brusacorci (c. 1516–1567) both natives of Verona. There is also a small room with later fresco work by the Venetian Giulio Carpioni (1611–74).

The photograph shows a wall of the Sophonisba Room. The episode depicting a gallant gentleman furtively embracing a young lady is attributed to Fasolo.

282 VILLA EMO, FANZOLO DI VEDELAGO

Palladio's *I Quattro Libri dell' Architettura* were published in 1570 and were to have a great and stimulating effect on European and, indeed, eventually American architecture. The Villa Emo, still entirely intact and in excellent condition, is one of the rare examples of a Venetian country villa whose design as executed corresponds exactly with Palladio's original published design. The farm buildings and offices are masked by the long arcaded wings on either side of the temple-fronted central portion which contained the owner's residential quarters.

284 SET FOR 'AIDA', ARENA OF VERONA

Verona offers the best open-air opera performances in Italy and Verdi's *Aida* is a favourite choice because its grandiose triumphal scene can be given on a suitable scale in the great Roman arena. This photograph was taken in the early hours of the morning after the Verdi centenary performance.

285 BASILICA OF ST ANTONY, PADUA

This great church was begun in 1232 to house the tomb of the Portuguese friar St Antony who had died in the preceding year in the Convent of Santa Maria outside the city. The building work continued for over one hundred years. The series of Byzantine domes imitates those of St Mark in Venice, but the interior lay-out follows the Gothic system; the form is a Latin cross. Nine chapels each built on a square plan radiate from the choir. Donatello designed the magnificent altar in 1450 but it has undergone changes and re-arrangements. This basilica attracts a vast number of visitors not only for its beauty but because of the immense popularity of St Antony.

287 ANATOMY THEATRE, UNIVERSITY OF PADUA

Padua University was founded in 1222 when a group of dissident students left the University of Bologna. From the first it specialized in anatomy and medicine. The famous Andreas Vesalius was professor here in the sixteenth century. The theatre for demonstrating dissections was the first in Europe, constructed in 1544, and used until a hundred years ago. Every spectator has a virtually vertical view down to the dissecting table. In the well at the bottom of the theatre was an adjustable mechanical table with a trap door for the quick disposal of the bodies.

FRESCOED HOUSES, VERONA

There are several attractive frescoed Renaissance houses in the Piazza delle Erbe, Verona, the most interesting being Nos. 21–23, 26, 30 and 36. The allegorical scene on the house seen here is by Alberto Cavalli of Mantua.

DETAIL FROM THE ALTAR OF RATCHIS, CIVIDALE DEL FRIULI

The reliefs of this altar constitute some of the very rare examples of the art of the Lombards, who entered Italy in 568, enjoyed a period of power during the seventh century and were finally crushed by Charlemagne in the eighth. The altar was made for the church of S. Martino between 734 and 737 under Duke Ratchis, and paid for (as the inscription records) by a Count Pemmo. The Christ in Glory, shown here, is crudely imitated from Byzantine models.

CLOISTER, BRESSANONE DUOMO

This cloister was built in the fourteenth century, replacing an earlier one in wood. The walls and ceilings are decorated with lively frescoes executed between the end of the fourteenth and beginning of the sixteenth centuries. Those shown are scenes from the Old and New Testaments – Reuben at the pit seeking Joseph, Mary Magdalen meeting Christ in the garden, David cutting off the head of Goliath, Samson and the lion, Samson carrying the doors of Gaza, and the Resurrection. They are signed by Jakob Sunter of Bressanone and date from the latter part of the fifteenth century. Both the style of painting, and such features as the *banderolles* with inscriptions, point to northern Europe rather than to Italy.

293 CHURCH OF OUR LADY, NOVACELLA

This convent was founded in the twelfth century with a hospice for pilgrims crossing the Brenner Pass on their way to or from Rome. The Church of Our Lady within the complex of the convent buildings is a mid-eighteenth-century Baroque reconstruction of an earlier church, designed by Josef Delai of Bolzano and Philip Apeller. The ceiling frescoes depicting scenes from the life of St Augustine are by the German painter Matthias Günther. The whole lavish ensemble of painted and gilded stucco, bright frescoes, polychrome marble and the ubiquitous putti has a panache that can be paralleled only in the Rococo churches of Austria and southern Germany.

295 AUTOSTRADA

Italy has an imposing network of fast motorways nearly all constructed in the last twenty years and now linking the Alps to the extremities of Calabria and the Ligurian coast and crossing from the Tyrrhenian Sea to the Adriatic. Many stretches of it are as imposing, and show as much sensitivity to the landscape, as works of Roman engineering.

296 TOBIAS AND THE ARCHANGEL RAPHAEL by the brothers Piero (1443–1496) and Antonio (c. 1432–1498) Pollaiuolo. Galleria Sabauda, Palazzo dell'Accademia delle Scienze, Turin

In this painting the figures are attributed to the Florentine painter Piero Pollaiuolo and the landscape background to his more famous brother Antonio, with whom he often collaborated. Piero, though a strong painter, was less vigorous than his brother and failed to achieve his evocative power of line. Antonio tended to sacrifice tonal effect to the strength of contour and he sought a harmony between figure and landscape to which he devoted considerable attention.

Acknowledgments

Those who have been patient and helpful during the many years of travel, research and editing required to realize this book are too many to name. Museums and their curators have been equally co-operative and understanding during a time when they are trying so desperately to preserve their great heritage. I must single out Prof. Bruno Molajoli, former Director of the Belle Arti for all of Italy who so kindly had the doors to museums and private collections throughout the country opened to me. Dr Vito Agresti, recently retired as Director of the Belle Arti, and Prof. Guido Gregorietti, Director of the Poldi Pezzoli Museum in Milan, who officially assisted my project in every way; and Prof. Mario Mondello and Dr Giovanni Carandente, Curator of the Palazzo Venezia, whose advice was invaluable. Among the individuals who gave me special privileges I wish to thank Donna Vittoria Leone, First Lady of Italy, who graciously allowed me to photograph special rooms in the Presidential Palace, the Quirinale. *Time-Life* Books, whose various editors commissioned me to photograph and contribute to their books, *Imperial Rome* and *Renaissance*, in their series *Great Ages of Man*, have kindly permitted me to reproduce several of the photographs taken when I have been on these assignments, including colour plate 34. Among friends who were always generous and encouraging during a long project I wish to thank Mrs Peggy Guggenheim, Count Francesco Guicciardini, the Hon. Lady Duff Assheton Smith, Princess Vittoria (Vicky) Alliata di Villafranca, Count and Countess Paolo Gaetani, Count and Countess de Rege, Marchesa Iris Origo, The Countess of Berkeley, Marchese Gondi, Donna Lelia Howard Caetani, Mrs Margaret Licht, Prof. Caprara, Countess Cristiana Brandolini d'Adda, Countess Anna Maria Cicogna Volpi, Countess Marina Luling Buschetti Volpi di Misurata, Count Carlo Cicogna Mozzoni, Mrs Margaret Donnelly, Mrs Evelyn Lambert, Marchesa Maria Teresa Ceschi a Santa Croce, and Baron Rubin de Cervin. In Rome itself there are many people who are to be thanked: Mrs Ann Natanson, Miss Dora Jane Hamblyn and Mr Erik Amfitheatrof from the *Time-Life* Bureau, and in my own studio Ann Lombardi assisted in the planning, Christine Imhof was a great help in the layout and design of the book and especially Shelley Donnelly who accompanied me almost from one end of Italy to the other. Franco Bugionovi was entirely responsible for the laboratory preparation and assisted in the creation of special effects. I am also deeply grateful to the following museums, galleries and private collectors who have given me permission to photograph and to reproduce: Uffizi, Florence: 2; National Museum, Syracuse: 48; Piazza Armerina Museum: 52, 53; Casina Cinese, Parco della Favorita, Palermo: 76; Campano Museum, Capua: 100; Paestum Museum: 101, 104; Ospedale degli Incurabili, Naples: 106, 107; National Museum of S. Martino, Naples: 109; Archaeological Museum, Florence: 122, 123; Borghese Gallery, Rome: 131; Museum of the Duomo, Ferrara: 159; Ducal Palace, Urbino: 171; Galleria dell'Accademia, Ravenna: 183; National Museum, Bargello, Florence: 184, 185, 186, 187; Bardini Museum, Florence: 188; Medici Chapel, S. Lorenzo, Florence: 189, 190; Biblioteca Communale Ariostea, Ferrara: 195; Pinacoteca Nazionale, Bologna: 203, 204; the Commune di Cremona: 221; Poldi Pezzoli Museum, Milan: 233, 243; Ducal Palace, Mantua: 249, 252; Villa Carlotta, Cadenabbia: 251; Castello Sforzesco, Milan: 224, 226, 227; the Stringa family, Nove: 286; Galleria Sabauda, Turin: 296; Dott. Giuseppe Nardini, Ponte Vecchio, Bassano del Grappa: 410; Weinreb and Douwma Ltd: map on pp. 13–14. Excerpts from W. H. Auden and Elizabeth Meyer's translation of Goethe's *Italian Journey* are printed by kind permission of Wm. Collins Sons & Co. Ltd.

Roloff Beny, Rome, February 1974.

Index of places illustrated